"CAMPUS Asia"

本报告获教育部"亚洲校园"专项经费资助

"亚洲校园"跨境高等教育项目质量报告

QUALITY REPORT OF
"CAMPUS ASIA" CROSS-BORDER
HIGHER EDUCATION PROGRAMS

教育部高等教育教学评估中心
HIGHER EDUCATION EVALUATION CENTER OF
THE MINISTRY OF EDUCATION, CHINA

周爱军　刘振天　郑　觅　主编
CHIEF EDITOR
ZHOU AIJUN, LIU ZHENTIAN, ZHENG MI

社会科学文献出版社
SOCIAL SCIENCES ACADEMIC PRESS (CHINA)

《"亚洲校园"跨境高等教育项目质量报告》
编 委 会

主　编：周爱军　刘振天　郑　觅

编　委：李利群　敬乂嘉　范士明　李红宇

　　　　陈多友　蔡玉平　丁相顺　李梅花

　　　　王　位　王　铄　樊路强　李　娜

　　　　徐　飞

Editorial Board

前　言

"亚洲校园"计划（CAMPUS Asia），全称为"亚洲大学学生交流集体行动计划"（Collective Action of Mobility Program of University Students in Asia），是根据中日韩领导人会议和《2020 中日韩合作展望》的精神，由中日韩三国政府主导、自上而下达成的教育交流计划。为保证"亚洲校园"计划的顺利实施，三国联合成立了由政府部门、大学、评估机构、产业界代表组成的"中日韩大学交流合作促进委员会"（以下简称"委员会"），并由三国质量保障机构负责对实施项目进行质量监控和保障。

2012 年，"亚洲校园"计划首批 10 个试点项目正式启动。试点项目结合自身资源优势，通过开展各种形式的大学交流活动，旨在探索出适用于亚洲地区大学交流与合作的模式和体系，并通过积累的经验和优秀实践，为开发不同类型和层次的交流项目、逐步拓展项目规模提供依据。为加强试点项目的过程监控，受教育部国际合作与交流司委托，教育部高等教育教学评估中心（以下简称"评估中心"）于 2014 年对 10 个试点项目质量进行了中期评估，编制完成了《"亚洲校园"试点项目质量监控中期评估报告》，同年，启动了"亚洲校园"试点项目优秀实践案例的遴选工作，编制完成《"亚洲校园"试点项目优秀实践案例集萃》。两份报告在"中日韩大学交流合作促进委员会"全体会议上，获得了三国政府部门、专家委员、高校代表和评估机构的一致肯定和好评，并获教育部推荐，在国家外交层面的"中日韩三国合作秘书处"

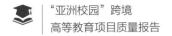
媒体见面会上进行宣传。

2015年，"亚洲校园"计划试点项目实施进入后期阶段。为对这一重要跨境高等教育合作计划进行全面"体检"，客观、翔实地反映项目的实施进展情况和教育教学质量，为计划正式实施提供参考，2015～2016年，评估中心在教育部国际合作与交流司的指导下，会同日本、韩国评估机构，对"亚洲校园"计划实施了终期质量评估。终期评估采取"联合"模式，即由三国质量保障机构推选三国高水平专家组成专家组，基于共同制定的联合评估标准，对10个参与项目进行联合材料评审和抽样现场考察，并形成终期质量评估报告。亚太地区最大的教育质量保障组织——亚太质量保障联盟（APQN）对此次三国质量保障机构的合作成果给予了表彰，并授予评估中心"质量保障国际合作奖"。

2016年，评估中心受教育部国际合作与交流司委托，并在教育部"亚洲校园"专项经费资助下，启动本报告的研制工作。本报告是在终期评估的基础上，对"亚洲校园"计划试点阶段的全面总结。我们本着特色性、示范性、持续性的原则，在充分尊重各自文化差异性和独特性的基础上，力图客观、翔实地反映"亚洲校园"各试点项目的实施质量和先进做法，希望能对"亚洲校园"计划的整体质量提升和可持续发展起到推动作用，为跨境教育的多边合作起到示范作用。

在报告的编制过程中，我们得到了教育部国际合作与交流司的悉心指导、大力支持和经费资助，并充分吸取了专家的宝贵意见，同时得到了中方各试点项目实施高校的大力支持与配合，在此一并表示诚挚的谢意。本次报告编制工作由周爱军指导，刘振天、李利群具体负责，郑觅对资料进行整理、分析并执笔，郑觅、王铄负责报告的英文校译，王位、樊路强参与报告研制前期与后期相关工作。限于我们的能力和水平，报告不足之处，望各界同仁批评指导，以便我们在今后工作中加以改进。

Preface

CAMPUS Asia, the abbreviation for the Collective Action of Mobility Program of University Students in Asia, is a top – down educational exchange initiative dominated by Chinese, Japanese and South Korean government based on Trilateral Summit Meeting in China, Japan and South Korea and the spirit of *Trilateral Cooperation Vision* 2020. To ensure the smooth implementation of "CAMPUS Asia" initiative, the three countries have jointly set up the Trilateral Committee for Promoting Exchange and Cooperation Among Universities (hereinafter referred to as the "Committee"), which consists of government authorities, universities, evaluation agencies and industry representatives. Quality assurance agencies of the three countries are responsible for quality control and assurance in implementing the project.

In 2012, student exchanges were officially initiated for the first 10 pilot programs of "CAMPUS Asia" initiative. In those pilot programs, program resources were made good use of and various forms of university exchange campaigns were organized, aiming to explore the patterns and systems suitable for cooperation and exchanges of universities in Asia. Also, exchange programs of different types and levels were developed based on the rich experience and good practices derived from pilot programs to gradually expand the program scale. To strengthen process monitoring of pilot programs, the Higher Education Evaluation Center of the Ministry of Education of the People's Republic of China ("HEEC"), entrusted by the Department of International Cooperationa and Exchanges of the the Ministry of Education, carried out the mid – term evaluation on 10 pilot programs in 2014 and completed the 1*st Quality Monitoring Report of CAMPUS Asia Pilot Programs.* Just in the same year, the selection of good practices of "CAPUS Asia" pilot programs was initiated and the *Collection of Good Practices of CAMPUS Asia Pilot Programs* was compiled. Both reports were well recognized and reviewed by government authorities, expert members, university representatives and evaluation agencies of China, Japan and South Korea at the plenary meeting of the Trilateral Committee for Promoting Exchange and Cooperation Among Universities. Also, they were recognized by the Ministry of Education of China for publicity at the press conference of Trilateral Cooperation Secretariat (TCS) at the level of foreign affairs.

The year 2015 marked the final stage of "CAMPUS Asia" pilot programs. In order to conduct an overall inspection on the important cross – border higher education cooperation initiative and describe the advancement and teaching quality of these programs in a detailed and objective manner so as to provide a reference for the formal implementation of the initiative, from the years 2015 to 2016, HEEC, together with Japanese and Korean evaluation agencies, conducted a final quality evaluation of the "CAMPUS Asia" initiative, and adopted a joint model in the final evaluation. Quality assurance agencies from China, Japan and South Korea recommended high – level experts of the three countries to form an expert team. Based on the joint evaluation criteria formulated by experts, the team made a joint material review and site sampling visit of 10 participating programs and formulated a final quality evaluation report. The cooperating accomplishments achieved by quality assurance agencies of the three countries were commended by Asia – Pacific Quality Network (APQN). Also, Higher Education Evaluation Center of the Ministry of Education (HEEC) was granted the "APQN Award of International Cooperation in QA".

This report represents a complete summary of the pilot stage of "CAMPUS Asia" initiative based on the final evaluation. We try to describe the implementing quality and leading practices of "CAMPUS Asia" pilot programs in a detailed, typical and objective manner in the principle of characteristics, demonstration and consistency by fully respecting the differences and uniqueness of their cultures. It is hoped that this report would facilitate the overall quality improvement and sustainable development of "CAMPUS Asia" initiative and play a demonstrating role in the multilateral cooperation of cross – border education.

During the preparation of this report, we have received guidance and support from the Department of International Cooperation and Exchanges of the Ministry of Education of China and fully integrated valuable advice of experts. We also got support and cooperation from Chinese universities involved in these pilot programs. Therefore, we would like to express our sincerest gratitude to them all. Zhou Aijun was responsible for guidance on the preparation of this report; Liu Zhentian, Li Liqun was specifically in charge of report preparation; Zheng Mi was responsible for sorting, analysis and preparation of data; Zheng Mi and Wang Shuo conducted English translation and proofreading; Wang Wei and Fan Luqiang participated in the pre – and post – preparation of this report. Due to the limitation of our abilities and skills, if there is any defect in our report, we hope our peers and colleagues could give criticism and guidance so that we can make improvements in our future work.

目录

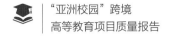

Table of Contents

"亚洲校园"计划及其质量保障

"亚洲校园"计划（CAMPUS Asia），全称为"亚洲大学学生交流集体行动计划"（Collective Action of Mobility Program of University Students in Asia），于2012年第五次中日韩领导人会议上，由时任中国国务院总理温家宝、韩国总统李明博、日本首相野田佳彦共同宣布正式启动。该跨境合作项目采取参与高校间的学分互认、学位互授等合作形式，旨在促进学生在亚洲校园间的自由流动，增进三国学生的相互了解，为增强学校竞争力、培养亚洲下一代杰出人才做出贡献。

一　"亚洲校园"计划的提出

　　2009年10月，中日韩三国领导人第二次会议提出关于加强三国大学交流合作的设想。为落实此共识，中日韩三国教育部门经过多次磋商，决定成立由政府部门、大学、评估机构、产业界代表参加的中日韩大学交流合作促进委员会，研究推进大学交流、学分互换、高等教育质量保障等问题。

　　2010年4月16日，中日韩大学交流合作促进委员会第一次会议在日本东京举行。会议就推动中日韩大学交流与合作达成以下共识：三国将联合开展大学交流项目，该项目被命名为"CAMPUS Asia"。

　　2010年12月10日，中日韩大学交流合作促进委员会第二次会议在中国北京举行。会议通过了《中日韩有质量保障的大学交流合作指导意见》和《中日韩大学交流"亚洲校园"计划框架》，两个指导性文件明确了政府、评估机构、大学、产业界等在大学交流项目中的职责任务，同时会议就试点项目的实施达成了共识。

2011年5月17日，中日韩大学交流合作促进委员会第三次会议在韩国济州岛举行。会议就实施"亚洲校园"试点项目相关具体细节进行了充分讨论，明确了试点项目参与院校范围、交流小组及学生数量、试点项目实施期限、政府及大学对项目给予的支持等事宜。

2012年5月13日，国务院总理温家宝、韩国总统李明博、日本首相野田佳彦共同启动了旨在增进中日韩大学交流合作的"亚洲校园"项目。

首批10个试点项目涉及中日韩三国共26所知名高校，实施期限为5年，三国计划每年各派遣和接收100名交换学生。这10个项目具体如下。

（1）BEST（北京—首尔—东京）商学院联盟—亚洲商业领袖项目（中国北京大学、日本一桥大学、韩国首尔国立大学，以下简称"商业领袖项目"）

表1　商业领袖项目

项目基本信息		
中方高校名称	北京大学	
合作高校名称	日方	一桥大学
	韩方	首尔国立大学
项目名称	中文	BEST（北京—首尔—东京）商学院联盟—亚洲商业领袖项目
	英文	BEST（Beijing–Seoul–Tokyo）Alliance–Asia Business Leaders Program（ABLP）
项目内容		
学术领域及参与院系	学术领域：工商管理	
	参与院系：北京大学光华管理学院、一桥大学国际企业战略研究院、首尔国立大学商学院	

续表

项目目标及预期成果	该项目始于北京大学光华管理学院（PKU）、首尔国立大学商学院（SNU）、一桥大学国际企业战略研究院（ICS）签署成立的 BEST（北京—首尔—东京）商学院联盟，该联盟致力于推动中日韩三国的领先商学院在教学科研等方面全位的合作与交流。"亚洲商业领袖项目"旨在将项目参与学生打造成为未来引领中、日、韩三国经济关系的商业领袖。2011 年 11 月，经过中日韩三国政府的严格筛选，该项目成为唯一入选"亚洲校园"计划的经济管理类合作项目						
项目计划（2012～2015）	交流类别		学生层次		交流期限		其他
	学位项目	√	本科	□	1 学年	√	
	学期交换	√	硕士	√	1 学期	√	
	短期交流	√	博士	□	寒暑期	√	

（2）国际关系及公共政策双硕士学位项目（中国北京大学、日本东京大学、韩国首尔国立大学，以下简称"国际关系项目"）

表 2　国际关系项目

项目基本信息							
中方高校名称	北京大学						
合作高校名称	日方	东京大学					
	韩方	首尔国立大学					
项目名称	中文	国际关系及公共政策双硕士学位项目					
	英文	BESETO Dual Degree Master's Program on International and Public Policy Studies（BESETO DDMP）					
项目内容							
学术领域及参与院系	学术领域：国际关系、法学及公共政策 参与院系：北京大学国际关系学院、东京大学公共政策大学院、首尔国立大学国际关系学院						
项目目标及预期成果	该项目通过设立以东亚问题研究为核心的三校国际关系、法学及公共政策的双硕士学位项目，促进青年学生交流，培养公共政策领军人才，强化高等教育合作，配合国家的外交政策						
项目计划	交流类别		学生层次		交流期限		其他
	学位项目	√	本科	□	1 学年	√	
	学期交换	√	硕士	√	1 学期	√	
	短期交流	√	博士	□	寒暑期	√	

（3）TKT 亚洲校园项目（中国清华大学、日本东京工业大学、韩国科学技术院，以下简称"TKT 项目"）

表3 TKT 项目

项目基本信息			
中方高校名称		清华大学	
合作高校名称	日方	东京工业大学	
	韩方	科学技术院	
项目名称	中文	TKT（中国清华大学—韩国科学技术院—日本东京工业大学）亚洲校园项目	
	英文	TKT Campus Asia Program（Tsinghua – KAIST – Tokyo Tech）	
项目内容			
学术领域及参与院系	学术领域：工科		
	参与院系：机械系、化工系、精密仪器系、工业工程系、电子工程系、航空航天学院、生命学院等		
项目目标及预期成果	该项目设置了联合学位、学期交换、暑期项目、联合培养科研等多种合作模式，涵盖了本科、硕士、博士等不同层次的学习项目，体现出项目实施的灵活性，满足了学生的多元化需求。其中参加清华和东工大双硕士学位项目学生如果满足双方要求，可获得两校硕士学位。参加学期交换的学生，如果满足要求，在对方学校获得的学分可在母校获得认可，双方学校学分互认。暑期项目都有明确的专业和主题		

项目计划	交流类别		学生层次		交流期限		其他
	学位项目	√	本科	√	1 学年	√	
	学期交换	√	硕士	√	1 学期	√	
	短期交流	√	博士	√	寒暑期	√	

（4）东北亚政策研究联合会项目（中国清华大学、日本政策研究大学院大学、韩国发展研究院公共政策与管理学院，以下简称"政策联合会项目"）

（5）培养东亚地区具有法律、政治理念共识，能够推动东亚共同体法制形成与发展的人才项目（中国中国人民大学、清华大学和上海交通大学，日本名古屋大学，韩国成均馆大学和首尔国立大学。以下简称"法律人才项目"）

表4 政策联合会项目

项目基本信息		
中方高校名称	清华大学	
合作高校名称	日方	政策研究大学院大学
	韩方	发展研究院
项目名称	中文	东北亚政策研究联合会
	英文	Northeast Asian Consortium for Policy Studies

项目内容		
学术领域及参与院系	学术领域：公共政策与管理 参与院系：公共管理学院	
项目目标及预期成果	"东北亚政策研究联合会"项目通过与周边国家的高校交流，服务于国家周边外交的整体工作。参与此项目，可使学生拥有更多国际交流的机会，拓宽学生视野；同时提高学院国际影响力，推动三国公共管理学科领域的合作，进一步提高国际化水平	

项目计划	交流类别		学生层次		交流期限		其他
	学位项目	□	本科	□	1学年	□√	
	学期交换	□√	硕士	□√	1学期	□√	
	短期交流	□√	博士	□√	寒暑期	□√	

表5 法律人才项目

项目基本信息		
中方高校名称	中国人民大学、清华大学、上海交通大学	
合作高校名称	日方	名古屋大学
	韩方	成均馆大学、首尔国立大学
项目名称	中文	培养东亚地区具有法律、政治理念共识，能够推动东亚共同体法制形成与发展的人才项目
	英文	Training Human Resources for the Development of an Epistemic Community in Law and Political Science to Promote the Formation of "jus commune" in East Asia

项目内容		
学术领域及参与院系	学术领域：法学 参与院系：法学院	

续表

项目目标及预期成果	该项目以三国六校学生交换为核心，选拔优秀本科生和研究生在中、日、韩三国合作院校间进行交换学习，课程涵盖三国的语言、文化、政治与法律，旨在培养东亚地区具有法律、政治理念共识，能够推动东亚共同体法制形成与发展的人才。此外，项目还辅以丰富的学生交流活动和多种形式的短期交流						
项目计划	交流类别		学生层次		交流期限		其他
	学位项目	□	本科	√	1学年	√	
	学期交换	√	硕士	√	1学期	√	
	短期交流	√	博士	□	寒暑期	√	

（6）东亚地区公共危机管理人才联合培养计划（中国复旦大学、日本神户大学、韩国高丽大学，以下简称"公共危机管理项目"）

表6　公共危机管理项目

项目基本信息		
中方高校名称	复旦大学	
合作高校名称	日方	神户大学
	韩方	高丽大学
项目名称	中文	东亚地区公共危机管理人才联合培养计划
	英文	Risk Experts in Asia
项目内容		
学术领域及参与院系	学术领域：公共管理（应急管理）	
	参与院系：国际关系与公共事务学院	
项目目标及预期成果	该项目旨在培养通晓亚洲风险管理问题的三国专家，促进各国应急管理学科的国际化发展。根据东北亚三国存在频繁的自然和城市灾害的特点，同时由于各国均在研究如何根据经济社会和自然条件的变化，扩大应急范围，增强应急管理能力，提高应急管理的韧性和效果，项目在建立之初，三校一致同意将项目定位于培养通晓亚洲风险管理问题的三国专家，要求学生通过系统学习风险管理和开展硕士论文研究，掌握风险管理基本原理和东北亚相关实践，为东北亚风险管理实践发展和区域内合作创造条件	

项目计划	交流类别		学生层次		交流期限		其他
	学位项目	√	本科	□	1学年	√	
	学期交换	√	硕士	√	1学期	√	
	短期交流	□	博士	□	寒暑期	□	

（7）中日韩能源与环境领域研究生教育合作计划（中国上海交通大学、日本九州大学、韩国釜山国立大学，以下简称"能源与环境项目"）

表7　能源与环境项目

项目基本信息						
中方高校名称	上海交通大学					
合作高校名称	日方	九州大学				
	韩方	釜山国立大学				
项目名称	中文	中日韩能源与环境领域研究生教育合作计划				
	英文	EEST Program				
项目内容						
学术领域及参与院系	学术领域：能源与环境 参与院系：机械与动力工程学院、环境科学与工程学院、研究生院					
项目目标及预期成果	项目旨在开发培养胜任全球环境与能源科学技术领域的人力资源的、具有质量保证的研究生教育体系，培养高水平下一代环境与能源方面的人才，使这些人才具有以下能力：①高水平的专业实践和科研能力；②理解和解决能源和环境问题的能力；③熟练运用英语能力；④全球化时代要求研究者和工程师应具备的专业道德素养以及对多元文化的理解能力					
项目计划	交流类别		学生层次		交流期限		其他
	学位项目	√	本科	□	1学年	□
	学期交换	□	硕士	√	1学期	√
	短期交流	□	博士	□	寒暑期	√

（8）可持续社会的亚洲教育合作门户项目——扩展化学、材料科学和技术的前沿（中国南京大学和上海交通大学、日本名古屋大学和东北大学、韩国首尔国立大学和浦项工科大学，以下简称"化学与材料项目"）

（9）核心人才培养项目：东亚地区共同利益的实现及传统文化的重视（中国吉林大学、日本冈山大学、韩国成均馆大学，以下简称"传统文化项目"）

表8　化学与材料项目

项目基本信息		
中方高校名称	南京大学、上海交通大学	
合作高校名称	日方	名古屋大学、东北大学
	韩方	首尔国立大学、浦项工科大学
项目名称	中文	可持续社会的亚洲教育合作门户——扩展化学、材料科学和技术的前沿
	英文	A Cooperative Asian Education Gateway for a Sustainable Society: Expanding the Frontiers in Science and Technology of Chemistry and Materials

项目内容		
学术领域及参与院系	学术领域：化学 参与院系：化工学院	
项目目标及预期成果	该项目计划在亚洲建立一个三边合作的化学教育中心，旨在通过合作教育和科研来推动可持续社会的发展。项目计划每年在成员学校之间合计交流30名在科研领域具有潜力的本科生或研究生，交流期限为3至12个月，旨在向这些学生教授环保材料的研究和发展方针。在接收方院校交流期间，研究生将学习体现每所成员学校优势的高级课程，并将所学知识应用到解决亲身实践的实际科研问题中。此外，计划举办短期讲座并进行讲师交流，鼓励成员学校的教师在合作科研领域增进互相理解并共同探索。该项目期望在相关联的材料领域培养未来领袖，他们将具备很好的理解和沟通能力，并将为了他们祖国的繁荣将此经验扩展至任何一个成员学校国家的学术或产业工作中。该项目也希望培养学生们在不使用母语的条件下，通过理解外国历史、文化和思考方式而提升全球意识和奉献精神。最后，计划在每个成员学校所在国加强化学和医药企业的合作，从而提供更多的特别讲座、实习及就业机会	

项目计划	交流类别		学生层次		交流期限		其他
	学位项目	□	本科	√	1学年	√	
	学期交换	√	硕士	√	1学期	√	
	短期交流	√	博士	√	寒暑期	□	

（10）中日韩三方联合培养东亚地区跨世代人文精英之流动校园工程（中国广东外语外贸大学、日本立命馆大学、韩国东西大学，以下简称"流动校园项目"）

表9 传统文化项目

项目基本信息		
中方高校名称		吉林大学
合作高校名称	日方	冈山大学
	韩方	成均馆大学
项目名称	中文	核心人才培养项目：东亚地区共同利益的实现及传统文化的重视
	英文	Program for Core Human Resources Development：For the Achievement of Common Good and the Re－evaluation of Classical Culture in East Asia

项目内容		
学术领域及参与院系	学术领域：人文与社会科学	
	参与院系：人文、社会科学学部，法学院、经济学院、行政学院、商学院、文学院、国际教育学院、外国语学院、哲学社会学院、公共外语教育学院、东北亚研究院等	

项目目标及预期成果：项目目的在于促进中日韩三国青年的相互理解，并加强人文资源合作和共同价值观的构建，为东北亚地区的发展培养具有广阔视野和理解能力的青年人才。项目参与三方在课程设置上考虑"传统文化"因素，给项目学生分别提供了解中、日、韩三国概况和传统文化的课程及文化体验活动机会，并积极组织由中日韩三国项目学生参与的学生交流活动，进一步加强相互理解

项目计划	交流类别		学生层次		交流期限		其他
	学位项目	□	本科	√	1学年	√	
	学期交换	√	硕士	√	1学期	√	
	短期交流	√	博士	√	寒暑期	√	

表10 流动校园项目

项目基本信息		
中方高校名称		广东外语外贸大学
合作高校名称	日方	立命馆大学
	韩方	东西大学
项目名称	中文	中日韩三方联合培养东亚地区跨世代人文精英之流动校园工程
	英文	Plan for a Joint Campus Representing Korea，China and Japan which will Foster Leaders in East Asian Humanities for the Next Generation

项目内容							
学术领域及参与院系	学术领域：人文学领域（文化、文学、历史等） 参与院系：东方语言文化学院日语、朝鲜语系，留学生教育学院，中国语言文化学院						
项目目标及预期成果	该项目整合中日韩三国有效资源，明确提出培养具有丰赡东亚文化学养、通晓国际规则、能够直接参与国际治理的复合型创新人才的目标，三国共同设计完整的课程体系，同时配备专门的教师队伍和管理队伍。这种由三国实施的"流动校园"模式在国内堪称首创。这种新形式的教学模式在保障教师资源上采取了"学生移动"和多媒体远程教学有机结合的办法。项目学生组成"国际班"，分两年四个学期，在中、日、韩三国的"流动校园"里共同学习与生活，领略不同国家文化下的教师风采						
项目计划	交流类别		学生层次		交流期限		其他
	学位项目	√	本科	√	1 学年	□	4 年制流动校园课程
	学期交换	□	硕士	□	1 学期	□	
	短期交流	□	博士	□	寒暑期	□	

注：项目的参与学校共同构成一个项目联合体。

从学科领域上看，10 个试点项目覆盖了管理学、哲学、文学、理学、工学、法学、经济学等相关学科，这些项目既发挥了学校学科建设和专业办学优势，同时也适应了东北亚区域性发展的需求。从培养层次上看，以研究生层次人才培养为主，个别项目明确定位于本科层次人才培养，特色也十分鲜明。从交流类型上看，主要有双学位项目（个别项目探索授予三学位或联合学位）、学期/学年交换项目和短期交流项目等。10 个试点项目结合自身资源优势，通过开展各种形式的大学交流活动，旨在探索出适用于亚洲地区大学交流与合作的模式和体系，并通过积累的经验和优秀实践，为开发不同类型和层次的交流项目、逐步拓展项目规模提供依据。

二 "亚洲校园"计划的质量保障

为推进"亚洲校园"计划大学交流、学分互认互换、质量保障与监控等各项工作，中日韩大学交流合作促进委员会专门设立两个工作组：大学交流工作组和质量保障工作组。其中，质量保障工作组的工作具体由中日韩三国质量保障机构协议会（以下简称"协议会"）负责组织实施〔中方：教育部高等教育教学评估中心（HEEC）；日方：日本大学评价与学位授予机构（NIAD－QE）；韩方：韩国大学教育协会大学评估院（KCUE－KUAI）〕。"亚洲校园"试点项目为期5年，对试点项目的质量监控工作分两轮进行，在试点项目实施中期进行第一轮（中期）质量监控，由三国质量保障机构分别对本国参与项目进行质量监控和评估；在试点项目实施结束时期进行终期质量评估，由三国质量保障机构组织专家对参与"亚洲校园"计划的10个试点项目联合体进行联合质量监控与评估。从2012年至2016年，三国协议会已先后完成对"亚洲校园"试点项目的两轮质量监控。

1. "亚洲校园"试点项目第一轮质量监控

2013年，在试点项目实施中期，三国质量保障评估机构基于各自制定的标准和流程，分别对本国参与项目进行质量监控。

中国教育部高度重视"亚洲校园"项目的质量保障工作，教育部国际合作与交流司在《关于实施"亚洲校园"试点项目有关要求的通知》（教外司亚〔2012〕365号）中明确提出，"中日韩三国教育部门将组织相关质量保障机构对项目实施情况进行中期评估和终期评估，加强质量检查，积累经验，确保项目健康有序推进"，并先后下发《关于加强"亚洲校园"试点项目质量监控工作的通知》（教外司亚〔2013〕1837号）和《关于提交"亚洲校园"试点项目自评报告的通知》（教外司亚〔2014〕1184号）等文件，为做好试点项目质量监控和评估工作提出了明确要求，也提供了行动指南。

2014年6月至7月，教育部高等教育教学评估中心（以下简称"评估中心"）对10个试点项目质量监控进行了中期评估。此次评估工作体现了"三个新"：一是树立了"学校为主、学生为本、侧重审核、关注产出"的新理念；二是制定了一套反映试点项目共性和特色、并把握影响质量六大核心要素的新标准（包括：目标设定、组织实施、教学活动、学生服务、质量保障、学习成果）；三是采取了高校自评、校际互评、专家评审相结合的既具创新性又简易可行的新方法。评估中心以高校自评材料、高校互评意见和专家评审意见为主要依据，用事实和数据说话，编制完成了《"亚洲校园"试点项目质量监控中期报告》（以下简称《报告》）。

《报告》中，我们通过对评分等级进行赋值加权计算及对数值进行标准化处理，得到了 10 个试点项目在各个标准项的单项得分，以及在综合各个标准项之后的整体得分，并据此对试点项目进行了单项和综合排行。总体来看，试点项目的目标设定能基本体现各校学术优势和跨国项目的特色；项目基本的组织实施和教学活动得以保证，大多数项目运行良好；项目基本建立了能够满足学生需求的服务支持体系，在学习环境、设备设施等硬件方面表现较好，学生对项目的满意度较高，但项目在学业指导、咨询服务等软件方面，以及质量保障和学习成果方面还有待加强，在实施过程中"以质量为核心"、"以学生发展为本位"、"以学习成果为导向"的意识有待增强。

2014 年 11 月至 2015 年 1 月，为进一步总结"亚洲校园"试点项目实践经验，落实中日韩大学交流与合作促进委员会第四次会议形成的三方共识中"选取优秀案例予以推广"的要求，基于各项目实施的阶段性成果，评估中心启动了"亚洲校园"试点项目优秀实践案例的遴选工作。我们采取学校自荐、专家评审和考察调研相结合的方式，遴选出"亚洲校园"试点项目优秀实践案例。这些优秀案例能够体现"亚洲校园"项目的宗旨、目标及多边合作模式的优势，具有典型性、创新性和实效性，特别注重在人才培养模式、课程教学、师资、学分互认与学位互授、质量保障等方面的探索，值得充分肯定。在充分调研基础上，评估中心编制完成《"亚洲校园"试点项目优秀实践案例集萃》，其中重点介绍的"流动校园"三边合作本科人才培养模式、学位项目＋暑期学校＋国际会议的三位一体培养形式、校企合作项目制教学研究、学校—学院—学生多级项目运行管理机制、多语言共同课程设计、信息化实验室教学平台、远程视频课程、多国导师联合授课、学分互换标准、学生成果评测及满意度调查等优秀实践案例，充分体现出"亚洲校园"项目在求同存异的实践中，各自凸显出来的独特性和创新性，值得在跨国大学多边合作中进行宣传和推广，这对于促进项目的可持续发展、探索东亚地区多边教育合作模式及教育一体化等方面具有重大意义和示范作用。

2. "亚洲校园"试点项目第二轮质量监控

中日韩大学交流合作促进委员会第五次会议于 2015 年 4 月在中国上海举行，会议达成共识，决定在试点项目结束阶段进行第二轮质量监控，即终期联合质量监控。

（1）联合质量监控的目的、原则和方针

"亚洲校园"试点项目联合质量监控，将通过对所有大学联合体的项目实施情况以及大学质量保障活动的合作程度进行检查，推进项目的质量持续改进；并将使用共同质量监控标准发布联合评估报告，宣传三国优秀实践；在此基础上，探索开发三国质量保障"共同指导方针"。

为此，我们遵循以下原则和方针来实施联合质量监控：

①促进试点项目整体质量提升；

②通过共同制定的标准进行联合质量监控；

③考察每个联合体取得的进步和成绩，总结各自的优秀实践；

④考察联合体在资源整合和质量保障等方面的合作程度；

⑤检查每个试点项目的质量持续改进情况；

⑥重视学生的意见和建议。

（2）联合质量监控标准

通过对三方机构开发的第一轮监控标准的比较和分析，我们在三方共同认可的核心指标的基础上，提出了包含五项一级指标的第二轮联合质量监控框架，其中每项指标都有两个二级指标。如表11所示，它包含以下内容。

表11　第二轮联合质量监控框架

一级指标	二级指标	一级指标	二级指标
1. 目标及实施	1.1　目标达成	3. 学生支持	3.1　学生选派
	1.2　组织管理		3.2　学习及生活支持
2. 学术项目的合作优势	2.1　课程整合	4. 项目增值	4.1　学生满意度
			4.2　学分转换及学位授予
	2.2　师资与教学	5. 内部质量保障	5.1　自我评估
			5.2　质量持续改进

该标准体系强调以下几点：

每个联合体目标达成情况、取得的成绩和值得宣传推广的优秀实践；

每个联合体在联合管理、资源整合、跨国质量保障等方面的合作情况；

学生支持和项目增值的情况；

每个试点项目的质量持续改进状况。

（3）联合质量监控专家组成及职责

由三国质量保障机构分别推选3名专家（其中1名为评估机构代表），共同组成联合质量监控委员会，该委员会主要有三项职责：审核10个联合体提交的自评报告；共同商定需要现场考察的联合体；形成联合质量监控总报告，全面反映10个试点项目质量监控情况。

从联合质量监控委员会中，三国各选派1～2名专家共同组成联合监控现场考察组，该考察组主要有两项职责：按照第二轮联合质量监控标准进校现场考察；考察结束后，形成现场考察报告，提交委员会审议。

（4）联合质量监控时间路线表

我们将 2016 年确定为"亚洲校园"试点项目结束期，联合质量监控按照以下流程实行（见表 12）。

表 12　联合质量监控流程

时　间	流　程
2015 年 4 ~ 6 月	编写自我评估报告 ——各大学联合体编写一份英文自我评估报告
2015 年 6 ~ 11 月	材料评审 ——来自中国、日本和韩国的联合监控专家组成员进行材料评审
2015 年 11 月至 2016 年 3 月	联合现场考察 ——来自中国人民大学（中国）、东京大学（日本）和东西大学（韩国）的中日韩联合监控专家组成员展开联合现场考察
2015 年 11 月至 2016 年 3 月	访谈或现场考察 ——各国家的专家组成员对本国大学展开访谈或实地考察
2016 年 10 月至 2017 年	联合监控委员会 ——《联合监控报告》定稿及发布

具体操作如下。

①三国评估机构相互合作，为各国大学提供内容相同或相似的有关质量监控目的及实施方式的培训。

②各联合体必须提交一份共同（联合）自评报告，该报告须由该联合体内所有参与大学联合撰写，从值得肯定之处、需要改进之处、优秀实践案例等方面总结项目实施质量。

③监控专家组成员进行材料评审，审读所提交的自评报告材料。

④监控专家组成员进行现场考察，问询材料评审中尚未证实的问题，采访项目负责人、参与该项目的教职人员以及相关学生。

⑤监控专家组成员根据评审材料及现场考察结果出具一份英文监控

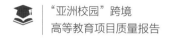

报告草案。

⑥评估机构督促联合体对监控报告草案进行审核，确保不含任何事实性错误。若存在事实性错误，监控分委会将对其进行审议。

⑦联合质量监控委员会委员共享三国评估机构联合体完成的监控报告。评估机构根据对所有联合体的监控报告，拟定终期评估报告草稿。利用包括书籍、网络及研讨会等形式广泛宣传联合监控报告。

与第一轮质量监控由三国分别对本国高校进行质量评估不同的是，第二轮质量评估采取"联合"模式，即由三国质量保障机构推选三国高水平专家组成专家组，基于共同制定的联合评估标准，对10个参与项目联合体进行联合材料评审和抽样现场考察，并形成终期质量评估报告。整个过程充分体现了三国在多个层面的"联合"，探索出了一套适合于"亚洲校园"项目质量保障的新模式：①联合评估标准。三方在共同认可的核心指标的基础上，提出了包含五项一级指标、十项二级指标的联合质量评估标准框架，这套专门适用于"亚洲校园"项目的评估标准体系，重点强调项目的三方合作程度和质量持续改进情况。②联合自评自查。三国参与学校参照联合评估标准共同查找问题、对项目实施整体情况进行自我评估，重视对项目的联合管理、资源整合和质量保障共建。③联合评估专家组。由三国质量保障机构推选具有高等教育国际化知识的专家学者以及质量保障机构的代表组成联合专家组，对项目自评报告进行联合材料评审，形成综合评审意见，遴选部分项目进行联合现场考察，并共同完成最终的质量报告。

5年来，在教育部的支持和指导下，通过各高校的自评自建工作，在两轮质量评估的保障下，"亚洲校园"各项目高校发挥自身优势、开拓创新，在资源整合、人才培养模式、质量保障、学分互换和学位互授等方面进行了积极探索，总结提炼了许多有益经验，取得了良好的阶段性成果。

在整合联合质量监控自评报告、专家组现场考察报告、实地调研报告、高校工作经验交流会等相关材料的基础上，评估中心会同日本、韩国评估机构，围绕联合质量监控五项指标，对"亚洲校园"试点项目中的优秀实践案例进行了充分挖掘，也对需要改进的问题进行了深入分析。

表 13　"亚洲校园"计划首批 10 个试点项目

中方高校	日方高校	韩方高校	项目名称	项目简称	项目类型
北京大学	一桥大学	首尔国立大学	商学院联盟—亚洲商业领袖项目	商业领袖项目	短期交流项目为主（硕士）
北京大学	东京大学	首尔国立大学	国际关系及公共政策双硕士学位项目	国际关系项目	硕士学期交换项目
清华大学	日本政策研究大学院大学	发展研究所	东北亚政策研究联合会项目	政策联合会项目	硕士学期交换项目
清华大学	东京工业大学	韩国科学技术院	TKT 亚洲校园项目	TKT 项目	双硕士学位项目
吉林大学	冈山大学	成均馆大学	核心人才培养项目：东亚地区共同利益的实现及传统文化的重视	传统文化项目	硕博学期交换项目

中方高校	日方高校	韩方高校	项目名称	项目简称	项目类型
中国人民大学 清华大学 上海交通大学	名古屋大学	成均馆大学 首尔国立大学	培养东亚地区具有法律、政治理念共识，能够推动东亚共同体法制形成与发展的人才项目	法律人才项目	本科长期交换项目
南京大学 上海交通大学	名古屋大学 东北大学	首尔国立大学 浦项工科大学	可持续社会的亚洲教育合作门户项目——扩展化学、材料科学和技术的前沿	化学与材料项目	硕士学期交换项目
上海交通大学	九州大学	釜山国立大学	中日韩能源与环境领域研究生教育合作计划	能源与环境项目	双硕士项目
复旦大学	神户大学	高丽大学	东亚地区公共危机管理人才联合培养计划	公共危机管理项目	双硕士项目
广东外语外贸大学	立命馆大学	东西大学	中日韩三方联合培养东亚地区跨世代人文精英之流动校园工程	流动校园项目	本科三学位项目

一 目标及实施

（一）经验总结

"亚洲校园"项目设计阶段，参与合作的大学在联合体内，结合自身学术优势和资源优势，共同商讨设定项目目标和基本框架，并在教职工和学生之间共享。大多数项目目标清晰阐述了对学生的知识、能力、素质等方面的培养要求，充分体现了跨国合作项目的特色性和附加值，为项目运行提供了指导。

在制度建设上，联合体从质量保障的角度出发，在书面合作协议中阐述了关于人才培养层次、跨校合作模式、组织管理机制、责任分工及配套的人员/经费/场地设施等支持系统方面的内容。参与高校普遍针对"亚洲校园"项目制定了专门的管理办法，或将项目纳入已有的教学管理制度规范中，严格按照统一标准进行管理。管理办法对课程设置、教学管理、学生服务等方面做出具体规定，权责明确、切实可行，通过建立多层面的工作机制和协作机制，为项目的正常开展提供了保障，促进了项目目标的有效达成，为参与学生有效维护自身权益提供了必要支持。在组织管理上，"亚洲校园"项目在多数参与高校都得到了校级层面的高度重视，均由校级领导牵头，成立专门的工作组，配备相应的人、财、物等资源，基本形成了利益相关方共同参与、院校两级分层落实的管理机制。健全的制度和规范的管理一方面保证了项目的运行在学校整体发展规划之内，能够充分利用校内外资源保障项目的实施；另一方面保障了项目实施的质量和水平，促进了高校自身在国际教育合作方面管理能力的提升。

（二）优秀实践

1. 共同确立项目目标和实施框架，阐明预期知识、能力和素质要求

公共危机管理项目的三所合作高校发挥了在"政府与公共治理"方面的学术优势，就项目培养目标进行了充分讨论，根据东北亚三国存在频繁的自然和城市灾害的特点，三方一致同意将项目目标定位于培养通晓亚洲风险管理问题的三国专家，促进各国应急管理学科的国际化发展。该目标对学生将应具备的知识、能力、素质做出了具体阐述，要求学生通过系统学习风险管理知识和开展硕士论文研究，对各国风险治理基本原理具有全面深入的认识，并从中获得扎实的学术分析与实践工作能力，为进入国内外公共应急部门从事风险管理工作奠定基础。联合体在学术框架搭建中充分发挥了三所大学的学术优势：神户大学提供自然灾害和减灾的危机管理教育；高丽大学提供安全问题及能源问题的危机管理教育；复旦大学从公共政策的角度提供危机管理教育。

流动校园项目在人才培养模式上，突破跨国教育中双边合作的传统，在国内首创三边合作新模式——"流动校园"模式。这种新形式

的教学模式在保障教师资源上采取了"学生移动"和多媒体远程教学有机结合的办法。项目学生组成"国际班",分两年四个学期,在中、日、韩三国间的"流动校园"里共同学习与生活,领略不同国家文化下的教师风采。这种办学模式不仅深化了中日韩三所大学的国际合作和交流,实现了优势互补和强强联合,还充分体现了"多边性"的特质,对我们探索三国高等教育一体化发展有着深远的影响。

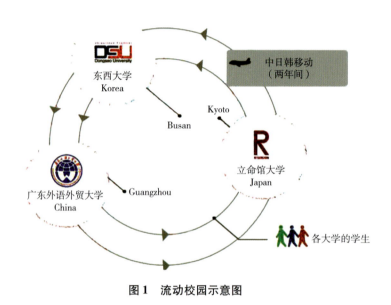

图1　流动校园示意图

该项目通过组织中日韩三国学生实现跨校国际流动,学习三国大学共同实施的课程和各大学设置的专门课程,强化学生外语技能,使其深化对中日韩三国政治、文化、历史等方面的理解,培养学生在文化、历史、政治及教育研究领域分析问题、解决问题的能力,使其成为东亚地区人文学方面的领军性人才。该项目的人才培养目标从知识、技能、沟通能力、实践能力等四个方面清晰地归结为以下四点:①培养掌握东亚传统文化基本知识,对不断发展变化的东亚局势及现状具备高度理解能力与把握能力的人才(认知高度);②具有高度的文献解析能力,通过对现代中国、日本、韩国的文化(文学、影视剧、动漫、语言等)的学习，实现对各国社会、生活、历史、媒体状况的理解（语言技能）；③通过中日韩三种语言的习得训练及留学实习、实践，培养具有突出的沟通能力，能够活跃在国际舞台上的人才（国际化沟通能力）；④培养能够和平解决东亚面临的各种问题的人才（实践能力）。

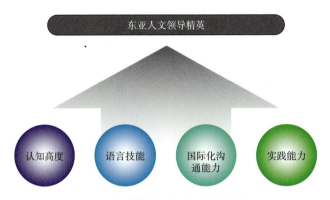

图2　流动校园项目人才培养目标

法律人才项目以三国六校学生交换为核心，选拔优秀本科生和研究生，在中日韩三国合作院校间进行交换学习，旨在"培养东亚地区具有法律、政治理念共识，能够推动东亚共同体法制形成与发展的人才"。项目对学生学习成果的具体要求如下：未来一代的法律专业人士具备必要的知识和能力，积极参与"共同体"的形成；他们乐于开启比较法研究的新趋势，促进法律信息区域共享的形成；他们有能力将这些结果运用于帮助其他亚洲国家（特别是寻求体制转型的国家）的发展，在法律合作和援助项目中给予这些国家更多的协助。

传统文化项目致力于促进中日韩三国青年间的相互理解，加强人文资源合作和共同价值观的构建。项目三方——吉林大学、冈山大学、成均馆大学地处东北亚地区核心地带，具有地缘、历史、文化上的亲近性，并有连续多年开展教学、科研及师生交流的合作基础。联合体充分考虑"传统文化"因素，为项目参与学生搭建了解中日韩三国国情和文化的学术框架，共同商议建设了东亚人文学科全球教育课程体系；该体

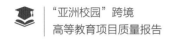
系由三所大学分工合作完成，其中，冈山大学组织实践考察活动，吉林大学提供国际关系课程，成均馆大学提供东亚经典和传统文化的课程。

能源与环境项目的三方高校共同确认了清晰的愿景和目标：整合三校的优质教育资源，在为能源和环境科学与工程领域的优秀研究生提供双学位教育的同时，以点带面，加强三校间优秀研究生的交流互动，扩大项目的影响力和受益面，立足亚洲培养具有全球视野的能源和环境科学与工程领域的杰出专业人才，并探索"建立一个在科学和工程相关领域具有先进性和多样性的示范性教育系统"。这一明确清晰的愿景和目标在项目的实施和持续发展过程中发挥了重要指导作用。

2. 项目目标在校内共享

商业领袖项目通过协议和谅解备忘录在参与大学之间共享项目目标，并将之作为实施教育内容的指导方针。谅解备忘录清楚地描述了目标及人力资源发展的愿景，声明"为了增强经济联系，中国、日本和韩国的商业领袖、教授和学生了解伙伴国家的经济、社会、文化等重要领域"，"参与学校将共同培养对东亚未来共同繁荣做出贡献的商业领袖"。

化学与材料项目通过联合体大学之间的定期会议分享项目目标。来自三个国家的六所大学商定轮流召开每年一次的"亚洲校园"研讨会，研讨会上重申项目的初始目标，即"在全球化学和材料领域培养具有全球视野的领先人才"，合作高校共同致力于推动学生交流和改善项目运作。

国际关系项目利用学生和教师的选派环节分享项目目标。项目对选派师生实行严格的英语面试，要求学生和老师熟知项目人才培养目标及毕业要求，明确学习和教学目的。该项目专门成立了由参与招生和课程研发等活动的教职工组成的委员会，定期根据项目目标开展教研活动。

3. 依据项目目标制定切实可行的实施办法

TKT项目通过协同发挥联合体高校的人才培养优势，确立了培养通晓三国语言、文化和习俗的亚洲科技和人文领域创新领军青年人才的目标。联合体依据项目目标制定了完备且切实可行的，包含组织实施、交流形式、学生资格、招生计划、申请程序、选派程序、培养方案、研究计划和学习记录、财务责任、学习成果证明、学分互认、质量监控等方面的实施办法。实施办法考虑到三国教育政策的差异，对部分环节进行了具体解释，例如，实施办法中详细列举了三国学分互认和学分转换政策的细微差别。

表 14　TKT 项目学分互认和转换政策

清华大学 Tsinghua University 清华大学	KAIST 韩国科学技术院	东京工业大学 Tokyo Institute of Technology 东京工业大学
在合作大学获得的类似或相关课程的学分可以在相关部门的学术办公室批准后转换和认可	学分是否可以转换，取决于教授类似课程的教授或主管部门的决定（通过/非通过）	离校前，学生需要向咨询部门主管或学术顾问咨询关于学分认可的事宜。返回国内大学后，学生必须提交学术成绩单和其他文件，如由主办大学颁发的课程大纲、课程表 在合作大学获得的学分由校长根据教师会议的评级决定是否认可，认可学分的评级是"通过"

4. 建立三方联动的工作机制

为保证项目顺利运行，能源与环境项目三所大学代表成立了计划—实施—检查—行动（PDCA）领导委员会，负责项目的规划、实施、自我评估和持续改进，形成了三方联动的闭环工作体系。在该领导委员会下，联合体内每个大学均建立了 PDCA 委员会和"亚洲校园"项目办公室，为学生提供日常支持。["PDCA"是英语单词 Plan（计划）、Do（执行）、Check（检查）和 Adjust（纠正）的第一个字母的组合，指的是一个循环过程，又称 PDCA 循环。PDCA 循环又叫质量环，是管理学中的一个通用模型。]

流动校园项目在课程管理上使用国际上先进做法，三所大学共同建

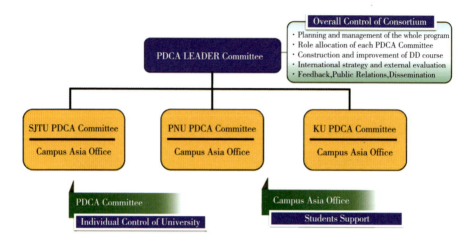

图 3　能源与环境项目 PDCA 工作机制

立中、日、韩三国语言的"亚洲校园"教务网站，发布课程信息。学生可以查看课程计划、成绩、授课老师信息，进行自主选课；教师可以在网上随时发布关于课程的信息，查看学生资料及选课情况，从而实现师生信息的及时交换，参见图 4、图 5。

图 4　"亚洲校园"教务网站教师管理页面

5. 构建多层面的磋商及沟通协作机制

法律人才项目通过在学院—项目—学生多个层面建立协作机制，加强项目质量保障建设。

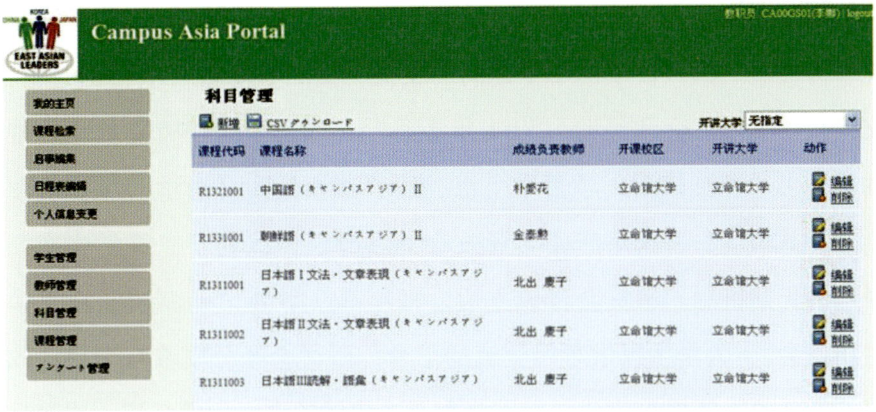

图5 "亚洲校园"项目教务网站上的项目课程列表

学院层面——"亚洲校园项目院长会议"协调机制

项目自启动以来，得到了中日韩三国六校合作伙伴院校领导的高度重视和大力支持，建立了由合作学院院长组成的"亚洲校园项目院长会议"协调机制。截至2017年，"亚洲校园项目院长会议"已先后举办了七次，对亚洲、特别是东亚法学教育的发展趋势、改革措施、人才培养标准、相关制度建设等问题展开了深入交流，成为探讨东亚地区法学教育与政策改革的重要平台，同时也对项目的发展、质量的保障发挥了重要作用。

项目层面——"亚洲校园项目质量保证委员会"

为了建立项目运行情况的定期协调机制，及时商讨并解决项目运行中出现的问题，由三国六校项目主任和分管教务人员组成了"亚洲校园项目质量保证委员会"。自2011年12月以来，项目质量保证委员会先后在日本名古屋，中国上海、北京，韩国首尔举行了近20次工作会议。会上，与会者既会分享已经接收学生的学习、生活情况，对下一期学生的选派提出建议，也会对现有课程设置及项目的发展计划做出深入讨论。定期协调机制对于精细化学生管理、将项目设计落到实处发挥了重要作用。

学生层面——"亚洲校园（法学）项目学友会"

为促进三国六校项目学生之间的交流，提高学生参与项目的热情，交换相关学习体会和经验，2014 年 2 月，在项目质量保障委员会的推动下，由"亚洲校园"项目学生组成的"亚洲校园（法学）项目学友会"正式成立，并选举产生了学友会的领导层，以利于完善学生交流学习的长期机制。学友会自成立后，每年都会举办"亚洲校园项目学生研讨会"，为学生提供学习交流的平台；研讨会既分享参与项目的收获、为项目发展提出建议，又围绕东亚法律话题进行学术交流，成效显著。2017 年 3 月，合作院校共同提议，增加学生职业发展方面的指导，将学生研讨会的内容范围扩展到学生职业发展方面的交流，并邀请中日韩的学者、律师、企业家等各个行业的杰出人士与学生共同交流，为学生毕业后的职业发展提供有益指导。学友会的成立，一方面可以为学生们的交流与相互学习搭建良好的平台，加强互动，发挥学生们的主观能动性；另一方面也激发了学生们参加该项目的积极性，使他们可以在结束交换学习后仍然可以保持紧密的联系，促进彼此学术能力的提高。

（三）问题剖析

目标设定方面，"亚洲校园"项目不同于大多数学生交换或联合培养项目之处在于，突破了双边合作的传统模式，强调中、日、韩多边合作，通过更紧密、更频繁的学生交流，树立亚洲地区共同体意识，探索区域教育一体化的可能，为亚洲地区更多学生的自由流动创造条件，培养下一代杰出人才。部分参与高校未能很好地理解"亚洲校园"项目的独特性和必要性，项目目标较少体现制度层面（例如多边合作模式、学分互认、学位联授等）的创新，仍停留在传统点对点合作的目标层面；部分项目目标较为宏观，未能体现出有别于双边合作的多边优势融合，合作项目内容不够聚焦；部分项目对学生的学习成果缺乏明确、具体的阐述。

组织实施方面，少数项目在实施过程中中、日、韩三边作用发挥不均衡，沟通机制不健全，未能形成联动机制，合作形式大于内容；一部分项目管理过于松散，涉及多个院系和职能部门，责任分工不明确，项目专员缺位，协调统筹难度较大，影响了项目的落实，另一部分项目由某一部门或学院归口管理，但缺乏学校层面的重视和其他相关部门的配合，执行力度不够，两种情况都对项目预期效果的达成造成了一定程度的影响；由于三国对项目投入经费的形式存在较大差异（日、韩采取年度专项经费拨款的形式，中国采取向来华学生提供政府奖学金资助的形式），部分项目未能采取有效措施筹措资金用于项目运营，项目活动的开展受到一定限制；部分项目的招生宣传力度不够，对学生遴选政策和办法亦未做明确说明，预期的交流学生数量未能得到保证，派出和接收学生不平衡。

二 学术项目的合作优势

（一）经验总结

"亚洲校园"项目联合体基于共同设定的项目目标，发挥各参与学校的学术优势，在充分整合资源的基础上，制定了体现跨国项目国际性、前沿性、特色性和附加值的课程体系。基于各项目在人才培养层次和所涉学科领域的不同，联合体在课程类型、教学内容、核心课程对接、教学方法、课程管理等方面开展了不同形式的创新，对国际项目课程开发进行了有益探索。

高水平大学的合作保障了参与"亚洲校园"项目教师的教学及研究水平，多数项目都有国际化的教师团队进行教学和指导，能够有效地达成项目教学目标。为体现跨国项目的合作优势，多数项目通过联合授课、教师互派、远程教学、专题讲座等方式实现教师资源的整合，确保了教育教学任务的有效完成。多语言的教学环境增加了"亚洲校园"项目为学生带来的附加价值，为学生未来积极投身东亚地区发展打下了坚实的基础。运用信息化手段实现的多种教学形式进一步促进了教学目标的达成。

（二）优秀实践

1. 基于合作优势共同开发适用于跨国教育的课程体系

流动校园项目整合中、日、韩三国高校有效资源，明确提出培养具有丰赡东亚文化学养、通晓国际规则、能够直接参与国际治理的复合型创新人才的目标，三国共同设计完整的课程体系，同时配备专门的教师队伍和管理队伍。在教学内容和课程体系上，开发了适用于跨国教育合作的"嵌入式"课程体系。中日韩三所大学共同开发出以"流动校园"（4～7学期）为核心，以短期研修（1～3学期）、共同实习项目（8～9学期）为必修课程的四年半制"嵌入式"课程体系（见图6）。在统一的课程体系中，中日韩三国大学除设置规定的涵盖听、说、读、写、译等各项知识技能训练的语言课程之外，还设置了社会、经济、历史、文学、文化及地域国别研究等范畴的人文学社会学专业科目，相互提供能够支撑人才培养目标的辅助性课程模块，共同实施学分互换，同时充分利用各大学的远程设备与技术开设远程教学科目，共享三方其他教育资源，培养能够在政治外交、社会文化、经济技术交流与合作以及教育研究领域发挥突出作用的优秀人才。通过流动、嵌入式的课程培养，三所大学共享教育教学资源，打破疆域、文化及学科藩篱，让不同国别、不同文化背景的青年学子通过"浸入式"的学习方式在同一个平台上充分交流，掌握相关知识与技能，获得三方学位，为学生最终成为可以在东亚乃至更宽广的国际舞台上具有通用价值的复合型人才打下坚实的基础。

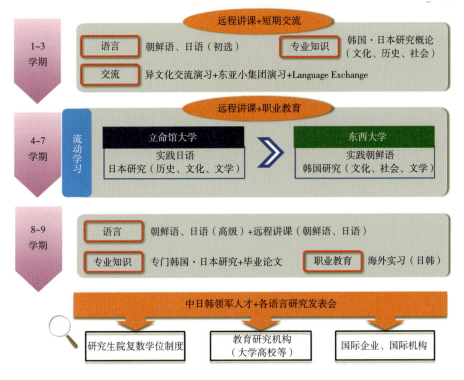

图6 流动校园项目四年半制"嵌入式"课程体系

公共危机管理项目中，复旦大学国务学院在 2012 年成立了"公共管理"全英文授课硕士学位项目，该学位项目除专门接收"亚洲校园"项目的韩日学位生和交流生外，也向全球开放招生。其中"亚洲校园"项目定位于培养通晓亚洲风险管理问题的三国专家，要求学生通过系统学习风险管理和开展硕士论文研究，掌握风险管理基本原理和东北亚相关实践。国务学院具有长期的国际化办学基础，该硕士项目开设近 30 门全英文课程，其中 6 门基础课程、8 门核心课程和约 15 门选修课程，并为留学生提供量身定制的汉语语言课程（分 6 个层次）。"亚洲校园"项目的课程"嵌入"这一学位课程之中，同时专门设立了中国应急管理、中国环境政策与可持续发展、公共创新、技术整合与新公共运营、公共政策、研究方法、中国社会、项目评估与政策分析等专业课程，并将风险管理学位教育置于公共管理和国际关系等基本教学体系内，形成跨学科的教学优势。在课程体系整体建构上，结合项目的整体定位，将所有课程分为三大类：合作课程、专门课程和拓展课程。中方还积极与日方和韩方沟通交流，对课程设置和体系建构进行了周密的部署和全面的协商，结合各个大学本身的办学特色，在推动东亚一体化风险管理体系建设的同时，兼顾各个国家本身应急实践的要求。

2. 深入开展校企合作育人

商业领袖项目含"亚洲商业经营方略"子项目，参与主体为工商管理硕士（MBA）项目和高层管理教育项目的学生。该子项目历时两周，由北京大学光华管理学院、首尔国立大学商学院及一桥大学战略企业研究院协同合作，共同制订项目内容、目标及小组作业，分别在北京、东京、首尔三地进行课程培训、企业现场参观、案例分析讨论等交流活动。

校企合作——中、日、韩三国顶尖商学院负责该项目的合作与具体执行。项目指导委员会与相关企业共同开发课程、讲义及公司案例，将涵盖近年三国经济等方面最热门话题，及从事联合研究教员的最新研究成果融入课程中，从亚洲商业模式和商业领导风格的视角来培养未来三国的商业领袖。项目为期两周，分别在三所院校所在地举行，每地都设有课程学习、企业拜访、文化体验等活动。学习期间，安排学生前往知名企业总部参观交流，并与企业负责人进行座谈。

项目制教学——该项目班级规模为30人，三方各自负责已方10名学生的选拔。在三地两周的学习期间，30名学员被分为5个小组，每个小组有6名学员（中、日、韩方各2名）。学员们围绕一个共同主题开展项目研究，并在课程结束时，以小组的形式进行汇报。以下列举一些特色项目教学课程。

跨文化管理项目教学。三方教授共同探讨制定了该期小组研究项目，即围绕星巴克的案例，研究跨文化管理中的客户关系管理及人才管理。星巴克亚太地区总部大力支持了这期研究项目，分别在北京、东京及首尔分部接待学员拜访，并请出各地高管与学生座谈，分享他们多年的从业经验。

东亚制造业的竞争与合作项目教学。学员参访了北京现代总部、东京优衣库总部及韩国三星总部。各企业高管人员的分享使课堂的学术知识不再只是书本上的文字，而是还原一个个生动的、体现了竞争与合作的博弈的案例。

东亚地区老龄化问题项目教学。根据老龄人口在各地所占比例，以及未来该数字的演变，指向该问题将给经济发展带来的巨大挑战。学员们在教授的引导下，逐渐地发现问题，寻求解决方案。

两周三地——在三国的通力协作之下，项目在短短两周之内，设置了目标明确、主题鲜明的教学内容，并安排学生前往三国进行文化体验。这种紧凑、浓缩的培养形式突破了传统短期项目流于浅层交流的限制。学生通过深入的学习和对不同文化的体验，增进了对亚洲经济、政府、社会体制、文化和商业活动的了解。这种形式对培养学生在跨国团队环境中学习工作技能和协作精神、正确理解东亚商业模式和商业领导方式起到了重要作用。

3. 多语言教学环境增加项目附加价值

法律人才项目联合体为该项目专门设计了六门共同课程，涵盖了三国语言、政治与法律的学习；这六门共同课分别是"社科汉/日/韩语（一）"、"社科汉/日/韩语（二）"、"中国法/韩国法/日本法概论"、"中国/日本/韩国政治"、"东亚比较法"和"东亚比较政治"。三国六校在项目工作会议上共同探讨课程的设计与教学，探索共同教材编写、远程教学等合作的可能性。除了六门共同课外，交换学生还将接受为期一年的当地语言培训，最大限度地提升语言水平，为今后深入开展学习研究打下语言基础。同时，项目开放全部的英文课程体系，以满足学生的学习需要，例如，体系中有依托于中国人民大学法学院的全英文中国法硕士项目课程，来华交换学生可以选修英文讲授的多门中国部门法课程，这有利于他们全面的学习、掌握中国法。

流动校园项目学生学习期间，各大学均针对学生开设汉语、日语、韩国语等语言教学课程，学生在课堂上使用当地语言共同学习，课后一起生活，加上在当地学习该国语言的优势，学生的语言能力得到极大的锻炼和提高。目前三国学生能够用熟练的汉、日、韩三语互相进行交流，共同开展课题研究与学习。该项目通过语言学习促进文化交流，在流动校园项目学习期间，三校均开设文化体验课程，例如广外（广东外语外贸大学的简称，下文同）开设的中国书法、中国武术、岭南文化等课程。在此过程中，三国学生互相学习、互相对比，为未来深入进行历史、文化等知识的研究与探讨奠定良好的基础。根据 2012～2015 年的统计，中日韩三方学员共计 30 名，其中广东外语外贸大学 10 名学生全部通过日语能力一级（最高级别）考试，7 人通过韩国语能力考试六级、2 人通过五级（最高级为六级）；立命馆大学 5 人通过韩国语能力测试六级，8 人通过 HSK 五级考试；东西大学 8 人通过日语能力一级考试，1 人通过 HSK 六级考试，8 人通过 HSK 五级考试。

4. 多种途径整合配置教师资源

流动校园项目在保障教师资源上采取了"教师不动学生动"和多媒体远程教学有机结合的办法。在教师资源保障上，该项目各大学均选派有丰富教学经验的教师进行授课，在开课前向教师下发学生档案，让教师充分了解学生情况，因材施教。该项目中日韩三所大学实施教师资源共享；截至 2017 年，中国广东外语外贸大学有 7 名专职教师，2 名外教，行政秘书 2 名；日本立命馆大学拥有专职教师 6 名，行政秘书 3

名；韩国东西大学拥有专职教师 6 名，行政秘书 2 名。授课教师职称结构较为合理，且均具有海外留学背景。学习期间，行政秘书定期与教师沟通，了解课堂情况，反馈学生意见，保证课堂教学质量、教育教学任务的高标准完成。学生共同组成"国际班"，每年分为三个学期，按照中、日、韩的顺序在广东外语外贸大学、立命馆大学、东西大学这个"流动校园"里沉浸式地共同学习与生活，领略不同国家文化下的教师风采。

TKT 项目的参与学生除依照各自大学培养方案完成基本课程外，还要到对方大学合作实验室进行为期 1 年的科研和学习工作，毕业时可获得双硕士学位。目前，项目参与院校已联合招生十期，互派学生 158 名，其中已毕业的研究生达 110 余名。此外，东京工业大学每年派遣资深教授中长期驻清华大学进行授课指导，并派遣中青年骨干教师以短期集中授课形式到清华大学进行教学活动。以下列举的是清华大学该项目核心课程的师资配置。

纳米方向开设课程科目：

"固体物理"，1 名东工大常驻教员授课；

"纳米电子材料"，2 名东工大教员授课；

"纳米科学特论"，2 名东工大教员授课；

"量子化学"，1 名东工大常驻教员授课；

"软性材料"，2 名东工大教员授课；

"纳米材料性能测试"，2 名东工大教员授课。

生化方向开设课程科目：

"生命工学特论"，1 名清华教员授课 8 周 +1 名东工大教员短期讲座；

"生命科学特论"，1 名清华教员授课 8 周 +1 名东工大教员短期讲座；

"生体分子科学特论"，1 名清华教员授课 8 周 +1 名东工大教员短期讲座。

人文社科方向开设课程科目：

"科技与社会"，1名清华教员全学期授课+3名东工大教员短期讲座。

图7　东工大教授在清华授课

此外，项目以三个学科方向为单位，每年举办资深教授与青年学者的互访型学术研讨会。迄今为止共有70人次以上的导师接收和派遣项目学生，超过300人次参加了三个方向举行的各种形式的学术研讨会，其中包括与国内其他高校共同举办的学术活动。教师们基于共同的研究兴趣合作申请课题等，并且通过互访讲学、联合授课等多种形式深入交流，真正实现了跨越国界的相互学习和共同研究。

除了致力于保障充足优质的师资和教学方法的革新外，流动校园项目的课程体系中，三校间教育资源进行了国际化共享——远程教学。三所大学在校内选派优秀教师或邀请学术界专家，利用远程教学视频开设特别讲座科目，供"亚洲校园"项目学生和大学其他学生听讲学习。同时，项目充分利用各大学的远程设备资源开设远程教学科目，实现了三所大学教育资源的共享与教育国际化。

公共危机管理项目与新西兰维多利亚大学、泰国国家发展行政研究

图8　流动校园项目学生在远程同传教室听讲座

图9　流动校园项目学生通过远程设备听讲韩国东西大学历史课程

所合作开设了"比较公共管理"三方视频课程，获得了日、韩、新、泰学生的热烈欢迎。学院与日、韩合作的三方视频课程，包括"全球治理"、"东北亚政治经济"、"东北亚国际关系"等传统课程，也使得"亚洲校园"项目学生充分受益。

图 10　流动校园项目学生在老师指导下通过远程设备进行研究发布

5. 促进项目目标达成的多种教学平台

（1）社会科学信息化实验室平台

该平台又称"公共决策实验室"平台。公共危机管理项目积极吸收国内外先进教学经验，尊重来自各个国家学生的教育和学习理念，采取讨论式教学与实时互动相结合的教育模式。复旦大学国务学院在国际化教学研究上的成果也应用到了"亚洲校园"项目的课堂上。图 11 是项目参与学生在"公共决策实验室"上课的情景。

图 11　"公共决策实验室"教学平台

该实验室将人、计算机、互联网、数据库有机结合，围绕"国家急需、世界一流"的议题开展研究、咨询和服务工作，旨在建设一流的政府绩效管理与公共决策的计算机仿真与展示平台，以定量分析和实验技术手段为主要特色，致力于推动政府管理、公共政策绩效、外交与国际关系的学科交叉和资源整合。该实验室的计算机仿真与展示平台是一种有效的研究公共问题的工具，也是一种有效的、低成本的政策实验平台。决策者可以在此平台上进行政策实验，然后通过可视化技术事先看到可供选择的决策结果及其比较。在课堂上，教师是平台的提供者、组织者和引导者，学生则扮演着主动探寻者、参与者和合作者的角色，实现了教学模式的转型。该实验室具有实景体验、案例分析、情景模拟、头脑风暴、协同工作、应急演练、复杂决策、仿真模拟、创新实验、行为分析等多种强大功能，是一个开放、平行、双向、实时、灵活的互动性实验室和教学平台，体现了该项目的前沿性和国际化水平。

（2）理工科导师制实验室教学平台

能源与环境项目特别注重实验室学习与课堂理论学习的相互结合。中、日、韩三国大学采取统一的做法，将一年级的研究生随机分配到不同的实验室进行学习，每个实验室由一名非常熟悉实验室环境的老师负责，确保每位研究生都能在负责老师的带领下，迅速融入实验室环境中。在实验室学习的过程中，首先，各实验室负责老师将利用半天的时间为研究生介绍自己课题的研究背景及领域的发展情况，之后为研究生选定具体的研究课题，并分组进行实验，最终根据研究生的实验表现，负责老师给出相应的考评意见。通过合作学习之后，经小组讨论，研究生需要将他们的学习成果进行公开展示，以听取其他老师及学生的意见。三校不定期组织学生到专业相关的工厂、企业、政府机构和非政府机构参观考察，不断加强同工业界、地方政府及其他非政府组织间的联系。

（3）人文学科研讨辩论式教学平台

在教学方法上，流动校园项目注重培养学生研究能力、思辨能力、实践能力。该项目倡导课堂上研讨和辩论、课后实践调研的形式为主，教师指导为辅的人才培养方法，发挥教师的指导作用，激发学生观察、

分析问题的能力，培养学生团队协作、创新、实践能力。通常，教师会组织学生围绕东亚地区政治、历史、人文等热点话题进行研讨和辩论，引导学生在思维的交流和碰撞中获得更深的见解。

（三）问题剖析

课程体系方面，部分派出和接收学生规模较小的参与学校并未针对"亚洲校园"项目设计专门课程，学校已有的课程组合缺乏系统性和针对性，并不能有效支撑"亚洲校园"项目培养目标的达成，也未能有效落实"亚洲校园"项目对学生知识、能力、素质的培养要求。部分项目在因材施教的个性化培养方面存在不足，选修课学分占总学分比例偏低，学生自主选课的灵活度不够，自主学习空间较小。由于沟通协商不够充分，部分合作高校没有就成绩评定、学分转换、实习实践学分认定等相关制度达成一致，一定程度上影响了学生的积极性和学业发展。同一联合体中出现合作程度不平衡的现象，部分项目双边（两两）合作开展课程体系建设较为深入，但三边高校资源整合力度不够。部分试点项目参与高校未能很好地将本校的学科优势、科研优势和教学资源优势转化为人才培养优势，未能完全体现出"亚洲校园"试点项目人才培养的创新性和高水平。

师资及教学方面，部分项目的师资在数量和结构上仍旧不能满足项目需要，多数项目缺乏激励教师投入教学、科研和学生指导的制度和措施，教师的奖励与支持系统并未建立，教师对学生学业指导、实习实践指导和就业指导的积极性未能有效激发。部分项目教师层面的交流机制不健全，三方教师在课程设置、教材选编、联合授课、合作研究等方面并未开展深入合作。部分项目仍停留在传统讲授的教学形式，对多媒体互动式教学方式应用不充分，教师根据教学目的灵活运用情景式教学法、讨论式教学法、任务式教学法等多种教学方法的实践不够，激发学生创造性思维方面效果不明显。

三 学生支持

（一）经验总结

"亚洲校园"项目制定了相应的招生制度，对甄选、录取、派送等环节做出了明确要求，多数项目能够按照高起点、高标准的要求，对学生的报名资格、学习动机、学习计划、语言能力、思想品德等方面严格把关，通过笔试、面试、学习能力测试等多种途径选拔优秀生源，并有相关制度保证选派环节公正、透明。多数项目制定了吸引优秀生源的制度，通过项目宣传、强化校企合作优势、完善奖助体系和学生服务、规范学业衔接制度、丰富第二课堂等措施，吸引优秀生源并保障招生规模的达成。部分派出学校为学生提供了有关留学目的地的民族文化、校园文化的行前辅导，保障派出学生更快适应留学学习与生活。

多数项目都为学生创造了良好的学习环境，提供准确及时的生活服务信息；部分项目为学生提供必要的语言补习，帮助学生解决语言和专业学习上的困难。多数项目开展了丰富的第二课堂和实习实践活动，促进学生跨文化交流和学习。所有参与高校均能充分尊重国外学生的民族文化、民族情感、宗教信仰，组织丰富多样的交流活动，增强学生对不同文化的理解和接纳，同时，避免对学生进行有倾向性的政治、宗教、价值观等方面的引导。

（二）优秀实践

1. 项目具有吸引优秀生源的政策措施

能源与环境项目在三校的共同努力下，创造性地为参与学生打造独特培养方案，更好地衔接三国学生的学业生活。项目通过对学期交换、

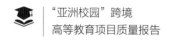
春季研讨会、国际暑期学校和秋季学术论坛的巧妙设计与安排，基本保证参加双硕士学位联合培养的研究生都可达到中、日、韩三国大学的学位申请要求，为探索"建立一个在科学和工程相关领域具有先进性和多样性的示范性教育系统"打下了坚实的基础。

流动校园项目自常态化实施以来，每年均有非常多的学生报名参加。项目选拔严格，只有为数不多的优秀学生才能通过选拔成为项目参与者。广东外语外贸大学的这一项目之所以在学生中有非常大的"魅力"，首先是源于其项目特色，即"流动校园"。大学就读期间学生可以赴日韩合作大学进行两年的流动学习，流动学习期间，有独特的课程体系与之匹配，并且可以和日韩学生一起学习、生活。这样的留学体验对学生有非常大的吸引力。其次，作为三国教育部主导实施的项目，三个国家和大学都为之配置了一定规模的资助，例如目前广东外语外贸大学学生出境学习均受留学基金委创新项目的资助。2018年起大学还将设置专门的奖学金资助"亚洲校园"项目学生出国学习。针对来华学习的学生，国家设立"亚洲校园"专项奖学金资助。对学生而言，获得奖学金资助出国，不仅是经济上的资助，更是一种荣誉，所以优秀的学生会积极报名参加项目。

传统文化项目高度重视"亚洲校园"计划的开展，冈山大学、成均馆大学、吉林大学将彼此列为全球战略中的重要战略伙伴，三所学校在"亚洲校园"项目框架下，为对方派来的师生提供经费支持，鼓励派出的优秀师生相互交流学习。三所大学选定若干重点合作学科领域，着力推动双边或三边实质性科研合作和人才联合培养，推动青年学生在三校之间自由流动，加深理解。

2. 项目具有完善的学生选派机制

流动校园项目采取校内新生选拔制度，选拔流程为报名—初审—笔试—面试。以参与学校广东外语外贸大学为例，该校每年针对新生群体，均会由"亚洲校园"教育中心通过大学官方网站、学校招生网站、教务处网站、大学微信公众号等平台进行"亚洲校园"项目招生宣传，推送关于"亚洲校园"项目的选拔信息。新生入学前，"亚洲校园"教育中心会从校方获取新生数据，经对各生源地录取分数、招生人数等数据进行分析后，确定报名条件。报名截止后，中心根据报名条件审核报考学生资格，符合条件的学生可以进入笔试环节。笔试由校方及学院相关专家命题，命题范围为东亚地区相关的政治、历史、人文等内容，主要考察考生的人文素质、思辨、写作等能力。笔试按照至少2∶1比例进行学生选拔，即选拔40～50名成绩优异的学生进入面试环节。面试教师为该校"亚洲校园"教育中心日、韩语专业教师，命题范围涉及政治、历史、语言、文化等内容，主要考察学生的语言表达、思辨及综合能力。通过以上环节，最终选拔20名学生进入"亚洲校园"项目。

能源与环境项目参与高校共同商议决定，一方可以向其他两方每年各派5名研究生参加双学位项目，即三校每年共选拔30名研究生参加双学位项目联合培养。该项目主要以硕士一年级学生为招募对象，鼓励各校在招生高校做招生宣传；在学生选拔方面，全面考察学生素质，着重关注学生的学术创新能力。例如，在上海交通大学，申请双硕士学位联合培养项目的学生由院系面试，之后面试结果须报送研究生院审核，并最终经合作院校确认录取后，申请者才能成为双硕士学位项目学生。申请到上海交通大学攻读硕士学位的其他二校学生，也须经就读学校审核选拔、向相关院系推荐，再经合作学校考核后确定是否录取。此外，为扩大项目的受益面，项目设计的春季研讨会、暑期学校和秋季学术论坛对非双学位项目的学生开放，三校各自选拔学生参加。

3. 重视学生服务工作，为学生发展构建科学的指导体系

流动校园项目面对的学生群体有两类，以参与高校广东外语外贸大学为例，一类是广外本校本科学生，另一类是合作大学派遣至广外的留

学生。对本校学生，广外"亚洲校园"教育中心组建了班主任导师、朋辈导师的指导体系。班主任导师主要从专业认同、学业规划、出国交流等方面对学生进行指导，朋辈导师主要从学习经验、奖学金申请以及出国留学经验等方面与学弟、学妹进行交流。对日、韩留学生，广外"亚洲校园"教育中心除了设置班主任导师负责其学业规划和学习指导以外，还为其配备了母语心理辅导教师。母语心理辅导老师主要负责日、韩留学生的心理健康。辅导老师经常与留学生交流，了解其在广外的学习与生活情况，以便及时把握学生心理动态，更好地帮助留学生完成在广外的学习任务。

国际关系项目、法律人才项目、传统文化项目、TKT项目、能源与环境项目等均建立了"Mentor"制度，即为每一位来华就读的日韩学生配一名语言基础较好、专业背景相近的中国学生作为学伴，帮助其适应在华留学生活，熟悉社会环境，提高中文水平，共同探讨学习和生活上的问题，从而加深三国青年间在思想、文化、观念上的沟通与交流，实现共同学习成长。

4. 加强校企合作，为学生提供实习实践支持和就业指导

公共危机管理项目定位于培养通晓亚洲风险管理问题的专家，要求学生通过系统学习风险管理知识、大量参与风险管理实践、开展硕士论文研究，为东北亚风险管理实践发展和区域内合作做出贡献。围绕这一培养目标，复旦大学着力于调动和整合校内、国内和国际的风险管理教学、学术与实践资源，以形成培养国际化风险管理人才的复合体系。该体系以丰富的实操、实训、实战资源为特色，以全英文专业课程为理论基础，以定期举办国际研讨会为有益补充。具体活动列举如下。

风险实地调研。项目组资助了留学生先后赴汉旺东汽地震遗址、汉旺居民区地震遗址、汶川大地震遗址和绵竹地震纪念馆实地调研。学生在受到地震破坏的工厂和居民区，仔细查看了地震对不同建筑材料和建

筑框架的破坏情况，听取了地震发生时的场景、地震造成的伤亡情况，以及灾后灾区人民自我救助及各省援建情况等内容的详细介绍。通过实地调研，学生进一步反思了地震发生的原因、不同震级地震可能造成的人员伤亡和物资损失以及给灾区生产生活带来的巨大影响。

图12　公共危机管理项目学员参加四川大地震遗址调研活动

应急管理实训。该项目积极组织留学生参加国际减灾应急与安全博览会。学生们参观了地震应急、火灾救援、城市安全应急以及应急后备物资及物流准备等多个分展区的顶级应急装备，还亲身体验了应急救援指挥车在自然灾害救援现场的中心决策指挥作用，对于灾害环境下管理能力的要求和应急决策时效性和紧迫性有了初步的认识。

应急救援实战。"发展中国家城市搜救能力培训"在中国召开之际，利用对三国官员进行应急管理体系建设和决策方法培训的契机，项目也组织留学生参加了理论培训。除此之外，学生们还参观了国家地震台网中心，参加了国家应急救援队的应急救援实战训练，亲身体验了国家应急救援的各个过程，以及我国应急救援管理组织体系，感受到实战性的应急管理培训和大学以理论为主的应急管理教育的差距。

流动校园项目中日韩合作大学共享实习基地资源。目前广东外语外贸大学"亚洲校园"教育中心在国内的签约基地有1个，每年可以接纳实习学生数为20名。日本、韩国的实习基地共有12个，分别是日本的保圣那（广州）人才服务有限公司、Aarata 会计师事务所（PWC Japan）、朝日新闻报社、每日新闻报社、京都市役所文化推进室、区役所、富士施乐、Mynavi、纪伊国屋书店、京都凯悦酒店、奈良酒店，以及韩国的新世界免税店。学生在四年级海外实习阶段，可以根据自己的优势和未来职业规划选择实习地点；广外学生在海外实习阶段有9名同学分别前往日本和韩国实习。此外，依托于广东地区活跃的国际交流，在广东地区举行的各类交易会也为本项目的学生提供了大量的实习机会。韩国学生在广外学习期间，就曾和中国学生一起参加中国化妆品交易会，为会场提供翻译。项目学生对中日韩三国语言的熟练使用、良好的沟通技巧，赢得了用人单位的高度评价。广东地区随着经济的发展，与日韩的合作也在进一步扩大，本项目的学生可以选择实习的场所和方式也不断增加。为了保证学生的实习和社会实践效果，本项目要求学生提交由用人单位提供的实习鉴定表，以及由学生自己进行总结的实习报告，以便及时掌握用人单位对本项目学生的评价和学生的实习成果。

（三）问题剖析

学生选派方面，部分项目的学生交流规模没有达到预期目标，派出和接收学生人数失衡，其中一个重要原因是参与学校对项目的宣传力度不够，未采取多种措施、利用多种形式和渠道对项目进行宣传，不注重在相关院系重点宣传，未在全校师生中形成共识。个别项目选拔机制不够严格，在遴选学生时对外语水平的考核不够严格，学生的外语能力达不到授课要求，而学校又未及时提供语言补习和辅导，导致学生的学习效果不佳。部分项目吸引优秀生源的措施和力度不够，通过校企合作为学生创造发展机会的措施不够，通过多种途径为学生学业发展筹措经费的力度不够。多数项目都为学生提供了行前指导，但普遍注重对学生生活及文化认知方面的指导，忽视对学业规划的指导，未提前告知培养方案、学习内容（课程及教学大纲）、学分转换及学位授予制度等重要信息。部分项目参与学生对自身的权利和义务并不明确，学生意见表达和反馈机制并未建立。

学习及生活支持方面，部分项目未能有效解决三国学生共同学习、共同生活的问题，项目参与学生的课外交流和融合不够深入。部分项目在整体组织机构建设上不够健全，导致在学生支持和服务方面人手短缺，对学生的咨询服务仅限于日常事务和行政手续办理，而在课业咨询、实习机会提供、就业支持与指导等方面较为薄弱。部分试点项目存在"生活服务多，学习支持少"的现象，学生除正常上课之外，能够获得的语言补习、补充课程、课后辅导、助教支持等机会比较少。

四　项目增值

（一）经验总结

部分项目使用问卷、采访等适当方式调查学生满意度水平及项目附加值，为项目的持续改进提供了参考。学分互换和学位互授是跨国教育合作项目的特殊需求，成熟的学分互换和学位互授体系是增强跨国教育合作项目吸引力、促进地区教育合作一体化的推动力。部分合作院校在充分沟通协商的基础上拟定学分互换制度，学分认定标准在三国间达成一致，同时，各项目通过核心课程对接、学时换算、科研活动学分化、成绩评级换算、学分上限管理等具体方式，保证了交换学分的实质等效以及所获学分质量。

在实施学位教育的项目中，合作大学之间对学位授予的通用方针、学位质量审查方法等进行了充分协商，基本达成共识。三国合作高校全面协作和对接，制定了完善的学位培养制度，形成了独特的工作机制和管理程序，在经费问题、入学标准、语言问题、学分互换、质量保障、论文审查、学位授予等方面制定了相应的制度规范，形成了鲜明的项目特色、强有力的组织实施体系、国际化的教学与实践安排、规范的学生交流和管理制度、情理相融的学生服务和发展体系，实现了项目增进三国学生和学者的相互了解和信任、推动知识交流和实践创新的战略目标。部分发展成熟的学位项目或交流项目，具备扩大到多边合作或联合授予学位的可能性的条件。

（二）优秀实践

1. 开展学生满意度调查与分析

商业领袖项目由三校联合制定该项目的评估计划，并且由联合学术委员会执行。此程序包括设计和实施学生调查问卷，并以其他调查方法收集学生、老师以及行政人员对该项目的评价和改进意见。该评估体系将收集与课程质量、服务的内容与质量以及行政效率相关的意见，完善合作交流计划。

能源与环境项目对学位课程和暑期课程的学生进行年度问卷调查。结果表明，大多数学生对课程内容和实验室的研究训练有很高的满意度。同时，参与学校也通过问卷调查收集到了学生对项目的意见和建议。问卷结果在参与大学间分享，并用于项目的持续改进。

除了实施和分析学生满意度调查和学生课程评估之外，政策联合会项目为院长/副院长提供与学生交谈的机会，鼓励学生建立一个交流沟通网络，广泛收集学生关于项目的意见和建议。

2. 通过核心课程对接、学时换算、科研活动学分化、成绩评级换算、学分上限管理等方式构建实质等效的学分体系

提供双学位课程的国际关系项目创建了一个核心课程对照表，明确

CAMPUS Asia Joint Meeting
Friday, June 28, 2013
Questionnaire

L Quality Assurance	To be answered by either professor or administrator. Please choose from the dropdpwn list. If you are practicing any of the examples, choose "yes."				Please write any comments. (Examples, reasons why not, etc)
Criteria	Examples of good practice	PKU	SNU	UT	Any Comment from Each School
Contents of Academlc Programs: Is a framework for achieving the program goals established and functioning effectively among the participating institutions?					
1 Contents of Academic Programs	The educational contets are configured in line with expected leaming outcomes (e.g. student kn owledge, skills, attitudes)—such as a need for global talent within East Asia. and have been systematically analyzed by the institution.				
2 Contents of Academic Programs	Information on the program contents, especially on curriculum stru cture and courses offerings, is shared among the participating institutions, with each program component inte grated and systematically structured.				
3 Contents of Academic Programs	It is clear that through intemational collaboration. the program adds value to education in the particlpating institutions and enhances their international competitveness.				

图 13   商业领袖项目三方联合评估问卷

了学生原就读大学提供的核心课程与合作大学的哪些课程实质等效，该对照表可作为学生学分转换的参考。通过使用该对照表（或称"映射表"），学生可以避免重复选择核心课程。

能源与环境项目自实施以来，一直致力于建立高质量的联合学分和学位授予体系；依据学生的成就，合作学校联合颁发能源与环境科学技术毕业证书和双硕士学位。为了达成双硕士学位联合培养的目的，上海交通大学、日本九州大学、韩国釜山国立大学召开了数十次三边会议，通过联合课程教学、统一教学方法、建立三国高校间有关学分转换的办法及体系，形成了一个严格的通过联合审查后方可毕业的学位授予政策，并在三校合作过程中，采用双硕士学位联合培养、国际暑期学校和国际论坛三大形式开展学生交流。该双学位项目设置了完善的学分制度，申请学位的总学分要求不少于 24 个学分，学分基本构成为"10 + 6 + X = 24"形

表 15 国际关系项目课程映射

	A 校	B 校
选择 4 门课程（8个课时）	公共管理简介	全球商业战略
	政策过程和谈判	多边贸易谈判或国际谈判模拟游戏
	公共政策的日本政治	日本政治和外交
	现代日本外交	当代日本政治中的理论与问题
	日本经济决策过程的比较分析	韩国和日本企业的比较研究
	东亚国际政治	东亚国际关系
	治理与发展	国际发展问题与合作，或全球社会治理，或国际合作
选择 2 门课程（10个课时）	国际冲突研究	国际合作，或国际冲突管理案例研究，或国际商务研讨会
	公共政策的宏观经济	国际经济关系，或汇率和国际宏观经济
	统计方法	研究方法和技能，或比较方法
必修（8 个课时）	案例研究（国际政治经济） 案例研究（日本对外经济政策） 案例研究（日本宏观经济政策：货币和财政政策的评估） 案例研究（日本宏观经济政策：货币和财政政策挑战的解决方案） 案例研究（日本的东亚政策）	商业谈判研究项目 国际合作特别研究 东亚区域合作与和平结构 东亚比较研究 国际商务研究项目 国际关系

式。其中，"10"代表日、韩留学生在交大需修读不少于 10 个学分的课程；"6"表示：该项目实行研究学习活动学分化，学生在学习期间参与两期国际暑期学校，每参加一期国际暑期学校，都将获得 3 个学分，共 6 个学分；"X"表示：日、韩学生在本国学校所修课程，可通过学分转换的方式，计入该学位项目。图 14 是上海交通大学与韩国釜山大学的双硕士学位项目学分构成图。

为规范对学生在国外高校学习成绩的认定及学分的转换，国际能源与环境项目严格依照学校的相关制度规范，对参与项目学生学分认定及成绩转换的要求和程序做了详细规定。若日、韩学生在本国获得的成绩

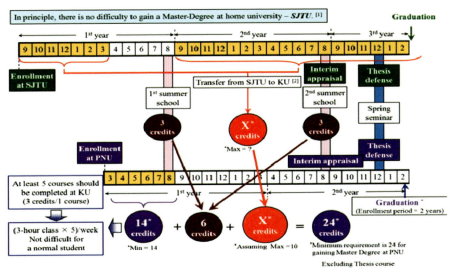

图 14　能源与环境双硕士学位项目学分构成
(上海交通大学与韩国釜山大学)

与上海交通大学有相同的评分等级，则直接以该等级登录；若为百分制，则换算成上海交通大学的评分等级后登录。每个参与大学都规定了学生可转换学分的上限。该项目开发了《成绩评级转换表》，显示如何将不同参与大学之间的不同评级标准转换为各自的百分制系统。项目要求日、韩学生在本国高校成绩在"B⁻"及"B⁻"以上的才具有参加学分转换的资格。换算标准如下。

表 16　能源与环境项目成绩评级转换

高丽大学		釜山国立大学		上海交通大学	
分　数	文字评级	分　数	字母评级	分　数	字母评级
90～100	秀	95～100	A⁺	96～100	A⁺
		90～94	A	90～95	A
80～90	优	85～89	B⁺	85～89	A⁻
		80～84	B	80～84	B⁺
70～80	良	75～79	C⁺	75～79	B
		70～74	C	70～74	B⁻

续表

高丽大学		釜山国立大学		上海交通大学	
分　　数	文字评级	分　　数	字母评级	分　　数	字母评级
		65～69	D$^+$	67～69	C$^+$
60～70	可	60～64	D	63～66	C
				60～62	C$^-$
＜60	不可	＜60	F	0～59	D

完成学分的双硕士学位生在第三年的春季学期开始向中方学校申请硕士学位，最终获得双硕士学位。该项目首批双硕士学位学生已于2015年3月取得双硕士学位。此外，该项目的三国合作也寻求建立国际联合研究生院，这个联合研究生院将实行统一的入学、课程和对外交流，探讨创新机制，建立一个在科学和工程相关领域具有先进性和多样性的示范教育系统。

法律人才项目中，参加大学要求合作方提前提供教学大纲，在详细讨论对方大学的学分制度和授课时间数等学分相关内容后，实施学分的互换认定。三国参加大学的计划负责人和教职员工参加定期质量保障（QA）会议，在该会议上对计划课程和质量保障交换意见，比较1学分的授课时间后再确定学分互换的方法。根据在QA会上确定的互换方式，三国学校确定日本和中国之间的1学分仍以1学分进行交换，而在韩国取得的3学分在日本将被作为4学分进行交换。此外，项目在实施系级交换留学的过程中实施学分互换的上限管理。例如，如从日本派遣到中国，半学期最多可互换22学分（必修科目和选择科目）；如从日本到韩国留学则半学期最多可互换21学分（必修科目和选择科目）。

流动校园项目中，参与学校根据项目培养目标，对流动校园期间提供的课程进行校际比较并调整。做出调整后，学生在其他大学取得的课程将被认可为原就读大学的语言课程或特殊课程。此外，由于每所大学的课程时间和学分认证标准不同，参与学校还努力调整教学时间以便更好地衔接，并通过补充课程的方式，确保学生在原就读大学获得适当的学分认证。大学之间的这些调整的结果被列入《"亚洲校园"项目指南》的学生手册。

TKT项目也在各参加大学的学校规则中，确定了在留学地取得的学分的移管或互换的上限数。并且，该项目中有双方导师联合授课的核心课程，经双方协商一致，其学分既可作为学生在清华大学获得的学分，也可以作为学生在东京工业大学获得的学分。关于研究活动的学分授予，本项目中的清华大学实施了一项政策，在暑假和寒假期间前往国外求学的本科学生，其研究成果可获得1个学分（最多5个学分）。

在同样关注基于实验室研究活动的化学与材料项目中，在合作大学的实验室活动可被视为研究实习。学生留学期间和原就读大学的学期相重合时，可以在原就读大学获得学分并获得认可。参加国际实习的学生可根据其回国后提交的报告内容获得学分确认。

3. 完善的结业和学位授予政策

在能源与环境项目中，联合体在合作备忘录中明确了双学位授予政策，包括选派学生、入学手续、课程提供、学分转换、双学位课程、奖学金和保险、计划—实施—检查—行动（PDCA）委员会和问题解决等。学生完成要求学分的学习后，三所大学的学术人员对双学位学生的硕士论文进行联合审查。除了论文联合评审之外，学生还需要按照其原就读大学的常规标准通过论文评审，并达到获得学位的要求。

公共危机管理项目对学生提出了较高的毕业要求，规定低于"C"（GPA2.0）的成绩不计入总学分；学生完成不少于30个学分后，通过中期考核，在硕士论文指导委员会的指导下按要求完成论文。如果学生

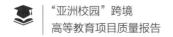
已经在原就读大学和留学大学获得必要的学分并通过论文答辩，则根据
两所大学的学位授予评审政策，授予其两所大学的学位。该政策的基础
是参与大学之间的双学位协议和各大学的规则。

（三）问题剖析

学生满意度方面，各参与学校通过经费、人员、资源的投入和保
障，为学生创造了较好的学习和生活环境，学生对在校学习、文化体验
基本满意。但部分学校信息收集手段和测评手段过于简化，未能全面深
入地了解学生的学习生活体验，对学生参加"亚洲校园"项目所获得
的附加值（即参加同类专业项目无法实现的价值）了解不够深入，也
未能从参与教师、用人单位的视角对满意度进行补充。学生对学习过程
体验和就业状况总体满意，但部分学生反映希望完善学分转换等相关制
度，同时加强就业指导。由于各项目在运行模式和人才培养方式上存在
较大差异，不同项目之间参与学生的满意度存在较大程度的不平衡现
象。多数项目还需要进一步将学生满意度测评结果有效运用于推进教学
和学习生活体验质量的改进。

学分转换及学位授予方面，部分项目联合体内协商沟通不充分，在
成绩评定、学分互换、实习实践学分认定等制度方面还存在不配套现
象，三边课程体系的一致性和等效性还有待进一步提高。目前，多数项
目采取的是学位互授的方式，很少项目探索学位联授；由于中日韩三国
教育部对学位授予的要求不同，部分项目的联合培养模式与成果虽趋于
成熟，但现阶段仍不能实现学位共同授予。如能实现三所大学联合授予
学位，不仅能更进一步地扩大三所大学在中日韩三国的影响力，也将启
发更多高校探索国际化合作办学的新模式，推动中日韩高等教育合作办
学，从而推动东北亚教育区域一体化的发展。与学分转换和学位授予等
相关的信息，应进一步在参与学生间分享，以便让学生合理规划学业。

五　内部质量保障

（一）经验总结

提高"亚洲校园"项目的质量，探索建立大学交流与质量保障的有效运行机制，是《中日韩有质量保障的大学交流与合作指导方针》中明确提出的要求。对于具体负责实施试点项目的各大学而言，建立有效的内部质量保障体系是三国大学达成的共识。

部分参与高校将"亚洲校园"项目纳入本校日常教学过程中的评教、评学等质量保障环节，多数高校同时考虑到了跨国教育合作项目的特殊性，注重项目整体质量的提升和学生学习体验。多数项目都通过联合体自我评估、学生反馈问卷报告、校—院—系三级委员会定期会议制度、管理人员信息交流平台、教职工联席会议以及学生学习成果测验机制等，采集和分析学生的学习情况和学习效果，定期对教学资源配置、课程设置、教学内容等重要事项进行审核，持续改进项目存在的问题，保证教学质量和教学目标的有效达成。这些措施均体现了三国高校对项目一体化管理和项目整体质量提升的重视，同时也体现了项目"以学生为中心"，重视学生就读体验、成果达成和满意度的基本原则。

"亚洲校园"项目虽然规模有限，但成效显著、经验丰富，部分高校采取了多种措施对其进行广泛宣传。例如，利用项目宣传手册、项目专题网站、报纸和电台等媒体报道、专刊专报、宣传视频等，面向社会广泛宣传项目的内容和成效。这些宣传措施有利于提高项目的吸引力，增强各参与方的积极性，促使高校总结项目实施经验，促进项目的可持续发展。

（二）优秀实践

1. 项目开展联合体自我评估

为了建立项目运行情况的定期协调机制，及时商讨并解决项目运行中出现的问题，法律人才项目由三国六校项目主任和分管教务人员组成了"'亚洲校园'项目质量保障委员会"（Campus Asia Project Quality Assurance Committee）。自2011年12月以来，项目质量保障委员会先后在日本名古屋，中国上海、北京，韩国首尔举行了近20次工作会议。会上，与会者既会分享已经接收学生的学习、生活情况，对下一期学生的选派提出建议，也会对现有课程设置及项目的发展计划做出深入讨论。定期协调机制对于精细化学生管理、将项目设计落到实处发挥了重要作用。

商业领袖项目要求学生完成联合体提供的密集课程后，针对项目提交改进意见和建议。由三国学术人员组成的课程委员会将对学生意见和建议进行审查，并充分讨论，以帮助改进下一期课程。

传统文化项目在项目运行阶段注重对项目质量及执行效果的关注和测评，定期召开研讨会汇报并讨论项目进展情况及各方关注的问题，协商制定下一步项目执行计划。三方大学从国际标准角度及教职员工发展角度进行项目检验，保证项目质量及项目参与人员的资质。此外，三方大学引入同行互审制度，在相互交流教学经验的同时保证教学质量。校内有关单位也已将"亚洲校园"项目的管理与教学纳入常态化、机制化的操作轨道，在明确项目细节、总结以往经验的基础上进一步加强对项目各环节的质量保障。在具体监管上，"亚洲校园"项目教学质量监控工作由主管校长领导，实行校院两级负责，建立教学管理组织协调系统，由研究生院、教务处、国际合作与交流处和相关教学科研单位对项目课堂教学及专项教学工作进行管理和监控，以及时解决教学中出现的问题，更好地适应项目学生的需求。

2. 校内外质量保障措施多举并行

流动校园项目内部质量保障措施

（1）广东外语外贸大学每学期及时跟进学生评教工作和教师评学工作，将涉及日韩学生的课程与合作大学实行数据共享，与之共同分析评价结果，及时发现、解决问题。此外，广外"亚洲校园"教育中心积极与学生、教师开展座谈活动，针对课程安排、教学方法、课外指导等进行具体交流，收集教师、学生意见，以不断改进教学模式，提高人才培养的效果。试点项目学生毕业后，"亚洲校园"教育中心对其开展跟进工作，及时了解学生毕业后的职业发展情况和用人单位对其的评价情况，了解毕业生对项目的满意度，以不断完善项目运营。

（2）广东外语外贸大学项目领导小组和学校职能部处定期对项目运营、课堂教学、办公室工作进行审查，听取"亚洲校园"教育中心工作汇报，与教师、项目学生座谈，了解学生培养工作的开展成果以及项目推进中遇到的问题，给予指导意见。

流动校园项目外部质量保障措施

（1）上级主管部门或同类院校来访时，广东外语外贸大学及时向其汇报项目推进的具体情况，介绍项目运营的成果，安排专家随堂听课，与师生座谈，派发项目报告书，共同探讨项目持续发展的方法。教育部学位评估中心、教育部留学基金委、中日韩三国合作秘书处等多次前来广外"亚洲校园"教育中心开展项目检查和调研工作，在肯定该项目运营成果的基础上，指出项目运营中可能出现的问题，并就项目的长远发展和示范推广等给予指导意见。

（2）广外"亚洲校园"教育中心及时整理汇总工作资料、运营成果，翻译中日韩三国语言资料，与日韩大学共同接受中日韩教育部的测评。在2014年举行的中日韩教育部中期测评中，流动校园项目获得日本文部省S级评价（最高级）、韩国教育部前三名的评价、中国教育部"优秀运营项目"评价。在2016年教育部进行的试点项目运营最终评价上，该项目获得了S级评价（最高级），三校被授予试点项目优秀运营单位。在进行扩大"亚洲校园"项目实施的院校征集阶段，教育部宣布该项目可无需参加遴选，直接作为正式项目继续运营。

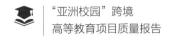

通过自上而下、内外共同监督的方式，流动校园项目的运营一直在科学规范的质量保障下推进，学生培养的质量、项目运营的模式也一直在不断提高、完善。

TKT项目联合培养研究生，在多年实践中形成了由多项措施推进的校内外质量保障机制。在校内环节，形成上级教育管理部门—学校—院系的多层管理监督机制，对教育质量、项目成效、师生参与等方面进行把控；在校外环节，由于有些项目都是教授联合培养、联合授课，所以由学校对学生培养质量进行评价和控制。该项目成果和质量还受到学生、家长以及社会相关部门的监督。该项目以联合运行工作委员会为支撑，每年召开一次全体工作会议，讨论联合培养中的重大问题，为项目的顺利实施提供了保证；以已有的学生培养平台为基础，建立联合项目学生和导师对项目效益及成果的评价及反馈机制。学生所到院系对学生的教学安排和日常质量进行管理，以定期检查、考试等环节检验学生的学习质量。同时，互认学分的交换项目还会出具成绩单供合作院校进行认定。学校规定学生完成项目后要提交一份学习总结，包括学习收获和感悟、对项目的意见和建议等。

3. 可持续发展与教学质量监控

公共危机管理项目自建立以来，形成了一系列专门的管理办法和制度，实现了与院校留学生管理制度的对接。项目通过有效的资金利用机制和信息定期汇报制度，保障了自身的可持续发展。同时，该项目还注重教学质量的提升和管理，形成了完备的教学质量监控措施。

资金保障。复旦大学国务学院将"亚洲校园"项目置于"公共管理"英文硕士学位项目中，通过后者招收自费留学生获得学费收入来补贴"亚洲校园"项目的运作，为项目的良性运行和可持续发展提供了长期的资金规划和费用保障。

项目信息公开。该项目建立了项目发展的专报制度，定期通过学校留学生办公室向教育部提供"亚洲校园"项目专报，目前已经累计提交了15份专报。

教学质量监控。项目除开展学院领导和项目主任听课制度外，还制定了学位项目评价表，全面系统地对项目设计、生源与录取、课程与培养、师资队伍以及项目管理的5个一级指标、16个二级指标开展自评与互评，并不断根据评估结果对教学质量监控相关措施进行调整和完善。项目建立了定期会议制度，分析项目建设中存在的问题并进行调整，以及明确下一步的工作重点和要求。三校之间也通过定期会晤，形成了制度化的合作机制和高度的相互信任。在每个学期课程结束后，项目请学生对教师的授课时间、授课内容、授课方式以及课程设计进行全面评估，并根据学生反馈给任课教师提供全面系统的授课评估报告，从而保证了授课教师与学生之间的需求沟通和良性互动。

4. 注重项目成果宣传

流动校园项目通过三方合作有效确保项目组织实施及运行质量，重视对学生学习成果的检验，并注重对项目信息的公开和项目成果的宣传，提升项目的吸引力。

三边合作。三国大学均设立"亚洲校园"办公室，办公室之间建立群邮、文件中转站等交流平台，及时共享信息，共同开展工作。为把握项目运营方向，三国办公室行政人员及主要参与教师每个月定期举行远程视频工作会议，汇报项目运营、学生的学习及活动等情况，总结项目实施过程中遇到的问题；三所大学每年定期举行三次三国教职工联席会议，就上一年度项目的运营进行总结，并就下一年度的课程设置、教学活动、学生服务等进行讨论协商，共同推进、完善项目的运营。

成果检验。三校通过举行演讲比赛，检验学生的语言能力；目前三国学生能够互相用熟练的中、日、韩三国语言进行交流。同时，项目通过不定期举办精英领导型人才论坛、人文学研究论坛、亚洲校园论坛等学术活动，安排学生进行专题发表，检验学生专业学术水平、团体协作能力等。

项目宣传。本项目独特的运营体制、人才培养的优秀成果得到了三国教育部门和教育机构的广泛且高度的认可。项目注重以适当方式向社会公开项目内容、取得成效等信息，提高了项目的吸引力。针对该项目的内容和成效，三国联合进行了广泛而有影响力的报道。以下是 2011 年至 2016 年期间，中国、日本、韩国的各大新闻报纸，以及电视、网络、杂志等社会媒体中部分有代表性的报道材料。

图15　《广州日报》大力宣传流动校园项目

中国在线> 华南地区

广东外语外贸大学"亚洲校园计划"每年提供百个奖学金名额

2012-03-27 14:36:46　来源:中国日报广东记者站

🖶 打印文章　📧 发送给我好友　　

　　3月26日下午,广东外语外贸大学"亚洲校园计划"项目领导小组会议举行,会议就如何建立和完善"亚洲校园计划"项目进行讨论和分工。

　　校长仲伟合在会议中指出,此次广外入选"亚洲校园"试点项目是学校近年来教育国际化努力的成果,能与北京大学、清华大学等国内名校一同入选,同时也说明教育部对广外的信任。"亚洲校园"项目中,试点学校每年有100个中国政府奖学金名额提供给在项目框架下来华学习的本科生、硕士研究生和博士研究生。希望广外能够把"亚洲校园"项目成功做下来并发掘真正优质的学生并且让他们受益。

　　副校长方凡泉布置了广外有关"亚洲校园"项目中各部门的分工内容后,各部门就课程设置、教学方案及应急预案等方面进行了进一步的讨论,并希望最快在明年2月份开始派送和接收"亚洲校园"项目的交换生。

　　来源:中国日报广东记者站　编辑:冯媛

图16　《中国日报》报道流动校园项目

表17　"亚洲校园"项目媒体报道

国别	报道媒体	时　　间	内　　容
中国	广州日报	2011 年 11 月 7 日	广外将与日韩两大学互认学位
中国 日本	中国日报 京都新聞	2012 年 3 月 27 日 2012 年 6 月 19 日	广东外语外贸大学"亚洲校园计划"每年提供百个奖学金名额
日本	京都新聞	2012 年 8 月 2 日	日・韓・中連携講座:フィールドワークの様子
日本	朝日新聞	2013 年 6 月 7 日	移動キャンパス紹介
韩国	朝鮮日報	2013 年 9 月 4 日	동서대학교에서개강한한중일 3국대이동수업
日本	読売新聞	2013 年 9 月 6 日	被災地研修
日本	【TV】每日放送（MBS）报道番组	2013 年 9 月 6 日	移動キャンパス2 学期特集
日本	日経ビジネス	2013 年 10 月 14 日	特集「世界のトップ大学」
韩国	파이낸셜뉴스	2013 年 11 月 29 日	캠퍼스아시아사업한국하기종강 장제국동서대총장특강

续表

国别	报道媒体	时　　间	内　　容
日本	日経新聞	2014 年 6 月 19 日	移動キャンパス紹介
韩国	东亚日报	2014 年 11 月 20 日	상대를보는시야와이해의폭을넓히는국적초월한뜨거운토론
日本	朝日新聞	2015 年 4 月 7 日	日中韓三国協力国際フォーラム
中国	人民网	2016 年 1 月 17 日	中日韩"亚洲校园"项目实现常态化毕业后或将拿三国证书

（三）问题剖析

自我评估方面，多数项目质量自我评估管理制度有待进一步健全，机构、人员、经费、责权落实尚不到位，质量标准缺乏针对性、执行不够刚性，影响了项目的高质量开展。联合体共同开展自我评估力度不够，对联合体内的资源整合与三边合作程度监控不深入，存在三国重视程度不一致的现象。项目自我评估方式较为单一，评教和问卷形式较为集中，缺乏对学生学习体验和学习满意度等方面的深度调查。参与高校的主体责任、质量意识和质量文化有待加强。

质量持续改进方面，部分项目缺乏对教学资源配置、课程设置、教学内容的定期审核机制，质量监控的反馈和持续改进尚未到位，决策、执行、评价、反馈、改进闭环系统衔接不够。多数项目接受同行评价和外部评审的意识和主动性不强，尚未建立起从外部对项目进行质量保障的长效机制。学校以适当的方式向社会公开项目内容、取得成效等信息，提高项目的吸引力和发展的可持续性等方面力度不够。

"亚洲校园"计划质量提升建议

伴随高等教育全球化的发展，跨境教育合作与交流日益频繁，学生、师资、理念、管理、制度等各类教育要素在全球和区域间的流动日益活跃，各国、各地区彼此相互影响和交融，逐渐向合作共赢的方向发展。《关于做好新时期教育对外开放的若干意见》指出，要进一步促进教育领域合作共赢，增进区域教育合作交流，推动大学联盟建设，深入推进友好城市、友好学校教育深度合作，深化双边多边教育合作。"亚洲校园"项目是一项对促进东亚地区高等教育合作与交流、深化东亚地区各国间的互利共赢合作具有重大意义的教育交流计划，计划的实施为东亚地区跨国教育合作和教育一体化发展进行了有益探索。"亚洲校园"项目实施五年以来，在教育部国际合作与交流司的大力推动、支持和指导下，有关高校精心策划和认真组织实施，教育部评估中心提供质量监控和评估的专业化服务，普遍取得了良好效果。项目高校克服了体制、文化、习俗差异的限制，在人才培养模式、课程教学、师资、学分互认与学位互授、质量保障等方面总结出一系列可借鉴、可推广的优秀实践，这对于促进项目的可持续发展、探索东亚地区多边教育合作模式及教育一体化等方面具有重大意义和示范作用。

　　"亚洲校园"项目参与方的积极探索和优秀实践，为进一步提升项目整体质量、扩大项目规模、深化项目建设提供了信心。在未来项目的持续发展过程中，应集中力量将好的项目做深、做实、做强、做精，使其更广泛、更有效地发挥效用、产生影响。同时，针对项目不足之处进行持续改进，着眼全球、面向世界，借鉴国际先进理念和经验，在推进多边合作、核心课程对接、学分互认互换、课程与联合学位授予及认证等工作方面取得实质性的突破与创新。基于上文的分析，我们对"亚洲校园"计划的质量提升提出以下建议。

一 注重项目全过程管理，完善项目进退机制

"亚洲校园"项目每五年为一个周期，每个周期包含项目宣传、项目遴选、合作计划、实施运行、质量控制和考核评价等重要环节，加强每一个环节的管理，对项目进行全过程指导与监控，对促进项目可持续发展、提升项目质量有着重要意义。项目宣传环节，政府部门应充分利用各种资源和渠道，鼓励并吸引高校参与项目，并面向校、院、系等多个层级的管理人员和学校师生广泛宣传项目，提高高校对项目的关注和重视程度。项目遴选环节，应进一步对项目的"高起点"、"特色"与"合作基础"进行把关，确保参选项目不流于传统交换学习和联合培养的一般形式，确保项目涉及的专业领域凸显并发挥三边学术优势，符合项目"为亚洲地区培养杰出人才"的目标定位，同时，确保项目三边学校具有一定的合作基础，校领导对教育合作比较重视。相关部门应针对上述一点严格把关，对不符合要求的项目不予批准。在合作计划拟定环节，政府部门应给予相应的指导，考察合作学校是否就项目目标进行充分沟通，并对人才培养在知识、能力、素质等方面有明确、具体的要求；参与学校应确保项目的质量基准，同时确保项目目标得到校内各方的认同、支持与配合。在实施运行环节，应进一步健全项目的组织机制建设，设置专人专岗负责项目具体工作，加强各相关职能部门和院系间的协调，明确各方职责，共同做好项目的组织实施、教学管理以及学生

服务等各项工作。在质量监控环节，应按照项目质量标准，建立健全内部质量管理制度，完善教学评价、学生满意度调查、毕业生质量跟踪调查等质量监控制度，定期主动接受外部质量评估，并根据内外部评估反馈意见进行持续改进，形成质量保障闭环系统。在项目考核评价环节，建议引入项目进退机制，基于对项目的质量监控与评估，对不重视（未设专人专岗，人、财、物保障严重不足，教师学生积极性不高）、不落实（项目的预期招生数常年存在较大缺口，教学活动未正常开展，学生服务体系未建立等）的项目，敦促其尽快整改，如改进不力，应及时停止对其拨款资助，经委员会商议批准后撤销其项目资格。对积极建设、成效明显的项目，应予以政策倾斜，例如提供更多专项活动经费保障特色项目的开展。

二 探索建立跨境高等教育学习成果互认制度

建立学习成果互认制度是跨境教育质量保障的关键环节，是实现各国间教育相认及教育国际化真正"落地"的前提保障。目前，各大学的学分制度规定如学习时间、修业年限、学期时间、成绩计算方式等因国家而有所不同，项目参与高校针对"亚洲校园"项目的学习成果互认管理主体不明，责任旁落，在实际操作中管理较为混乱。校级教育部门或外事管理部门或针对交流学习、联合培养中涉及的学分互认、学位互授问题统一管理并进行质量监控，或督促项目合作方针对项目特殊情况签订学习成果互认协议形成最终管理方案，鼓励合作方签署学位互授、学位联授、双重或多重学位等的发展协议，摸索学校层面跨境教育互认的各种策略。通过制度的健全，明确责任主体、认可标准及程序，提高学分转换和成绩评定的科学性、等效性、程序性和透明性，让不同教育系统的学生在交换学校所修的学分能做有效的转换，学习成绩能够获得实质等效的评定，减少学习成果互认过程中的阻碍，进而促进区域

内学生的流动。一套健全的学习成果互认制度，也有效保证了学生学习交流活动的质量，使区域内的人员流动有更实质的意义，同时也提升项目的吸引力。相关部门及人员须紧密合作，才能有效监督与确保成果互认系统的运作及发挥功能。

三　深化中日韩三国大学跨国协同培养机制

"亚洲校园"项目与区域内的传统的双边合作模式不同，强调中、日、韩三边高校作为一个联合体，在联合体内优势互补、强强联合。这种多边合作模式的困难程度远超传统模式，在文化、语言、教育制度等方面均存在不一致、不对接的问题；而一旦克服困难，做深、做精，项目的影响和带给学生的附加价值也将远超传统模式。三边应进一步深化整合中日韩三国大学的优势资源，同时借助中日韩三国政府、非政府组织、企业、研究机构等社会力量，共同培养人才。创新人才培养模式，推动课程体系的联合开发，充分挖掘教师资源，促进教师团队联合授课，增强校企协作，安排学生实习或进行职业体验，加强学生的社会实践能力。三边应通过学校层面、学院层面、师生层面的跨国培养协同机制的建设，确保在项目各环节同一理解，同步发展，同频共振，共同发声，最终产生 1 + 1 + 1 > 3 的效果。

四　建立激励支持机制，提升师生积极性

教师的投入和学生的参与是确保"亚洲校园"项目持续开展的重要因素。对"亚洲校园"项目的两轮质量监控显示，部分教师和学生参与项目的积极性不高，主要原因是激励支持机制的缺乏。对教师而言，绝大多数项目都是借助已有的教师资源为"亚洲校园"项目学生授课，教师除了要完成基本工作外，还要将大量科研时间投入"亚洲校园"项目的教学工作。为此，应建立相关激励支持机制，将与"亚

洲校园"项目相关的工作纳入教师考评和考核，使之形成竞争优势，提升教师参与的积极性，吸引更多优秀学术人才和高水平教师参与课程研发和项目教学。对学生而言，由于三边学习时间、修业年限、学期时间等存在差异，学分认定和转换存在障碍，部分学生在外研修学分得不到认定，返校后需要花费大量精力来达到本校学分要求；学生留学期间参加科研项目、学术发表、社会实践等活动，但缺乏相关制度将这些课程以外的学习活动转换成等效学分；项目为学生就业带来的附加值还有待进一步提升。为此，应建立学分转换，社会活动学分认定，提供区别于传统分数成绩单、而是增强学生就业竞争力的"综合成绩单"等激励支持机制和措施，让更多学生积极、安心地参与项目学习并学有所获。

一 引言

根据中国、日本、韩国达成的三方共识,"亚洲校园"试点项目旨在开拓亚洲更美好的未来。该项目促进了中日韩三国大学在质量保障领域的合作与交流,在东北亚建立历史和文化方面创建区域意识,通过三国教育交流活动,培养未来领导者对区域和平以及共存的愿景。

中日韩三国质量保障机构,包括中方的教育部高等教育教学评估中心、日本的大学评价与学位授予机构(现为大学学位授予与质量提升机构)以及韩方的韩国大学教育协会大学评估院,设立了中日韩质量保障机构协作会。由于国际教育质量保障模式是各国面临的共同问题,协会协商共同实施"亚洲校园"试点项目质量监控。

不同于判断学术项目是否符合最低质量标准的评价体系,"亚洲校园"监控待考察项目当前的状态及概况,从教育质量的角度出发选择优秀实践案例,同时在国内外广泛宣传这些案例。

三国的质量保障机构对 10 个学术项目进行了两轮监控。2013 ~ 2014 年,对各国项目分别实施第一轮监控,将各国的相关规定及评估体系和方法考虑在内;随后,对各国的监控标准及方法进行比较分析。2015 ~ 2016 年,三国的质量保障机构联合建立了统一的质量保障框架,

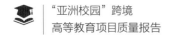
包括相关标准、原则及流程等，并实施了第二轮监控。在联合监控过程中，来自中日韩三国的专家根据各联合体提供的自评报告开展了材料评审及现场考察活动，对包含优秀实践案例的监控结果进行汇编并广泛宣传。

2015年试点项目结束之后，2016年秋，三国政府启动了以第二轮监控模式为模板的较为成熟的"亚洲校园"计划。三国基于长期发展的愿景，决定持续讨论将"亚洲校园"计划扩展到整个东盟地区的可行性。同时，在此模式下，三国质量保障机构参考这些指导方针实施监控，进一步确保质量保障活动，根据第一种模式中积累的丰富经验以及三国开展的密切合作，进一步加强监控，同时与各国政府开展合作。

我们希望，优秀实践案例的监控和宣传对国际合作学术项目（包括"亚洲校园"计划）的质量保障有加强和巩固作用，为取得相应学习成果的优秀学生提供支持，同时促进各质量保障机构之间的国际合作。

二　目的

三国质量保障机构从制定传统质量保障方法过程中获得经验，制定联合指导方针，来开展未来的"亚洲校园"计划质量保障活动。

联合指导方针的第一个目的是，具体说明国际合作学术项目（"亚洲校园"计划）的监控方法，确保质量保障机构及专家能够清晰了解监控标准、流程及方法，并在"亚洲校园"计划的下一模式中以传统方式落实。

第二个目的是，其他质量保障机构在实施国际合作学术项目监控/评估时（特别是与其他国家机构合作时），及为高等教育机构进行国际合作教育的内部质量保障时提供参考。

凭借在"亚洲校园"计划联合监控方面的经验，三国的质量保障机构制定了本指导方针所述的联合质量保障框架，建立了互信关系。从这个意义上讲，这使三国的质量保障机构采取共同的质量保障框架。在某一质量保障机构实施质量监控时，可由三国的联合监控委员会做出最终决定。

我们希望本指导方针能够提高中日韩三国及其他国家质量保障活动的水平。根据全球质量保障的趋势以及各大学国际合作教育的情况，三国的质量保障机构将致力于不断完善并改进本指导方针。

三 质量监控指导方针

1. 总原则

（1）促进国际合作学术项目质量提升；

（2）基于三国联合标准及程序实施监控；

（3）考察所有联合体的进展和成绩，确定各自的优秀实践案例；

（4）考察参与大学在国际合作教育项目资源整合和质量保障方面的合作程度；

（5）检查每个"亚洲校园"试点项目的持续质量改进情况；

（6）重视学生对"亚洲校园"项目的意见和建议。

2. 执行监控人员组成

（1）联合监控委员会是实施监控的决策主体机构。委员会根据实际流程的执行情况设立了监控专家组。

（2）联合监控委员会委员和监控专家组成员无权就任何与他们自身相关的项目进行决策。

（3）联合监控委员会由3名专家组成（其中1名来自质量保障机构），由各国的质量保障机构指定，负责：①确认及完成最终联合监控报告；②公布官方最终联合监控报告。

（4）联合监控委员会委员最好具备有关国际合作学术项目和质量

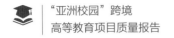
保障方面的知识和经验。

（5）监控专家组成员由各国质量保障机构指定，负责：①评审自评报告，撰写材料评审报告；②进行现场考察；③编写联合体监控报告。

（6）监控专家组成员最好具备有关国际合作学术项目、质量保障以及各项目专业领域的知识和经验。

（7）各质量保障机构最好指定监控专家组的至少一名成员。在各质量保障机构无法指定成员的情况下，监控专家组最好安排了解相关国家的成员。

（8）最好对监控专家组成员安排相关培训，以便监控专家组成员了解质量保障活动的实施标准。在对各国监控专家组成员进行培训期间，三国质量保障机构应相互配合，确保培训内容相同。

（9）监控专家组内部成员（例如主席和协调员）应予以说明。

3. 监控流程

总体监控流程如下。

（1）推荐为联合体提供有关质量保障（监控）目的及实施方式的培训，以便其对这些内容充分了解。三国质量保障机构应相互合作，为各国大学提供相同或相似内容的培训。

（2）各联合体必须联合撰写及提交一份该联合体所有参与大学出具的共同（联合）自评报告，描述其优秀实践案例及十个标准中需要改进的问题。

（3）监控专家组成员审读所提交的自评报告材料。

（4）监控专家组成员进行现场考察，问询材料评审中尚未证实的问题，采访项目负责人、参与该项目的教职人员以及需被纳入现场考察计划的学生。建议各国参与大学代表都在场时进行现场考察。

（5）监控专家组成员根据评审材料及现场考察结果出具一份联合体报告草稿。如果报告草稿采用当地语言，应给出对应的英文版本。

（6）质量保障机构督促联合体对监控报告草稿进行审核，确保不含任何事实性错误。若存在事实性错误，监控分委会将对其进行审议。

（7）联合监控委员会委员共享三国质量保障机构联合体完成的监控报告。质量保障机构根据所有联合体的监控报告，拟定总联合监控报告草稿。

（8）联合监控委员会完成总联合监控报告。

（9）利用包括书籍、网络及研讨会等形式广泛宣传总联合监控报告。

4. 监控标准及观测点

质量保障的相关监控标准及观测点如下所述，用于确定项目的现状及其质量改进活动。在对各个标准进行监控时，参见优秀实践案例确定的观测点。

所预见的观测点包括但不限于下列项。

（1）目标

通过参与大学之间展开讨论，明确定义人才培养的愿景。

清晰阐述目标，包括与学生知识、技能及态度习得相关的预期学习成果。参与大学一致认可项目目标。

参与大学师生共同分享项目目标，各机构都一致理解这些目标。

项目目标作为学术项目建立及执行的指导方针。

项目目标根据五年规划实现，项目可产生优质的活动及成果。

（2）组织管理

参与大学之间达成的书面协议中清晰阐述了关于跨校组织结构、各大学与学生相关的责任以及相关费用的分配情况方面的基本政策，并由这些参与大学执行这些政策。

各参与大学定期召开会议，建立关于项目执行情况及相关问题的评审机制，共同承担解决共同问题的责任。

在学术监督适用的情况下，各参与大学相互配合建立及执行相应的

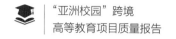
监督体系。

清晰确定各大学执行国际合作项目的责任以及涉及其他部门（如国际部、学生支持部及评估事务部）的支持系统。

参与大学同意基于过去五年来的经验来支持该项目，并正在考虑支持该项目所需的组织结构及计划。同时，各大学获得关于支持该项目的大学范围内的同意。

（3）课程

课程由各参与大学联合设计。

各参与大学之间共享每个大学的课程信息。

教学内容适用于项目目标的实现。

教学内容与预期学习成果相符（如学生的知识、技能及态度）。

教学内容和方法适用于国际合作教育。

澄清项目方法/内容与其学习成果之间的关系。

（4）师资

保证提供充足的合格教师以支持跨国合作项目的执行。

建立规定教学内容（如调配教师的联合监督、远程学习）以及合作大学教师参与的体系。

开展以获得国际能力为目的的教师发展与能力培养工作。

提供激励和支持系统，吸引对项目持续实施起积极促进作用的国际优秀教师。

教育教学方法符合要求，适合留学生（即采用双语教材、英文授课、课后或业余辅导教材）。

（5）学生录取

广泛宣传项目信息，招收有上进心的学生。

学生选拔流程（选择标准及体系）以项目的教学目的及内容为基础，由各参与大学联合确定并开展。

保证学生的预期数量。

被录取学生的学术水平适合项目目标及课程。

（6）学习及生活支持

参与大学共享课上所需的必要的信息，同时向学生提供足够的离境前课程指导。

向参与项目的学生提供各种学习支持，包括教学助理提供的语言培训、辅助课程及支持。

向参与项目的学生提供各种生活支持，包括入学指导、辅导、风险灾害管理及职业支持。

向参与项目的学生提供足够的学习环境，包括图书馆、IT 设备及实验设施。

向参与项目的学生提供足够且适当的奖学金及住宿支持。

参与大学支持学生和校友之间的交流及互动。

（7）学习成果

根据预期学习成果，确定适当的学习成果衡量方法，持续衡量学习成果。

分析学生课程报名、学分获取及其学习成果之间的关系。

基于项目目的取得相应的学习成果。

学生对项目内容非常满意，且取得很大的进步。

各参与大学共享学生满意度及学习成果调查结果。

通过国际合作项目获得要实现的学习成果（增值成果）。

持续跟进毕业生的状况，并与参与大学共享。

（8）学分转换、评分系统以及学位授予

各合作大学相互了解各自的学分体系，建立基于项目的学分转换系统。

在双学位项目中，各大学共享学位授予标准及评审方法，同时讨论

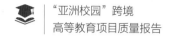
评审标准和方法。

协调各参与大学的评分方法，各大学进行严格评估，确保被授予学分的有效性。

就双学位项目而言，所取得的学习成果适用于“亚洲校园”项目。

（9）内部质量保障

通过调查问卷、采访及学生参与评审委员会等方式定期获得学生反馈，同时进行相应的项目评估。

根据对学生的学习进度、所取得的学习成果、课程、教学及教学内容等信息的分析进行项目评估。

通过咨询委员会等方式进行外部评估。

各参与大学共享及讨论评估结果，以实现各大学的进一步发展。

参与大学根据自我评估结果讨论及考虑质量改进措施及日后活动。

各参与大学共享评估结果，并将其用于项目改进。

各大学的国际事务部、质量保障部及学生支持部审核评估结果，同时在大学层次上采取必要措施。

参与大学同意根据最近五年积累的经验，保持及巩固项目，并对其质量进行改善。同时，各大学获得大学层次关于持续项目的许可。

在未参与的学生中发现项目执行的一些效果。

5. 监控注意事项

（1）质量保障机构注意事项如下：

充足、适当的资源（含人力资源和财务资源）。准备开展有效监控所需的充足、适当的人力资源和财务资源。

目的性、透明度及独立性。保持质量保障机构的目的性、透明度及独立性，同时还需确保专家在开展客观、公平监控时的独立性。

积极沟通、合作。在实施监控时，三国的质量保障机构、参与大学及相关组织进行有效沟通与合作。

持续改进。建立质量保障活动持续改进的系统。

（2）专家注意事项如下：

积极沟通与合作。在评审过程中，来自三国的专家进行积极的沟通与合作。

监控文件与信息。监控期间获得的文件及信息不用于除监控活动之外的任何其他目的。

联络及协调。如果对"亚洲校园"项目提供者不确定或需要查询，请联系负责查询工作的质量保障机构，不得直接接触项目提供者。

客观公正的评审。评审应保持客观、公正。

现场考察期间的谈话。

• 在每次采访之前，现场考察团应召开会议，全面讨论要确认的事实以及在采访期间要发表的评论。

• 就现场考察期间来自项目提供者的咨询而言，原则上，各现场考察专家应约定回复内容。如果需要表述个人观点，请告知陈述时间。

• 切勿询问被采访对象个人问题。

• 注意被采访对象不要受到其回复的负面影响，同时确保保密性。

• 切勿与被采访对象争论或批评项目提供者。

• 如果被采访对象批评"亚洲校园"项目或监控，倾听他们给出的意见的理由，避免提出任何相反的论据。但是，如果存在误解，传达正确信息。

• 现场考察结束后，现场考察团应全面讨论应纳入报告中的内容。

撰写报告（材料评审报告、现场考察报告及最终报告）时要注意的几点。所撰写的报告应客观、公平，以材料评审和现场考察期间调查的事实为依据；特别是在提出负面的观察结果时，确保增加关于观察结果的详细、客观的理由；确保报告中不存在任何矛盾内容。

附 录

"亚洲校园"跨境
高等教育项目质量报告

附录一
中日韩有质量保障的大学交流与合作指导方针

（"中日韩大学交流合作促进委员会"第二次会议，
2010 年 12 月，北京）

根据中日韩领导人会议和《2020 中日韩合作展望》的精神，三国确认通过学分互认、联合学位等合作项目，切实提升大学之间的交流。同时，推动三国教育质量保障机构合作，确保交流项目质量。为此，"中日韩大学交流合作促进委员会"（以下简称"委员会"）在充分沟通和达成共识的基础上，提出本指导意见。

一　总则

1. 目的。本指导意见旨在进一步推进中日韩大学交流合作，保障和提高交流项目的质量，共同提升大学的国际竞争力；同时，探索建立大学交流与质量保障的有效运行机制，保障学生及其他相关者的利益，促使参与方各尽其责、通力合作；以此，促进三国教育的全面合作，加深三国人民的睦邻互信。

2. 内涵。本指导意见中的"大学交流合作"，可以通过三国共同商定的"亚洲校园"计划（CAMPUS Asia, Collective Action of Mobility Program of University Students）来组织实施，其框架及具体交流项目另

有文件陈述。此外，不强迫开展其他任何特定的大学教育或交流活动，也不涉及由大学自愿自发开展的交流项目。

3. 原则。鉴于各国国情和法律体系的不同，大学交流合作与质量保障活动的推广，必须坚持开放性、广泛性、渐进性、灵活性、示范性的原则。在共同探索研制某种通用性体系时，要尊重多样性及互惠互利，允许各自在体制、习俗、文化等方面的差异性和独特性。

4. 对象。本指导意见主要适用于三国参与大学交流合作与质量保障的各相关方——政府、大学、质量保障机构及包括产业界在内的其他相关单位。并希望各相关方密切协作，共同致力于大学交流项目的实施，确保所授学分、学位的应有质量。

二 分则

（一）对政府的建议

1. 建立全面、连贯、透明的质量保障框架

政府应根据相关法律法规，明确高等教育体系中的学校类型、学术水平、文凭颁发等内容，以及与中等教育体系、职业教育体系和其他非正规教育体系的相互关系。要明确对大学招生的条件，以及对授予学位的具体要求。尽可能明确高等教育质量标准（或资历框架），提供高等教育质量保障的信息包。

2. 鼓励相关大学参与交流项目

对于相关大学开展的交流项目，政府应充分利用其自身权限和政策，通过各种资源、渠道加以支持。特别是在启动"试点交流项目"阶段，应得到政府的推动和财政及其他方面的支持。

3. 支持质量保障机构开展活动

政府应充分发挥质量保障机构对提高质量的作用，支持"中日韩

质量保障机构协议会"开展相关活动，对其围绕交流项目开展的质量保障活动，应确保相对独立性，并在政策、经费等方面给予大力支持。

（二）对大学的建议

1. 建立内部质量保障体系

相关大学应建立有效的内部质量保障体系，以确保交流项目的质量。"内部质量保障体系"的内涵，可能会因各国教育体制和学术实践的不同而存在差异，但下述内容是三国大学应当共同遵守的：

（1）公布学校教育教学的基本信息，以及提供交流项目的详细信息；

（2）构建规范、系统化的课程体系，适度考虑教学大纲的标准化和成绩评价制度的连贯性；

（3）有健全的教学制度和规范的管理，确保学分授予、学业成绩判定及学分转换的程序均符合本国法律法规的要求。

2. 确保交流项目的有效实施

参与交流项目的大学应制定实施细则和应急预案，合作大学就重要事项和交流细节达成一致后可签订协议，并公布于众和定期采取跟进措施；在注重质量保障的同时，要探索建立学分转换的办法，为制订中日韩三国乃至东南亚地区学分转换和累积系统奠定基础；大学之间还可以建立合作伙伴关系，共同提供教育资源，并通过大学与学生确认的"学习协议"等制度框架，保证交流学生的学习结果（如：学分、学位证书等）被有关方面承认，以便回国后能顺利继续学习。

3. 为学生提供周到的服务

向学生（包括项目申请者）提供完整、正确的信息，以便其对自己的学业生涯做出选择；交流项目实施的流程及要求等做到内容明确、公开透明和易于理解；大学要尽可能提供"一站式服务"，方便国际学生获得信息、申请、咨询等多种服务，以便其专注于自身学业。项目实施时可为交流学生提供必要的语言补习，以及学习过程中给予持续性支持、指导和提供"文化交流"的机会；可通过学生顾问、助教、志愿者与国际学生保持沟通，并依托校内各方面的力量共同做好服务工作。

（三）对质量保障机构的建议

1. 确保程序明确和信息公开

必须清楚地认识到，即使三国具有相似的大学评估体制，各自质量保障机构的作用不尽相同。因此，质量保障机构应更加关注对方质量保障机制中的差异性和多样性，并通过"中日韩质量保障机构协议会"（以下简称"协议会"）建立质量保障信息交流平台，实现三国间的质量保障信息交流与共享。

2. 探索共同标准和联合评估

三国质量保障机构在加强交流项目质量保障的同时，还应注意三国大学评估的通行做法和共同特征（如：通用的指标体系、共同的评估方法），特别是利用协议会开展跨国教育质量保障体系研究的成果，今后在三国大学交流项目中寻求某些通用的指标框架，联合开展大学评估活动。

3. 加强员工的能力建设

加强评估机构员工的能力建设，对提高大学评估工作水平十分重要。根据国际交流项目的要求，有必要使相关人员具有跨国交流的知识和经验，以胜任大学交流项目的质量保障工作。要充分利用协议会开展员工交流和能力建设，使大学交流合作能够共享能力建设的成果。

（四）对其他相关单位的建议

大学交流项目培养的是具备跨国沟通和工作能力的国际化人才，这是未来东亚经济发展的中坚力量，对促进中日韩及整个东亚地区的经济发展和共同繁荣具有深远意义。因此，希望其他相关单位（包括产业界）能对三国大学交流项目给予必要的支持（如：合作开办实习实践课程、联合开展科研项目等）。

三　附则

1. 本指导意见的效力

本指导意见于 2010 年 12 月 10 日，在中国北京召开的委员会第二次会议上讨论通过。文本分别用中文、日文、韩文和英文四国语言书写，对不同语言版本理解有分歧时以英文版本为准，若需修订由委员会商定。本指导意见由参与交流合作的有关方面参照执行，尊重三国高等教育体系的独特性，不强迫任何国家对其条例规定等进行修改。

2. 相关的宣传和推广

政府应把本指导意见和"亚洲校园"计划框架，作为一项非约束性的、但具有重要意义的指导文件，向国内及国际社会进行宣传和推广。同时，还建议各国政府公开发布各大学和质量保障机构的先进经验和做法，包括将要推行的"试点交流项目"。

附录二
“中日韩大学交流合作促进委员会”第四次会议
三方共识

2013 年 8 月 6 日在东京召开的“中日韩大学交流合作促进委员会”（以下简称“委员会”）上，达成以下共识。

一、“亚洲校园”项目扩大委员会共同确认了“亚洲校园”项目在亚洲高等教育中的重要意义、开放性及发展潜力。为贯彻 2012 年 5 月在中国北京召开的第五次中日韩领导人会议《联合宣言》的精神，委员会确认，未来将在试点项目的基础上进一步推动“亚洲校园”项目发展，从而进一步扩大该项目的规模和范围，为本地区培养更多、更好的优秀人才。

《关于提升全方位合作伙伴关系的联合宣言》，第五次中日韩领导人会议（2012 年 5 月 13 日，中国北京）提出：“我们鼓励三国通过该试点项目为建立一个共同的亚洲质量保障体系做出贡献并进一步扩大该项目的规模和范围，为本地区培养更多、更好的优秀人才。”

二、“亚洲校园”试点项目的监控活动。

委员会共同认可了目前进行的试点项目质量监控的意义和重要性，监控促进了“亚洲校园”项目的质量保障，并将形成一套对于项目扩大及未来持续有效开展具有重要意义的标准。委员会对监控活动的基本体系及进度安排确认如下。

1. 监控活动由三国质量保障机构认定大学质量保障活动，并按教育质量从中选取优秀案例予以推广。

2. 三国质量保障机构通过两轮监控活动，旨在比较、分析三国质量保障活动，形成面向质量保障机构的、关于教育国际合作质量保障的共同指导方针。

三、下一次中日韩会议"中日韩大学交流合作促进委员会"第五次会议将于 2014 年秋季在中国上海举办。

附录三
"中日韩大学交流合作促进委员会"第五次会议
三方共识

2015 年 4 月 10 日，三方在中国上海召开了"中日韩大学交流合作
促进委员会"（以下简称"委员会"）第五次会议，会上达成以下共识。

一 "亚洲校园"项目的质量保障与监控

1. 根据《中日韩有质量保障的大学交流与合作指导方针》以及
委员会第四次会议达成的共识，三国质量保障机构在相互认可质量监
控标准和程序的基础上，分别在各自国家对 10 个试点项目进行了中
期质量监控。委员会认可三国质量保障机构所给出的中期质量监控
结果。

2. 对于三国质量保障机构共同遴选出的"亚洲校园"试点项目优
秀实践案例，委员会给予高度认可，并决定在三国乃至更广范围内予以
宣传推广，促进"亚洲校园"的项目扩大和整体质量提升。

3. 委员会讨论通过了"亚洲校园"试点项目终期联合质量监控
标准及实施框架，并支持三国质量保障机构在试点阶段结束之前
（2015 年至 2016 年）据此对项目进行终期共同质量监控，形成终期
质量报告。

4. 委员会同意，充分利用"中日韩质量保障机构协议会"网站，加强三国间质量保障与监控信息交流共享，及时向社会公布质量监控标准、程序和结果，确保信息公开透明，更好地发挥社会支持和监督作用。

二　"亚洲校园"项目的扩大与可持续发展规划

1. 委员会商定，为实现"亚洲校园"计划关于开放、灵活、渐进的宗旨，将逐步采取三种方式推进项目扩大。第一种方式：扩大项目的开放度，以促进更加灵活的学生流动，比如不同项目间的流动，这要由成员院校来决定；第二种方式：吸收中日韩三国新的项目院校加入；第三种方式：将项目院校扩大到其他亚洲国家和地区。

2. 委员会同意，为保证"亚洲校园"项目的可持续发展，将分三个时间段实施项目扩大方案。其中2015年至2016年，采用第一种扩大方式，对试点阶段表现突出的优秀示范性项目和有较大发展潜力的项目，扩大学生交流数量；2015年至2016年，研究制定更加灵活、多样的新增项目准入标准，并遴选出新增参与高校。第二种扩大方式将在2016年9月份启动；实施第二种方式后，委员会应总结经验，讨论第三种方式的可行性方案。

3. 委员会同意为有利于"亚洲校园"项目交流持续发展提供服务，在完全实施了第二种模式之后，进一步讨论专门的"亚洲校园信息平台"（网站），发布委员会活动信息，提供三国交流项目信息，收集发布交流发展情况、经验，并形成数据分析结果。为政府、教师和学生服务。具体方案请交流工作组在工作级别会议商讨。

4. 委员会鼓励建立三国资历互认、学分互认合作机制，为更加灵活的学生流动提供良好环境，增强"亚洲校园"项目的发展能力。鼓励"亚洲校园"计划项目院校召开三国相关高校（校长、教师、学生）

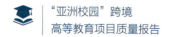
研讨会，交流探讨项目交流、质量保障与监控经验，促进大学交流顺利
务实开展，确保"亚洲校园"项目具有长久的吸引力与影响力。

三　下一次会议

委员会决定于 2016 年在韩国举行"中日韩大学交流合作促进委员
会"第六次会议，具体时间、会议主题等由三方事务层面沟通。

附录四
"中日韩大学交流合作促进委员会" 第六次会议
三方共识

（草案）

中日韩大学交流合作促进委员会（以下简称"委员会"）第六次会议于 2017 年 11 月 23 日在韩国首尔举行。作为成果，达成了以下共识。

一 "亚洲校园" 项目的可持续发展与扩张

1.（继续推动"亚洲校园"项目）根据"大学交流与合作指导方针"和委员会第六次会议的共识，委员会高度赞赏 2016 年成功启动了正式阶段项目，并同意三方更加紧密地合作，以期在试点项目取得成功的基础上追求"亚洲校园"项目的持续发展。为此，三国分享了各项目的成果，并就如何进一步改进的方式进行了讨论。此外，委员会确认，还需要进一步深入的讨论，通过包括第二次三边教育部长会议在内的各种途径来规划好该计划的未来之路。

2.（模式 3 的扩大）在上次委员会会议上，三国同意通过引入三种方式的扩大计划来扩大亚洲校园。委员会还重申，推动该项目促进高等教育领域的流动仍是他们继续追求的目标；目前的"亚洲校园"计划是模式 2，委员会决定在下次会议上讨论模式 3。

二 "亚洲校园" 项目的质量保障与监督

（共同原则）为了支持项目对子之间学生的活跃交流，委员会同意制定共同原则，以实施“亚洲校园”项目。共同原则将包括与计划运作有关的各种事宜，包括短期和长期交流的概念，平衡的学生交流的原则，负责提供资助的单位，以及奖学金的范围和规模（包括金额，期限和接收人数）。这三个国家也同意积极向项目对子告知共同原则，以协助项目的成功运作。

（监控）在第一届三边校长论坛上发布的第二次监控结果再次在第六次委员会会议上分享，并得到成员们的通过。基于结果，委员会决定建立“亚洲校园”项目第三期质量监控框架。对于将要进行的、包括监测标准和指导方针在内的第三次监测的总体方向进行了讨论，并决定于 2018 年开展。监控的具体内容将由政府指定机构经过进一步讨论后确定。

三 为活跃的学生交流和能力建设创造有利环境

1.（联合政策研究的启动）根据委员会第五次会议的共识，委员会成员就支持“亚洲校园”项目对子之间的活跃交流达成一致，并开始讨论启动三国高等教育体系联合研究项目及其资历认可，以促进高等教育领域的流动。此外，委员会也认为这项研究应有助于促进三国在高等教育方面的双/联合学位和流动性。

2.（相关交流活动的扩大）在第五次委员会会议上，同意举办更多的定期研讨会，邀请校长、教师和学生就与其他大学交流以及实现质量保障所付出努力的经验交换意见。委员会成员确认要加倍努力，注意“亚洲校园”项目的积极成果，并通过开展这些活动，包括定期组织三国项目对子和校友的会议，扩大其进展。

四 下一次会议

委员会决定第七次委员会会议将于 2019 年在日本举行。

附录五　"亚洲校园" 试点项目学生交流情况统计

1. 商业领袖项目

表1　学生接收（日本/韩国→中国）

序号	项目持续时间		学生参与情况（来自日本/韩国）	流动项目类型	是否授予双学位	国内高校认可的最高学分	接收学生人数
	开始日期	结束日期					
1	2012年2月	2012年6月	韩国	学期交流项目（MBA，4个月）	否	18	2
2	2012年9月	2012年12月	日本	学期交流项目（MBA，4个月）	否	18	2
3	2012年9月	2012年12月	韩国	学期交流项目（MBA，4个月）	否	18	1
4	2013年9月	2013年12月	韩国	学期交流项目（MBA，4个月）	否	18	1
5	2014年9月	2014年12月	日本	学期交流项目（MBA，4个月）	否	18	1
6	2015年9月	2016年6月	韩国	双学位项目（MBA，1年）	是	36	4
7	2013年9月	2014年6月	日本	双学位项目（MBA，1年）	是	36	1
8	2014年9月	2015年6月	日本	双学位项目（MBA，1年）	是	36	1
9	2012年8月20日	2012年9月1日	日本和韩国	暑期项目（2周，MBA）	否	2	20
10	2013年8月15日	2013年8月30日	日本和韩国	暑期项目（2周，MBA）	否	2	20
11	2014年8月12日	2014年8月28日	日本和韩国	暑期项目（2周，MBA）	否	2	20
12	2015年8月11日	2015年8月26日	日本	暑期项目（2周，MBA）	否	2	8

表 2　学生派出（中国→日本/韩国）

序号	项目持续时间		学生参与情况（派至日本/韩国）国	流动项目类型	是否授予双学位	国内高校认可的最高学分	派出学生人数
	开始日期	结束日期					
1	2013 年 9 月	2014 年 6 月	日本	双学位项目（MBA，1 年）	是	22	2
2	2012 年 9 月	2013 年 6 月	韩国	双学位项目（MBA，1 年）	是	22	1
3	2013 年 9 月	2013 年 6 月	韩国	双学位项目（MBA，1 年）	是	22	1
4	2015 年 1 月	2015 年 6 月	韩国	双学位项目（MBA，5 个月，两个模块）	是	22	5
5	2014 年 2 月	2014 年 6 月	日本	学期交流项目（MBA，4 个月）	否	18	1
6	2015 年 9 月	2015 年 12 月	日本	学期交流项目（MBA，4 个月）	否	18	2
7	2012 年 8 月 20 日	2012 年 9 月 1 日	日本和韩国	暑期项目（2 周，MBA）	否	1	8
8	2013 年 8 月 15 日	2013 年 8 月 30 日	日本和韩国	暑期项目（2 周，MBA）	否	1	8
9	2014 年 8 月 12 日	2014 年 8 月 28 日	日本和韩国	暑期项目（2 周，MBA）	否	1	8
10	2015 年 8 月 11 日	2015 年 8 月 26 日	日本	暑期项目（2 周，MBA）	否	1	10

2. 国际关系项目

表 3　学生接收（日本/韩国→中国）

序号	项目持续时间		学生参与情况（来自日本/韩国）国	流动项目类型	是否授予双学位	国内高校认可的最高学分	接收学生人数
	开始日期	结束日期					
1	2012 年 9 月 1 日	2015 年 5 月 1 日	韩国	交流项目（研究生项目，6 个月）		9	17
2	2012 年 9 月 1 日	2015 年 5 月 1 日	日本	交流项目（研究生项目，6 个月）		9	9
3	2012 年 9 月 1 日	2015 年 5 月 1 日	日本	双学位项目	是	10	5

表 4　学生派出（中国→日本/韩国）

序号	项目持续时间		学生参与情况	流动项目类型	是否授予双学位	国内高校认可的最高学分	派出学生人数
	开始日期	结束日期	（派至日本/韩国）				
1	2012年9月1日	2015年5月1日	韩国	交流项目（研究生项目，6个月）		9	27
2	2012年9月1日	2015年5月1日	日本	交流项目（研究生项目，6个月）		6	25
3	2012年9月1日	2015年5月1日	日本	双学位项目	是	24	4

表 5　学生接收（日本/韩国→中国）

序号	项目持续时间		学生参与情况	流动项目类型	是否授予双学位	国内高校认可的最高学分	接收学生人数
	开始日期	结束日期	（来自日本/韩国）				
1	2012年2月20日	2012年7月15日	韩国	交流项目	否	9	1
2	2013年3月1日	2013年7月15日	韩国	交流项目	否	9	1
3	2013年3月1日	2014年1月31日	韩国	交流项目	否	9	1
4	2014年2月21日	2014年6月30日	韩国	交流项目	否	27	3
5	2013年8月7日	2013年9月3日	日本	暑期项目	否	—	2
6	2014年8月7日	2014年9月3日	韩国	暑期项目	否	15	5
7	2014年9月22日	2015年1月31日	韩国	交流项目	否	9	1
8	2015年9月22日	2015年8月31日	韩国	交流项目	否	9	1
9	2015年3月1日	2015年8月31日	韩国	交流项目	否	18	2
10	2015年7月28日	2015年8月25日	韩国	暑期项目	否	15	5
11	2015年8月31日	2016年1月31日	韩国	交流项目	否	9	1
12	2016年3月1日	2016年7月15日	韩国	交流项目	否	27	3

3. 政策联合会项目

表6 学生派出（中国→日本/韩国）

序号	项目持续时间		学生参与情况	流动项目类型	是否授予双学位	国内高校认可的最高学分	派出学生人数
	开始日期	结束日期	（派至日本/韩国）				
1	2013年7月13日	2013年10月31日	日本	交流项目	否	9	1
2	2013年8月1日	2013年8月31日	韩国	暑期项目	否	9	4
3	2013年8月7日	2013年8月22日	日本	暑期项目	否	9	5
4	2014年10月1日	2014年3月31日	日本	交流项目	否	9	1
5	2013年10月1日	2014年9月30日	日本	交流项目	否	9	1
6	2014年8月4日	2014年9月5日	韩国	暑期项目	否	9	5
7	2014年8月12日	2014年8月25日	日本	暑期项目	否	9	4
8	2015年7月30日	2015年9月23日	日本	暑期项目	否	9	4
9	2015年10月1日	2016年2月5日	日本	交流项目	否	9	2

4. TKT 项目

表7 学生接收（日本/韩国→中国）

序号	项目持续时间		学生参与情况	流动项目类型	是否授予双学位	国内高校认可的最高学分	接收学生人数
	开始日期	结束日期	（来自日本/韩国）				
1	2012年9月1日	2013年7月31日	日本	长期交流（研究生项目）	否	10	1
2	2012年9月1日	2013年2月1日	日本	长期交流（研究生项目）	否	10	1
3	2012年9月1日	2013年7月31日	日本	长期交流（本科生项目）	否	60	1
4	2012年9月3日	2013年1月30日	韩国	长期交流（研究生项目）	否	36	3

续表

序号	项目持续时间		学生参与情况（来自日本/韩国）	流动项目类型	是否授予双学位	国内高校认可的最高学分	接收学生人数
	开始日期	结束日期					
5	2013 年 3 月 1 日	2014 年 1 月 31 日	日本	学位项目（研究生项目）	是	10	1
6	2013 年 9 月 1 日	2014 年 7 月 31 日	日本	学位项目（研究生项目）	是	10	2
7	2013 年 3 月 1 日	2013 年 7 月 31 日	韩国	长期交流（研究生项目）		18	1
8	2013 年 9 月 1 日	2014 年 1 月 31 日	韩国	长期交流（本科生项目）		36	4
9	2013 年 9 月 1 日	2014 年 1 月 31 日	韩国	长期交流（研究生项目）		18	1
10	2014 年 1 月 1 日	2014 年 3 月 31 日	日本	短期交流（研究生项目）		10	1
11	2014 年 2 月 1 日	2014 年 6 月 30 日	日本	长期交流（研究生项目）		10	1
12	2014 年 9 月 1 日	2014 年 11 月 30 日	日本	短期交流（研究生项目）		10	1
13	2014 年 9 月 1 日	2015 年 1 月 31 日	日本	长期交流（研究生项目）		10	1
14	2014 年 9 月 1 日	2015 年 8 月 31 日	日本	长期交流（研究生项目）		10	1
15	2014 年 9 月 1 日	2015 年 7 月 15 日	韩国	长期交流（本科生项目）		36	3
16	2015 年 2 月 27 日	2015 年 6 月 26 日	韩国	长期交流（研究生项目）		18	1

表 8　学生派出（中国→日本/韩国）

序号	项目持续时间		学生参与情况（派至日本/韩国）	流动项目类型	是否授予双学位	国内高校认可的最高学分	派出学生人数
	开始日期	结束日期					
1	2012 年 7 月 1 日	2012 年 8 月 31 日	日本	暑期项目		无限制	3
2	2012 年 8 月 1 日	2013 年 1 月 31 日	日本	长期交流（研究生项目）		11	2
3	2012 年 10 月 1 日	2013 年 2 月 28 日	日本	长期交流（本科生项目）		无限制	2

续表

序号	项目持续时间		学生参与情况	流动项目类型	是否授予双学位	国内高校认可的最高学分	派出学生人数
	开始日期	结束日期	（派至日本/韩国）				
4	2012年9月1日	2012年12月31日	韩国	长期交流（本科生项目）		无限制	4
5	2013年7月1日	2013年8月31日	日本	暑期项目（本科生项目）		无限制	4
6	2013年9月1日	2014年2月28日	日本	长期交流（研究生项目）		11	1
7	2013年9月1日	2014年9月30日	日本	学位项目（研究生项目）	是	11	3
8	2013年1月1日	2013年2月20日	韩国	短期交流（本科生项目）		无限制	2
9	2013年8月1日	2013年8月31日	韩国	暑期项目		无限制	6
10	2013年9月1日	2013年12月31日	韩国	长期交流（本科生项目）		无限制	8
11	2013年12月1日	2014年2月19日	韩国	短期交流（本科生项目）		11	5
12	2014年1月1日	2014年2月28日	韩国	短期交流（本科生项目）		无限制	1
13	2014年1月1日	2014年2月28日	韩国	短期交流（研究生项目）		无限制	1
14	2013年12月1日	2014年2月16日	韩国	短期交流（研究生项目）		无限制	1
15	2014年7月1日	2014年8月31日	日本	暑期项目（本科生项目）		无限制	3
16	2014年10月1日	2015年2月28日	日本	长期交流（研究生项目）		11	2
17	2014年9月1日	2014年9月30日	日本	短期交流（研究生项目）	是	11	1
18	2014年9月1日	2015年8月1日	日本	长期交流（研究生项目）	是	11	2
19	2015年3月1日	2015年8月1日	日本	长期交流（研究生项目）	是	11	1
20	2014年8月1日	2014年8月29日	韩国	暑期项目（本科生项目）		无限制	4
21	2014年8月1日	2014年8月29日	韩国	暑期项目（研究生项目）		11	9
22	2015年3月1日	2015年5月9日	韩国	短期交流（研究生项目）		11	1

5. 传统文化项目

表 9　学生接收（日本/韩国→中国）

序号	项目持续时间		学生参与情况（来自日本/韩国）	流动项目类型	是否授予双学位	国内高校认可的最高学分	接收学生人数
	开始日期	结束日期					
1	2012 年 3 月	2013 年 2 月	日本	长期交流项目			4
2	2013 年 3 月	2014 年 2 月	日本	长期交流项目			5
3	2014 年 3 月	2014 年 8 月	日本	长期交流项目			1
4	2014 年 3 月	2015 年 2 月	日本	长期交流项目			4
5	2015 年 3 月	2016 年 2 月	日本	长期交流项目			5
6	2012 年 3 月 1 日	2012 年 8 月 31 日	韩国	长期交流项目			2
7	2012 年 3 月 1 日	2013 年 2 月 28 日	韩国	长期交流项目			1
8	2012 年 8 月 4 日	2012 年 9 月 2 日	日本	暑期项目			10
9	2012 年 8 月 4 日	2012 年 9 月 3 日	韩国	为期 4 周的汉语项目			10
10	2012 年 9 月 1 日	2013 年 2 月 28 日	韩国	长期交流项目			4
11	2013 年 3 月 1 日	2013 年 8 月 31 日	韩国	长期交流项目			1
12	2013 年 3 月 1 日	2014 年 2 月 28 日	韩国	长期交流项目			3
13	2013 年 8 月 5 日	2013 年 8 月 31 日	日本	暑期项目			10
14	2013 年 9 月 1 日	2014 年 2 月 28 日	韩国	长期交流项目			2
15	2014 年 3 月 1 日	2014 年 8 月 31 日	韩国	长期交流项目			2
16	2014 年 3 月 1 日	2015 年 2 月 28 日	韩国	长期交流项目			3
17	2014 年 8 月 7 日	2014 年 8 月 31 日	日本	暑期项目			10

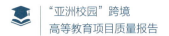

续表

序号	项目持续时间		学生参与情况	流动项目类型	是否授予双学位	国内高校认可的最高学分	接收学生人数
	开始日期	结束日期	(来自日本/韩国)				
18	2014年9月1日	2015年2月28日	韩国	长期交流项目			2
19	2014年9月21日	2014年9月27日	日本	研讨会			22
20	2015年3月1日	2015年8月31日	韩国	长期交流项目			5
21	2015年8月24日	2015年8月27日	日本	短期交流			10
22	2015年9月	2016年2月28日	韩国	长期交流项目			3

表 10 学生派出（中国→日本/韩国）

序号	项目持续时间		学生参与情况	流动项目类型	是否授予双学位	国内高校认可的最高学分	派出学生人数
	开始日期	结束日期	(派至日本/韩国)				
1	2012年10月	2013年3月	日本	长期交流项目			6
2	2013年10月	2014年3月	日本	长期交流项目			5
3	2013年4月	2013年9月	日本	长期交流项目			5
4	2014年10月	2015年3月	日本	长期交流项目			5
5	2015年10月	2016年3月	日本	长期交流项目			5
6	2015年4月	2015年9月	韩国	长期交流项目			5
7	2012年9月1日	2013年2月28日	韩国	长期交流项目			6
8	2013年8月4日	2013年8月24日	韩国	为期3周的韩语项目			10
9	2013年8月6日	2013年8月20日	日本	暑期项目			5
10	2013年9月1日	2014年2月28日	韩国	长期交流项目			7

续表

序号	项目持续时间 开始日期	项目持续时间 结束日期	学生参与情况（派至日本/韩国）	流动项目类型	是否授予双学位	国内高校认可的最高学分	派出学生人数
11	2014年3月1日	2014年8月31日	韩国	长期交流项目			2
12	2014年4月	2014年9月	日本	长期交流项目			5
13	2014年8月3日	2014年8月16日	日本	暑期项目			5
14	2014年9月1日	2015年2月28日	韩国	长期交流项目			3
15	2015年3月1日	2016年2月28日	韩国	长期交流项目			5
16	2015年8月9日	2015年8月18日	日本	暑期项目			10

6. 法律人才项目

表11　学生接收（日本/韩国→中国）

序号	项目持续时间 开始日期	项目持续时间 结束日期	学生参与情况（来自日本/韩国）	流动项目类型	是否授予双学位	国内高校认可的最高学分	接收学生人数
1	2012年9月1日	2013年6月30日	日本	交流项目（本科生，1年；4名到中国人民大学学习，1名到上海交通大学学习）		34	5
2	2012年9月1日	2013年6月30日	韩国	交流项目（4名本科生，1年；1名研究生，1学期）		36	5
3	2013年9月1日	2014年6月30日	日本	交流项目（5名本科生，1年；3人到中国人民大学学习，2人到上海交通大学学习）		28	5
4	2013年9月1日	2014年6月30日	韩国	交流项目（4名本科生，1年&1名研究生，1学期；4人到中国人民大学学习，1人到上海交通大学学习）		36	5

续表

序号	项目持续时间		学生参与情况（来自日本/韩国）	流动项目类型	是否授予双学位	国内高校认可的最高学分	接收学生人数
	开始日期	结束日期					
5	2014年9月1日	2015年6月30日	日本	交流项目（5名本科生，1年；3人到中国人民大学学习，2人到上海交通大学学习）		尚未认可	5
6	2014年9月1日	2015年6月30日	韩国	交流项目（4名本科生，1年 &2名研究生，1学期；4人到上海交通大学学习）		36	6

表12 学生派出（中国→日本/韩国）

序号	项目持续时间		学生参与情况（派至日本/韩国）	流动项目类型	是否授予双学位	国内高校认可的最高学分	派出学生人数
	开始日期	结束日期					
1	2012年9月22日	2013年8月30日	日本	交流项目（本科生，1年；4名来自中国人民大学，1名来自上海交通大学）		38	5
2	2012年8月28日	2013年8月1日	韩国	交流项目（2名本科生&1名研究生，1年）		22	3
3	2012年8月5日	2012年8月31日	日本	暑期项目（5名本科生&4名研究生，5人来自中国人民大学，2人来自清华大学，2人来自上海交通大学）			9
4	2013年9月22日	2014年8月30日	日本	交流项目（4名本科生&1名研究生，1年；3人来自中国人民大学，2人来自上海交通大学）		26	5

续表

序号	项目持续时间		学生参与情况（派至日本/韩国）	流动项目类型	是否授予双学位	国内高校认可的最高学分	派出学生人数
	开始日期	结束日期					
5	2013年8月28日	2014年8月1日	韩国	交流项目（3名本科生 &2名研究生，1年；4人来自中国人民大学，1人来自上海交通大学）		11	5
6	2013年8月5日	2013年8月23日	日本	暑期项目（5名本科生 &4名研究生；5人来自中国人民大学，2人来自清华大学）			9
7	2014年9月22日	2015年8月31日	日本	交流项目（5名本科生，其中，2人学习1学期，3人学习1年；1名研究生，1年。这6名学生中，4人来自中国人民大学，2人来自上海交通大学）		尚未转学分	6
8	2014年8月1日	2015年8月28日	韩国	交流项目（5名本科生，1学期；1名研究生，1年）		尚未转学分	6
9	2015年8月4日	2015年8月25日	日本	暑期项目（5名本科生 &4名研究生；5人来自中国人民大学，2人来自清华大学）			9

7. 化学与材料项目

表 13 接收学生（韩国/中国→日本）

序号	交流期限		交流项目类型			可获得学分数	交流学生人数
	开始日期	结束日期		交流项目类型			
1	2012 年 3 月 4 日	2012 年 5 月 31 日		中国→日本	日本东北大学	1	1
2	2012 年 6 月 12 日	2012 年 9 月 11 日		中国→日本	日本东北大学	1	1
3	2012 年 8 月 20 日	2012 年 8 月 23 日	短期交流	中国→日本	日本东北大学	0	3
4	2012 年 9 月 26 日	2012 年 10 月 28 日	短期交流	中国→日本	日本东北大学	1	1
5	2012 年 10 月 15 日	2012 年 12 月 20 日	短期交流	中国→日本	名古屋大学	1	1
6	2012 年 10 月 24 日	2012 年 11 月 25 日	短期交流	中国→日本	日本东北大学	1	1
7	2012 年 11 月 1 日	2013 年 1 月 31 日		中国→日本	名古屋大学	4	1
8	2012 年 11 月 5 日	2013 年 2 月 6 日		中国→日本	名古屋大学	4	5
9	2012 年 11 月 5 日	2013 年 1 月 19 日		中国→日本	名古屋大学	4	1
10	2012 年 11 月 11 日	2013 年 11 月 10 日		中国→日本	日本东北大学	1	1
11	2013 年 4 月 1 日	2013 年 6 月 30 日		中国→日本	日本东北大学	1	1
12	2013 年 7 月 1 日	2013 年 9 月 30 日		中国→日本	日本东北大学	1	1
13	2013 年 8 月 1 日	2013 年 10 月 31 日	短期交流	中国→日本	名古屋大学	4	3
14	2013 年 8 月 29 日	2013 年 8 月 30 日		中国→日本	日本东北大学	0	1
15	2013 年 9 月 3 日	2014 年 1 月 5 日		中国→日本	名古屋大学	4	1
16	2013 年 9 月 3 日	2013 年 12 月 5 日		中国→日本	名古屋大学	4	1
17	2014 年 3 月 1 日	2014 年 5 月 28 日		中国→日本	日本东北大学	1	1

续表

序号	交流期限			交流项目类型		可获得学分分数	交流学生人数
	开始日期	结束日期					
18	2014 年 3 月 29 日	2014 年 3 月 30 日	研讨会	中国→日本	名古屋大学	0	2
19	2014 年 4 月 1 日	2014 年 9 月 30 日		中国→日本	日本东北大学	1	1
20	2014 年 5 月 7 日	2014 年 8 月 6 日		中国→日本	名古屋大学	4	3
21	2014 年 5 月 7 日	2014 年 9 月 6 日		中国→日本	名古屋大学	4	1
22	2014 年 5 月 7 日	2014 年 8 月 31 日		中国→日本	名古屋大学	4	1
23	2014 年 5 月 14 日	2014 年 8 月 13 日		中国→日本	日本东北大学	1	1
24	2014 年 5 月 28 日	2014 年 8 月 31 日		中国→日本	名古屋大学	4	1
25	2014 年 7 月 1 日	2014 年 9 月 30 日		中国→日本	名古屋大学	4	1
26	2014 年 7 月 1 日	2014 年 9 月 30 日	短期交流	中国→日本	名古屋大学	1	1
27	2014 年 8 月 25 日	2014 年 8 月 26 日		中国→日本	日本东北大学	0	5
28	2014 年 9 月 24 日	2014 年 12 月 24 日		中国→日本	名古屋大学	4	1
29	2014 年 9 月 24 日	2015 年 1 月 23 日		中国→日本	名古屋大学	4	1
30	2014 年 10 月 1 日	2014 年 12 月 31 日		中国→日本	名古屋大学	4	1
31	2014 年 11 月 26 日	2014 年 11 月 27 日	CA 座谈会	中国→日本	日本东北大学	0	12
32	2015 年 3 月 2 日	2015 年 6 月 2 日		中国→日本	日本东北大学	1	1
33	2015 年 5 月 1 日	2015 年 7 月 31 日		中国→日本	日本东北大学	1	4
34	2015 年 6 月 1 日	2015 年 8 月 31 日	短期交流	中国→日本	名古屋大学	4	4
35	2015 年 8 月 27 日	2015 年 8 月 28 日		中国→日本	日本东北大学	0	6
36	2015 年 9 月 24 日	2016 年 1 月 23 日		中国→日本	名古屋大学	4	5

续表

序号	交流期限		交流项目类型			可获得学分数	交流学生人数
	开始日期	结束日期					
37	2015 年 9 月 24 日	2015 年 12 月 22 日		中国→日本	名古屋大学	4	1
38	2012 年 7 月 30 日	2012 年 8 月 25 日	短期交流	韩国→日本	日本东北大学	1	3
39	2012 年 8 月 20 日	2012 年 8 月 23 日	短期交流	韩国→日本	日本东北大学	0	2
40	2012 年 9 月 24 日	2013 年 2 月 8 日	短期	韩国→日本	名古屋大学	4	1
41	2013 年 1 月 13 日	2013 年 8 月 13 日		韩国→日本	日本东北大学	1	1
42	2013 年 7 月 1 日	2013 年 9 月 30 日		韩国→日本	名古屋大学	4	1
43	2013 年 8 月 1 日	2013 年 12 月 3 日		韩国→日本	名古屋大学	4	1
44	2013 年 8 月 5 日	2013 年 9 月 1 日	短期交流	韩国→日本	日本东北大学	1	2
45	2013 年 8 月 29 日	2013 年 8 月 30 日	短期交流	韩国→日本	日本东北大学	0	2
46	2013 年 10 月 1 日	2014 年 2 月 28 日		韩国→日本	名古屋大学	4	1
47	2014 年 3 月 29 日	2014 年 3 月 30 日	研讨会	韩国→日本	名古屋大学	0	2
48	2014 年 5 月 7 日	2014 年 8 月 31 日		韩国→日本	名古屋大学	4	1
49	2014 年 7 月 7 日	2014 年 10 月 8 日		韩国→日本	日本东北大学	1	1
50	2014 年 7 月 7 日	2014 年 8 月 6 日	短期交流	韩国→日本	日本东北大学	1	1
51	2014 年 8 月 25 日	2014 年 8 月 26 日	短期交流	韩国→日本	日本东北大学	0	2
52	2014 年 11 月 26 日	2014 年 11 月 27 日	CA 座谈会	韩国→日本	日本东北大学	0	3
53	2014 年 12 月 15 日	2015 年 3 月 14 日		韩国→日本	名古屋大学	4	1
54	2015 年 5 月 7 日	2015 年 12 月 31 日		韩国→日本	名古屋大学	4	1
55	2015 年 8 月 27 日	2015 年 8 月 28 日	短期交流	韩国→日本	日本东北大学	0	1
56	2015 年 9 月 1 日	2015 年 12 月 23 日		韩国→日本	名古屋大学	4	0

表 14　学生派出（日本→韩国/中国）

序号	交流期限 开始日期	交流期限 结束日期		交流项目类型	可获得学分数	交流学生人数
1	2013 年 3 月 11 日	2013 年 3 月 13 日	CA 座谈会	日本→中国　名古屋大学/日本东北大学	0	19
2	2013 年 6 月 11 日	2013 年 9 月 11 日		日本→中国　日本东北大学	2	1
3	2013 年 9 月 4 日	2013 年 12 月 3 日		日本→中国　名古屋大学	4	1
4	2014 年 3 月 13 日	2014 年 3 月 15 日	教育交流	日本→中国　名古屋大学	0	10
5	2014 年 3 月 14 日	2014 年 3 月 14 日	教育交流	日本→中国　名古屋大学	0	12
6	2014 年 6 月 1 日	2014 年 6 月 1 日	教育交流	日本→中国　名古屋大学	0	2
7	2014 年 6 月 25 日	2014 年 9 月 24 日		日本→中国　名古屋大学	4	1
8	2014 年 8 月 31 日	2014 年 11 月 30 日		日本→中国　日本东北大学	2	1
9	2015 年 6 月 25 日	2015 年 9 月 24 日		日本→中国　名古屋大学	4	4
10	2015 年 9 月 1 日	2015 年 11 月 30 日		日本→中国　日本东北大学	2	1
11	2015 年 11 月 5 日	2015 年 11 月 6 日	上海交通大学座谈会	日本→中国　名古屋大学/日本东北大学	0	16
12	2012 年 7 月 2 日	2012 年 7 月 31 日	短期交流	日本→韩国　日本东北大学	1	5
13	2012 年 8 月 9 日	2012 年 11 月 13 日		日本→韩国　日本东北大学	2	1
14	2012 年 8 月 31 日	2013 年 8 月 29 日		日本→韩国　日本东北大学	2	1
15	2013 年 1 月 20 日	2013 年 1 月 25 日	教育交流	日本→韩国　名古屋大学	0	5
16	2013 年 4 月 5 日	2013 年 7 月 5 日		日本→韩国　日本东北大学	2	1
17	2013 年 6 月 18 日	2013 年 9 月 17 日		日本→韩国　名古屋大学	4	1
18	2013 年 6 月 19 日	2014 年 3 月 3 日		日本→韩国　日本东北大学	2	1

续表

序号	交流期限		交流项目类型			可获得学分数	交流学生人数
	开始日期	结束日期					
19	2013 年 7 月 1 日	2013 年 9 月 30 日		日本→韩国	日本东北大学	2	1
20	2013 年 7 月 8 日	2013 年 8 月 5 日	短期交流	日本→韩国	日本东北大学	1	3
21	2013 年 7 月 19 日	2013 年 10 月 19 日		日本→韩国	名古屋大学	4	1
22	2013 年 9 月 2 日	2013 年 12 月 6 日		日本→韩国	日本东北大学	2	1
23	2013 年 11 月 7 日	2013 年 11 月 9 日	CA 座谈会	日本→韩国	名古屋大学/日本东北大学	0	18
24	2014 年 6 月 25 日	2014 年 9 月 24 日		日本→韩国	名古屋大学	4	1
25	2014 年 7 月 7 日	2014 年 8 月 7 日	短期交流	日本→韩国	日本东北大学	1	2
26	2014 年 7 月 24 日	2014 年 10 月 23 日		日本→韩国	名古屋大学	4	1
27	2014 年 8 月 17 日	2014 年 8 月 23 日	暑期学校	日本→韩国	名古屋大学	2	6
28	2014 年 8 月 17 日	2014 年 8 月 23 日	暑期学校	日本→韩国	日本东北大学	0	3
29	2014 年 12 月 1 日	2015 年 2 月 28 日		日本→韩国	日本东北大学	2	1
30	2015 年 2 月 25 日	2015 年 3 月 25 日	短期交流	日本→韩国	日本东北大学	1	1
31	2015 年 5 月 4 日	2015 年 8 月 4 日		日本→韩国	日本东北大学	2	1
32	2015 年 6 月 25 日	2015 年 9 月 24 日		日本→韩国	名古屋大学	4	4
33	2015 年 7 月 5 日	2015 年 7 月 11 日	暑期学校	日本→韩国	名古屋大学	2	0
34	2015 年 7 月 6 日	2015 年 7 月 11 日	暑期学校	日本→韩国	日本东北大学	0	0
35	2015 年 7 月 6 日	2015 年 8 月 4 日	短期交流	日本→韩国	日本东北大学	1	1

8. 能源与环境项目

表15　学生接收（日本/韩国→中国）

序号	项目持续时间		学生参与情况（来自日本/韩国）	流动项目类型	是否授予双学位	国内高校认可的最高学分	接收学生人数
	开始日期	结束日期					
1	2012年9月1日	2013年1月31日	韩国	交流项目		0	2
2	2012年9月1日	2013年1月31日	日本	交流项目		0	3
3	2013年9月1日	2014年1月31日	韩国	双学位项目	是	10	3
4	2013年9月1日	2014年1月31日	日本	双学位项目	是	10	5
5	2013年11月25日	2013年11月27日	日本	CSS 国际会议		0	50
6	2013年11月25日	2013年11月27日	韩国	CSS 国际会议		0	61
7	2014年8月11日	2014年8月22日	韩国	暑期学校	是	3	28
8	2014年8月11日	2014年8月22日	日本	暑期学校	是	3	44
9	2014年9月1日	2015年1月31日	韩国	双学位项目	是	10	4
10	2014年9月1日	2015年1月31日	日本	双学位项目	是	10	6
11	2015年9月1日	2016年1月31日	韩国	双学位项目	是	10	5
12	2015年9月1日	2016年1月31日	日本	双学位项目	是	10	5
13	2016年4月6日	2016年4月8日	韩国	春季研讨会		0	
14	2016年4月6日	2016年4月8日	日本	春季研讨会		0	
15	2016年9月1日	2017年1月31日	韩国	双学位项目	是	10	
16	2016年9月1日	2017年1月31日	日本	双学位项目	是	10	

表 16 学生派出（中国→日本/韩国）

序号	项目持续时间 开始日期	项目持续时间 结束日期	学生参与情况（派至日本/韩国）	流动项目类型	是否授予双学位	国内高校认可的最高学分	派出学生人数
1	2012 年 8 月 16 日	2012 年 8 月 24 日	韩国	暑期学校		0	9
2	2012 年 9 月 1 日	2013 年 1 月 31 日	韩国	交流项目		0	3
3	2012 年 9 月 1 日	2013 年 1 月 31 日	日本	交流项目		0	3
4	2012 年 11 月 20 日	2012 年 11 月 23 日	日本	CSS 国际会议		0	22
5	2013 年 2 月 1 日	2013 年 7 月 1 日	日本	双学位项目	是	10	5
6	2013 年 2 月 22 日	2013 年 2 月 26 日	日本	春季研讨项目		0	10
7	2013 年 8 月 17 日	2013 年 8 月 29 日	韩国	暑期学校	是	3	18
8	2013 年 9 月 1 日	2014 年 1 月 31 日	韩国	双学位项目	是	10	2
9	2014 年 2 月 1 日	2014 年 7 月 1 日	日本	双学位项目	是	10	6
10	2014 年 2 月 22 日	2014 年 2 月 26 日	日本	春季研讨会		0	8
11	2014 年 9 月 1 日	2015 年 1 月 31 日	韩国	双学位项目	是	10	6
12	2014 年 11 月 13 日	2014 年 11 月 15 日	韩国	CSS 国际会议		0	22
13	2015 年 2 月 1 日	2015 年 7 月 1 日	日本	双学位项目	是	10	8
14	2015 年 8 月 17 日	2015 年 8 月 27 日	日本	暑期学校	是	3	33
15	2015 年 9 月 1 日	2016 年 1 月 31 日	韩国	双学位项目	是	10	8
16	2015 年 11 月 13 日	2015 年 11 月 15 日	日本	CSS 国际会议		0	8
17	2016 年 2 月 1 日	2016 年 7 月 1 日	日本	双学位项目	是	10	
18	2016 年 8 月 17 日	2016 年 8 月 27 日	韩国	暑期学校	是	3	
19	2016 年 9 月 1 日	2017 年 1 月 31 日	韩国	双学位项目	是	10	

9. 公共危机管理项目

表 17 学生接收（日本/韩国→中国）

序号	项目持续时间		学生参与情况（来自日本/韩国）	流动项目类型	是否授予双学位	国内高校认可的最高学分	接收学生人数
	开始日期	结束日期					
1	2012 年 9 月 1 日	2013 年 7 月 15 日	韩国	双学位项目（研究生项目，1 年）	是	10	2
2	2012 年 9 月 1 日	2013 年 7 月 15 日	日本	双学位项目（研究生项目，1 年）	是	10	2
3	2012 年 9 月 1 日	2013 年 1 月 31 日	韩国	交流项目（研究生项目，6 个月）		10	2
4	2012 年 9 月 1 日	2013 年 7 月 15 日	日本	交流项目（研究生项目，1 年）		10	1
5	2013 年 9 月 1 日	2014 年 7 月 15 日	韩国	双学位项目（研究生项目，1 年）	是	10	3
6	2013 年 9 月 1 日	2014 年 7 月 15 日	日本	双学位项目（研究生项目，1 年）	是	10	2
7	2013 年 9 月 1 日	2014 年 1 月 31 日	韩国	交流项目（研究生项目，6 个月）		10	2
8	2013 年 9 月 1 日	2014 年 1 月 31 日	日本	交流项目（研究生项目，6 个月）		10	2
9	2014 年 9 月 1 日	2015 年 7 月 15 日	韩国	双学位项目（研究生项目，1 年）	是	10	1
10	2014 年 9 月 1 日	2015 年 7 月 15 日	日本	双学位项目（研究生项目，1 年）	是	10	4
11	2014 年 9 月 1 日	2015 年 7 月 15 日	日本	交流项目（研究生项目，1 年）		10	1
12	2014 年 9 月 1 日	2015 年 1 月 31 日	韩国	交流项目（研究生项目，6 个月）		10	4
13	2015 年 3 月 1 日	2015 年 7 月 15 日	韩国	交流项目（研究生项目，6 个月）		10	3
14	2015 年 9 月 1 日	2016 年 7 月 15 日	韩国	双学位项目（研究生项目，1 年）	是	10	3
15	2015 年 9 月 1 日	2016 年 7 月 15 日	韩国	交流项目（研究生项目，1 年）		10	1
16	2015 年 9 月 1 日	2016 年 1 月 31 日	日本	交流项目（研究生项目，6 个月）		10	1

表 18　学生派出（中国→日本/韩国）

序号	项目持续时间		学生参与情况		流动项目类型	是否授予双学位	国内高校认可的最高学分	派出学生人数
	开始日期	结束日期	（派至日本/韩国）					
1	2012 年 9 月 1 日	2013 年 7 月 15 日	韩	国	双学位项目（研究生项目，1 年）	是	10	2
2	2012 年 9 月 1 日	2013 年 1 月 31 日	韩	国	交流项目（研究生项目，6 个月）		10	2
3	2012 年 9 月 1 日	2013 年 7 月 15 日	日	本	双学位项目（研究生项目，1 年）	是	10	3
4	2013 年 9 月 1 日	2014 年 7 月 15 日	韩	国	双学位项目（研究生项目，1 年）	是	10	2
5	2013 年 9 月 1 日	2014 年 1 月 31 日	韩	国	交流项目（研究生项目，6 个月）		10	3
6	2013 年 9 月 1 日	2014 年 7 月 15 日	日	本	双学位项目（研究生项目，1 年）	是	10	2
7	2013 年 9 月 1 日	2014 年 1 月 31 日	日	本	交流项目（研究生项目，6 个月）		10	4
8	2014 年 9 月 1 日	2015 年 7 月 15 日	日	本	双学位项目（研究生项目，1 年）	是	10	3
9	2014 年 9 月 1 日	2015 年 1 月 31 日	日	本	交流项目（研究生项目，6 个月）		10	3
10	2014 年 9 月 1 日	2015 年 7 月 15 日	韩	国	双学位项目（研究生项目，1 年）	是	10	1
11	2014 年 9 月 1 日	2015 年 1 月 31 日	韩	国	交流项目（研究生项目，6 个月）		10	4
12	2015 年 9 月 1 日	2016 年 1 月 31 日	日	本	交流项目（研究生项目，6 个月）		10	4

10. 流动校园项目

表 19 学生接收（韩国/日本→中国）

序号	项目持续时间		学生参与情况（来自日本/韩国）	流动项目类型	是否授予双学位	国内高校认可的最高学分	接收学生人数
	开始日期	结束日期					
1	2012 年 8 月 4 日	2012 年 8 月 10 日（日本）/ 2012 年 8 月 11 日（韩国）	日本/韩国	短期交流		2/0	32
2	2013 年 2 月 16 日	2013 年 4 月 29 日（日本）/ 2013 年 4 月 30 日（韩国）	日本/韩国	长期交流（本科生项目）		10/16	18
3	2014 年 2 月 15 日	2014 年 4 月 28 日（日本）/ 2014 年 4 月 29 日（韩国）	日本/韩国	长期交流（本科生项目）		13/18	20
4	2015 年 3 月 7 日	2015 年 5 月 28 日	韩国	实习生		0/0	7
5	2012 年 2 月 19 日	2012 年 2 月 24 日	日本/韩国	短期交流		2/0	29
6	2014 年 2 月 18 日	2014 年 2 月 22 日	日本/韩国	短期交流		2/2	23
7	2013 年 8 月 31 日	2014 年 7 月 12 日	韩国	长期交流（硕士项目）		0	2
8	2014 年 9 月 9 日	2015 年 7 月 25 日	韩国	长期交流（硕士项目）		0	1
9	2014 年 9 月 9 日	2015 年 7 月 25 日	日本	长期交流（硕士项目）	是	10	1

表 20 学生派出（中国→韩国/日本）

序号	项目持续时间		学生参与情况（派至日本/韩国）	流动项目类型	是否授予双学位	国内高校认可的最高学分	派出学生人数
	开始日期	结束日期					
1	2012 年 8 月 13 日	2012 年 8 月 20 日	韩 国	短期交流		0	20
2	2012 年 8 月 21 日	2012 年 8 月 27 日	日 本	短期交流		0	20
3	2012 年 8 月 24 日	2013 年 1 月 27 日	韩 国	长期交流（硕士项目）		0	5
4	2013 年 2 月 26 日	2013 年 12 月 31 日	韩 国	长期交流（硕士项目）		12	4
5	2013 年 5 月 6 日	2013 年 8 月 8 日	日 本	长期交流（本科生项目）		14	10
6	2013 年 9 月 3 日	2013 年 12 月 7 日	韩 国	长期交流（本科生项目）		14	10
7	2014 年 2 月 27 日	2014 年 7 月 31 日	韩 国	长期交流（硕士项目）		6	4
8	2014 年 5 月 1 日	2014 年 8 月 4 日	日 本	长期交流（本科生项目）		20	10
9	2014 年 9 月 14 日	2014 年 12 月 25 日	韩 国	长期交流（本科生项目）		8	10
10	2014 年 8 月 27 日	2015 年 1 月 27 日	韩 国	长期交流（硕士项目）		6	4
11	2015 年 2 月 27 日	2015 年 7 月 29 日	韩 国	长期交流（硕士项目）		6	4
12	2012 年 7 月 28 日	2012 年 8 月 3 日	日 本	短期交流		2	20
13	2013 年 2 月 19 日	2013 年 2 月 23 日	韩 国	短期交流		2	13
14	2013 年 7 月 30 日	2013 年 8 月 3 日	日 本	短期交流		2	16
15	2014 年 7 月 27 日	2014 年 8 月 1 日	日 本	短期交流		2	12
16	2015 年 2 月 3 日	2015 年 2 月 7 日	韩 国	短期交流		2	17

Chapter I

"CAMPUS Asia" Initiative and Quality Assurance

Quality Report of "CAMPUS Asia" Cross-border Higher Education Programs

CAMPUS Asia, the abbreviation for Collective Action of Mobility Program of University Students in Asia, was jointly announced and initiated by Wen Jiabao, the premier of the State Council of China, Lee Myung – bak, the Korean president and Yoshihiko Noda, the prime minister of Japan at the fifth China – Japan – ROK Leaders' Meeting in 2012. Through mutual credit recognition and degree granting among universities, the cross – border cooperation program aims to promote the free flow of students among Asian campuses, increase the mutual understanding of students in the three countries and contribute to the enhancement of universities' competitiveness and training of next – generation distinguished talents in Asia.

I. Introduction of the "CAMPUS Asia" Initiative

In October 2009, the idea of enhancing exchange and cooperation among universities of China, Japan and South Korea was proposed at the second China – Japan – ROK Leaders' Meeting. In order to implement the consensus, through negotiations, education authorities of the three countries decided to establish the Trilateral Committee for Promoting Exchange and Cooperation among Universities which consists of government authorities, universities, evaluation agencies and industry representatives. The Committee focused on promotion of university exchange, mutual credit transfer, higher education quality assurance and other issues.

On April 16, 2010, the first meeting of the Committee was held in Tokyo, Japan. A consensus was reached at the meeting on facilitating the exchange and cooperation among universities of the three countries. The three countries intended to initiate a university exchange initiative, which is called "CAMPUS Asia".

On December 10, 2010, the second meeting of the Committee was held in Beijing, China. The *Guiding Ideas on China – Japan – South Korea University Exchange and Cooperation with Quality Assurance* and the *Framework of "CAMPUS Asia" Initiative for China – Japan – South Korea University Exchange* were passed at the meeting. Both guidelines specified tasks and responsibilities of governments, evaluation agencies, universities and the industry in the university exchange initiative. Also, a consensus on the implementation of pilot programs was reached at the meeting.

On May 17, 2011, the third meeting of the Committee was held in Jeju Island. At the meeting, details regarding implementation of "CAMPUS Asia" pilot programs were fully discussed and matters about pilot programs were determined, including scope of participating universities, number of communication groups and students, period of pilot programs, program support offered by governments and universities, etc.

On May 13, 2012, "CAMPUS Asia", aiming to facilitate exchange and cooperation among Chinese, Japanese and Korean universities, was jointly initiated by Wen Jiabao, the premier of the State Council of China, Lee Myung – bak, the Korean president and Yoshihiko Noda, the prime minister of Japan.

The first 10 pilot programs cover 26 well – known Chinese, Japanese and Korean universities, with an implementation period of 5 years. Each year, three countries plan to send and receive 100 exchange students respectively. The 10 programs include:

(1) BEST (Beijing – Seoul – Tokyo) Alliance – Asia Business Leaders Program (Peking University, Hitotsubashi University, Seoul National University, Hereinafter referred to as the "ABLP")

Program Information		
Chinese university		Peking University
Partner universities	Japanese university	Hitotsubashi University
	Korean university	Seoul National University
Program title	Chinese	BEST（北京—首尔—东京）商学院联盟—亚洲商业领袖项目
	English	BEST（Beijing – Seoul – Tokyo）Alliance – Asia Business Leaders Program（ABLP）
Program Content		
Academic field/participating school and department	Academic fields: Business Administration; Participating schools: Guanghua School of Management, Peking University (China); Graduate School of International Corporate Strategy of Hitotsubashi University (Japan); Business School of Seoul National University (South Korea)	
Objectives and expected results	The program originates from BEST (Beijing – Seoul – Tokyo) Alliance, which is signed by Guanghua School of Management, Peking University, Business School of Seoul National University and Graduate School of International Corporate Strategy of Hitotsubashi University. The Alliance devotes itself to promoting the cooperation and exchange among leading business schools of China, Japan and South Korea. ABLP aims to develop the participating students into business leaders that lead the economic relations of China, Japan and South Korea in the future. In November 2011, subject to rigorous selection by Chinese, Japanese and South Korean governments, the program became the sole economics and management program that was chosen for the "CAMPUS Asia" initiative.	

continued

	Exchange type		Students' level		Exchange period	Others
Program plan (2012 – 2015)	Degree program	√	Undergraduate	□	One academic year	√
	Semester exchange	√	Master	√	One semester	√
	Short – term exchange	√	Doctor	□	Summer and winter vacations	√

（2）BESETO Dual Degree Master's Program on International and Public Policy Studies（Peking University, University of Tokyo, Seoul National University, Hereinafter referred to as the "BESETO DDMP"）

Program Information		
Chinese university		Peking University
Partner universities	Japanese university	The University of Tokyo
	Korean university	Seoul National University
Program title	Chinese	国际关系及公共政策双硕士学位项目
	English	BESETO Dual Degree Master's Program on International and Public Policy Studies（BESETO DDMP）
Program Content		
Academic field/participating school and department	Academic fields:	International Relations, Law and Public Policy
	Participating schools:	School of International Studies, Peking University Graduate School of Public Policy, University of Tokyo Graduate School of International Studies, Seoul National University
Objectives and expected results		Through the establishment of the dual degree Master's Program in International Relations, Law and Public Policy which focuses on the research on issues of East Asia, the program aims to facilitate exchanges among young students, train leading talents in public policy, strengthen higher education cooperation and provide support to national foreign policies.

	Exchange type		Students' level		Exchange period	Others
Program plan	Degree program	√	Undergraduate	□	One academic year	√
	Semester exchange	√	Master	√	One semester	√
	Short – term exchange	√	Doctor	□	Summer and winter vacations	√

(3) TKT Campus Asia Program

(Tsinghua University, Tokyo Institute of Technology, Korea Advanced Institute of Science and Technology, Hereinafter referred to as the "TKT Program")

Program Information		
Chinese university	Tsinghua University	
Partner universities	Japanese university	Tokyo Institute of Technology
	Korean university	Korea Advanced Institute of Science and Technology
Program title	Chinese	TKT（中国清华大学—韩国科学技术院—日本东京工业大学）亚洲校园项目
	English	TKT Campus Asia Program (Tsinghua – KAIST – Tokyo Tech)
Program Content		
Academic field/participating school and department	Engineering; Department of Mechanical Engineering, Department of Chemical Engineering, Department of Precision Instrument, Department of Industrial Engineering, Department of Electronic Engineering, School of Aerospace Engineering, School of Life Sciences, etc.	
Objectives and expected results	In this program, joint degree, semester exchange, summer vacation program, joint training and research and other cooperation modes are established and academic programs at undergraduate, master and doctor levels are offered, which reflects flexible program implementation and satisfies students' diversified demands. Any student who is enrolled by the dual degree program of Tsinghua University and Tokyo Institute of Technology may obtain master's degrees of both universities if he/she satisfies the requirements specified by the two. For any student who participates in the semester exchange program, his/her credits obtained at his visiting university will be recognized by the home university if he/she meets relevant requirements. That means credits of both universities are mutually recognized. A summer vacation program often has clear specialties and themes.	

Program plan	Exchange type		Students' level		Exchange period		Others
	Degree program	√	Undergraduate	√	One academic year	√	
	Semester exchange	√	Master	√	One semester	√	
	Short – term exchange	√	Doctor	√	Summer and winter vacations	√	

(4) Northeast Asian Consortium for Policy Studies

[Tsinghua University, National Graduate Institute for Policy Studies (GRIPS), School of Public Policy and Management, Korea Development Institute (KDI), Hereinafter referred to as the "Policy Consortium Program"]

Program Information		
Chinese university	Tsinghua University	
Partner universities	Japanese university	National Graduate Institute for Policy Studies (GRIPS)
	Korean university	Korea Development Institute (KDI)
Program title	Chinese	东北亚政策研究联合会
	English	Northeast Asian Consortium for Policy Studies
Program Content		
Academic fields/participating schools and departments	Public Policy and Management; School of Public Administration	
Objectives and expected results	The Northeast Asian Consortium for Policy Studies Program serves the overall foreign affairs of neighboring countries through exchanges with universities of such countries. The program may enable students to obtain more opportunities for international exchanges and expand students' vision. Also, it can increase the international influence of schools, facilitate the cooperation of China, Japan and South Korea in management disciplines and further improve internationalization level.	

Program plan	Exchange type		Students' level		Exchange period		Others
	Degree program	□	Undergraduate	□	One academic year		□√
	Semester exchange	□√	Master	□√	One semester		□√
	Short – term exchange	□√	Doctor	□√	Summer and winter vacations		□√

(5) Training Human Resources for the Development of an Epistemic Community in Law and Political Science to Promote the Formation of "jus commune" in East Asia (Renmin University of China/Tsinghua University/Shanghai Jiao Tong University, Nagoya University, SungKyunKwan University, Seoul National University, Hereinafter referred to as the "Legal Talent Program")

Program Information		
Chinese university	Renmin University of China, Tsinghua University, Shanghai Jiao Tong University	
Partner universities	Japanese university	Nagoya University
	Korean university	SungKyunKwan University, Seoul National University
Program title	Chinese	培养东亚地区具有法律、政治理念共识，能够推动东亚共同体法制形成与发展的人才项目
	English	Training Human Resources for the Development of an Epistemic Community in Law and Political Science to Promote the Formation of "jus commune" in East Asia
Program Content		
Academic field/participating school and department	Law; School of Law	
Objectives and expected results	With a focus on student exchanges among six universities from China, Japan and South Korea, the program selects excellent undergraduates and graduates from partner universities of China, Japan and South Korea to participate in exchange learning. Courses cover language, culture, politics and law of the three countries. The program aims to train talents who have a common understanding of legal and political concepts and could facilitate the forming and development of legal systems in East Asia. Also, diversified student exchanges and various forms of short – term exchanges are offered in the program.	

Program plan	Exchange type		Students' level		Exchange period		Others
	Degree program	☐	Undergraduate	√	One academic year	√	
	Semester exchange	√	Master	√	One semester	√	
	Short – term exchange	√	Doctor	☐	Summer and winter vacations	√	

(6) Program for Joint Training of Public Risk Management Experts in East Asia (Fudan University, Kobe University, Korea University Hereinafter referred to as the "Risk Experts in Asia")

Program Information		
Chinese university	Fudan University	
Partner universities	Japanese university	Kobe University
	Korean university	Korea University

continued

Program Information		
Program title	Chinese	东亚地区公共危机管理人才联合培养计划
	English	Risk Experts in Asia
Program Content		
Academic field/participating school and department	Public Administration (Emergency Management); School of International Relations and Public Affairs	
Objectives and expected results	The program aims to train the experts in China, Japan and South Korea who are familiar with risks management issues in Asia and promote the international development of emergency management disciplines in the three countries. In view of frequent natural and urban disasters in the three countries, the three governments are studying how to expand emergency scope, enhance the capacity of emergency management and improve the effect and robustness of emergency management according to the changes in economic society and natural conditions. At the beginning of the program, it was agreed by the three universities that the program would identify its position as training trilateral experts that have a good knowledge of risk management issues in Asia. Students are required to understand basic principles of risk management and related practices of Northeastern Asia by systematically learning risk management and conducting master's thesis research in order to create conditions for the development of risk management practices and regional cooperation of Northeastern Asia.	

Program plan	Exchange type		Students' level		Exchange period		Others
	Degree program	√	Undergraduate	□	One academic year		√
	Semester exchange	√	Master	√	One semester		√
	Short – term exchange	□	Doctor	□	Summer and winter vacations		□

(7) Co – operational Graduate Education Program for the Development of Global Human Resources in Energy and Environmental Science and Technology (Shanghai Jiao Tong University, Kyushu University, Pusan National University, Hereinafter referred to as the "EEST Program")

Program Information		
Chinese university		Shanghai Jiao Tong University
Partner universities	Japanese university	Kyushu University
	Korean university	Pusan National University
Program title	Chinese	中日韩能源与环境领域研究生教育合作计划
	English	EEST Program
Program Content		
Academic field/participating school and department		Energy and Environment; School of Mechanical Engineering, School of Environmental Science and Engineering, Graduate School
Objectives and expected results		The program aims to develop a postgraduate education system with quality guaranteed that can satisfies the requirements for human resources in the energy and environmental science and technology field and train next – generation high – level environment and energy talents. After participating in the program, participants are expected to have: (1) the ability of high – level professional practice and research; (2) the ability to understand and solve energy and environmental issues; (3) ability to skillfully apply English; (4) professional moral quality and understanding of pluralistic culture to be equipped by researchers and engineers in the era of globalization.

Program plan	Exchange type		Students' level		Exchange period		Others
	Degree program	√	Undergraduate	☐	One academic year	☐	
	Semester exchange	☐	Master	√	One semester	√	
	Short – term exchange	☐	Doctor	☐	Summer and winter vacations	√	

(8) A Cooperative Asian Education Gateway for a Sustainable Society: Expanding the Frontiers in Science and Technology of Chemistry and Materials (Nanjing University/Shanghai Jiao Tong University, Nagoya University/Tohoku University, Seoul National University/ POSTECH, Hereinafter referred to as the "Chemistry and Materials Program")

Program Information		
Chinese university		Nanjing University, Shanghai Jiao Tong University
Partner universities	Japanese university	Nagoya University, Tohoku University
	Korean university	Seoul National University, POSTECH

continued

Program Information	
Program title	**Chinese** 可持续社会的亚洲教育合作门户——扩展化学、材料科学和技术的前沿
	English A Cooperative Asian Education Gateway for a Sustainable Society: Expanding the Frontiers in Science and Technology of Chemistry and Materials

Program Content	
Academic field/participating school and department	Chemistry; School of Chemical Engineering
Objectives and expected results	The program plans to build a trilateral chemical education center in Asia and aims to facilitate the development of a sustainable society via cooperative education and research. Each year, 30 undergraduates or postgraduates in total with potential in research are planned to be exchanged among member universities, with a period of 3 to 12 months. It aims to teach students research and development guidelines on environment – friendly materials through exchanges. During the exchanges at the receiving university, postgraduates would study the advanced courses that may reflect the advantages of each member university and apply the knowledge into actual research issues. Additionally, it is intended to conduct exchanges among short – term lecture teachers, encouraging teachers of member schools to facilitate mutual understanding and joint exploration in the joint research field. The program is expected to train prospective leaders in the related materials field, who would acquire a good ability of understanding and communication and extend their experience to the academic or industry work of any partner country for the prosperity and benefit of their homeland. It is also hoped that each student would understand the history, culture and thinking modes of foreign countries without using his/her native language so as to improve his/her global awareness and spirit of devotion. Finally, it is planned that cooperation in chemical and medical enterprises will be enhanced in the each partner country so as to offer more opportunities for special lectures, internship and employment.

Program plan	Exchange type		Students' level		Exchange period		Others
	Degree program	□	Undergraduate	√	One academic year	√	
	Semester exchange	√	Master	√	One semester	√	
	Short – term exchange	√	Doctor	√	Summer and winter vacations	□	

(9) Program for Core Human Resources Development: For the Achievement of Common Good and the Re-evaluation of Classical Culture in East Asia (Jilin University, Okayama University, SungKyunKwan University, Hereinafter referred to as the "Traditional Culture Program")

Program Information		
Chinese university		Jilin University
Partner universities	Japanese university	Okayama University
	Korean university	SungKyunKwan University
Program title	Chinese	核心人才培养项目：东亚地区共同利益的实现及传统文化的重视
	English	Program for Core Human Resources Development: For the Achievement of Common Good and the Re-evaluation of Classical Culture in East Asia
Program Content		
Academic field/participating school and department	Humanities and Social Science; Faculty of Arts and Humanities, Faculty of Social Sciences; School of Law, School of Economics, School of Public Administration, School of Business, College of Arts, College of International Education, College of Foreign Languages, School of Philosophy and Sociology, School of Foreign Language Education, Northeast Asia Research Institute, etc.	
Objectives and expected results	The purpose of this program is to facilitate mutual understanding of the youths of China, Japan and South Korea, enhance the cooperation in human resources and the building of common values and train youth talents with broad vision and understanding for the development of Northeast Asia. While adding the "traditional culture" factor in curriculum setting, the participating universities offer participants the courses to understand the overall conditions of China, Japan and South Korea and the opportunities to get engaged in cultural experience activities. Also, exchanges among participating students of China, Japan and South Korea are actively organized to further enhance their mutual understanding.	

Program plan	Exchange type		Students' level		Exchange period		Others
	Degree program	☐	Undergraduate	√	One academic year	√	
	Semester exchange	√	Master	√	One semester	√	
	Short – term exchange	√	Doctor	√	Summer and winter vacations	√	

（10）Plan for a Joint Campus Representing Korea, China and Japan which will Foster Leaders in East Asian Humanities for the Next Generation（Guangdong University of Foreign Studies, Ritsumeikan University, Dongseo University, Hereinafter referred to as the "Mobile Campus Program"）

Program Information		
Chinese university	Guangdong University of Foreign Studies	
Partner universities	Japanese university	Ritsumeikan University
	Korean university	Dongseo University
Program title	Chinese	中日韩三方联合培养东亚地区跨世代人文精英之流动校园工程
	English	Plan for a Joint Campus Representing Korea, China and Japan which will Foster Leaders in East Asian Humanities for the Next Generation
Program Content		
Academic field/participating school and department	Humanities（Culture, Literature, History, etc.）Department of Japanese Language and Literature & Department of Korean Language and Literature, Faculty of Asian Languages and Cultures; Institute for International Education; Faculty of Chinese Language and Culture	
Objectives and expected results	The program integrates effective resources of China, Japan and South Korea. It is expressly specified that the program aims to train interdisciplinary innovative talents who have rich accomplishments in Eastern Asian culture, get familiar with international rules and be able to directly get involved in international governance. A complete circumlunar system was jointly designed by the three countries and special faculty and management teams were formed. The "Mobile Campus" mode implemented in the three countries can be called a pioneer in China. It combines the "mobile students" and long-distance multimedia teaching in an organic manner. An international class is formed by participating students and covers four semesters in two years. Students live and study in the "Mobile Campus" program among China, Japan and South Korea and appreciate the charm of teachers under different cultures.	

Program plan	Exchange type		Students' level		Exchange period		Others
	Degree program	√	Undergraduate	√	One academic year	□	Four-year mobile campus courses
	Semester exchange	□	Master	□	One semester	□	
	Short-term exchange	□	Doctor	□	Summer and winter vacations	□	

Note: The universities that participate in each program form a consortium.

In terms of academic field, the 10 pilot programs cover Management, Philosophy, Arts, Science, Engineering, Law, Economics, etc. These programs not only bring the advantages of discipline development and professional school operation into full play and also meet the demand for regional development of Northeast Asia. In terms of academic level, most of these programs highlight graduate talent training and some programs expressly focus on undergraduate talent training, with distinguished characteristics. In terms of exchange type, there are dual degree programs (tri – degree or joint degrees are pilot in some programs), semester/academic year exchange programs and short – term exchange programs. In the 10 pilot programs, program resources were made good use of and various forms of university exchange campaigns were organized, in order to explore the patterns and systems suitable for cooperation and exchanges of universities in Asia. Also, exchange programs of different types and levels were planned to develop based on the rich experience and good practices derived from pilot programs so as to expand program scale.

Number of Student exchanges in the "CAMPUS Asia" pilot programs is listed in Appedix:

II. Quality Assurance of "CAMPUS Asia" Initiative

In order to facilitate university exchanges, mutual credit transfer and recognition, quality assurance and monitoring and other work of the "CAMPUS Asia" initiative, two working groups are established by the Trilateral Committee for Promoting Exchange and Cooperation among Universities (hereinafter referred to as the "Committee"): university exchange working group and quality assurance working group. The China – Japan – South Korea Quality Assurance Council (hereinafter referred to as the "Council") is responsible for specific work of the quality assurance working group [Chinese party: Higher Education Evaluation Committee of the Ministry of Education of China (HEEC); Japanese party: National Institute for Academic Degrees and University Evaluation (NIAD – UE); Korean party: Korean Council for University Education, Korean University Accreditation Institute (KCUE – KUAI)]. The pilot programs of "CAMPUS Asia" last 5 years. Quality monitoring on pilot programs was conducted in two rounds. In the first round of quality monitoring for the mid – term of the pilot programs, quality assurance agencies of the three countries conducted quality monitoring and evaluation of the programs of their own countries. In the final period of pilot programs, final quality evaluation is made, and the experts of quality assurance agencies of the three countries organized joint evaluation on the 10 pilot program consortiums that participate in "CAMPUS Asia" programs. From the year 2012 to 2016, the Council had completed two rounds of quality monitoring of pilot programs of "CAMPUS Asia" successively.

1. First Round of Quality Monitoring of "CAMPUS Asia" Pilot Programs

In 2013, during the mid – term of pilot programs, quality assurance evaluation agencies of the three countries conducted quality monitoring of the programs of their countries based on the criteria and procedures they formulated.

The quality assurance of "CAMPUS Asia" Initiative is paid high attention by the Ministry of Education of China. It is expressly specified in the *Notice on the Implementation Requirements Regarding "CAMPUS Asia" Pilot Programs* (Jiao Wai Si Ya [2012] No. 365) published by the Department of International Cooperation and Exchange that, "Education authorities of China, Japan and South Korea would organize relevant quality assurance agencies to carry out mid – term and final evaluations on the implementation of pilot programs, enhance quality inspection and accumulate experience so as to facilitate the healthy and orderly advancement of these programs". Also, the Department issued the *Notice on Enhancing the Quality Monitoring of "CAMPUS Asia" Pilot Programs* (Jiao Wai Si Ya [2013] No. 1837) and the *Notice on Submitting the Self – assessment Report of "CAMPUS Asia" Pilot Programs* (Jiao Wai Si Ya [2014] No. 1184), which provides guidelines and specific requirements for quality monitoring and evaluation of pilot programs.

From June to July in 2014, the Higher Education Evaluation Center of the Ministry of Education (hereinafter referred to as HEEC) carried out midterm round quality monitoring of the 10 pilot programs. The quality monitoring features with three new principles that go as follows: first, new philosophy featuring "university centered", "student oriented", "audit focused" and "outcome based" were set up; second, new criteria reflecting both commonness and diversities of the pilot programs and focusing on six essential dimensions of quality were created; third, new methodology with a combination of self – evaluation of universities, mutual peer evaluation between the universities, and expert panel review were adopted, being creative, simple and feasible. In line with the principle of "evidence – and – data – based", and in light of the materials of self – evaluation, judgments from mutual peer evaluation, and reports of the expert panel review, HEEC has drafted and finalized the *Midterm Quality Monitoring Report of CAMPUS Asia Pilot Programs*.

In the *Report*, the scores or ratings were assigned with values or weights. Values were subject to normalization. Then, individiual scores of 10 pilot programs as well as total score after all standard items were combined. Also, individual and comprehensive rankings of pilot programs were given. On the whole, the objectives of pilot programs can basically reflect the academic strength and characteristics of transnational programs. Basic organization implementation and teaching activities of programs are guaranteed and most programs run well. A service support system that can satisfy students' demand is basically built in programs. Programs are better in hardware aspects including learning environment and facilities, and students are greatly satisfied with these programs. However, the programs remain to be developed in software aspects such as academic tutoring and consulting service, as well as quality assurance and learning outcome. The awareness of "quality focused", "student development based" and "learning outcome oriented" is to be enhanced.

During the period from November 2014 to January 2015, in order to further summarize the practice experience of "CAMPUS Asia" pilot programs and to implement the requirements for "selecting good practices for promotion" specified in the Agreement of the 4th Meeting of Korea – China – Japan Committee for Promoting Exchange and Cooperation among Universities, HEEC initiated the selection of good practices for HEEC pilot programs based on staged deliverables obtained by each program. A combination of university self – nominations, expert review and field research was adopted to select good practices of "CAMPUS Asia" pilot programs. These good practices can reflect the aim, objectives and advantages of multilateral cooperation mode. Being typical, innovative and effective, the practices pay special attention to explorations in terms of talent training mode, curriculum teaching, qualified faculty, mutual credit recognition and mutual credit grating, quality assurance, etc. , which are worthy of recognition. Based on full survey, HEEC finalized the *Collection of Good Practices of CAMPUS Asia Pilot Programs* and briefly introduced good practices of CAMPUS Asia, such as trilateral joint bachelor talent training mode, trilateral training mode of degree program + summer school + international conference, teaching research of university – enterprise cooperation system, university – school – student program operation management mechanism, multi – language joint course design, information lab teaching platform, long – distance video course, transnational supervisors joint teaching, credit transfer criteria, student result test and satisfaction survey. These good practices fully reflect the unique and innovative characteristics displayed in the practice of seeking common ground while reserving differences and are worthy of publicity and promotion in multilateral cooperation of transnational cooperation. They are of important significance, demonstrating effect for facilitating sustainable development of programs, and exploring multilateral education cooperation mode and education integration of East Asia.

2. Second Round Monitoring of CAMPUS Asia Pilot Programs

The 5th Meeting of the China – Japan – Korea Committee for Promoting Exchange and Cooperation among Universities was held in April, 2015 in Shanghai, China. At the meeting, these three parties reached a consensus and decided to conduct the second round monitoring or final round monitoring at the conclusion of pilot programs.

Goals, Principles and Guildlines for the Joint Quality Monitoring

In the joint quality monitoring of "CAMPUS Asia" pilot programs, we facilitate the continuous quality improvement of these programs by looking at the implementation of the programs by consortiums and the degree of collaborative activities in quality assurance of consortiums; publish joint reports by joint criteria which include collections of good practices in the three countries; and explore the "joint guidelines" for quality assurance of the three countries.

Thus, we conduct a joint quality monitoring by observing the following principles and guidelines:

Promote overall quality enhancement;

Conduct monitoring by joint criteria;

Look at consortium – wide progress and achievement to identify good practices of each party;

Look at the degree of collaboration of consortiums in respect of resource integration and quality assurance activities;

Examine continuous quality improvement of each CAMPUS Asia pilot program; and

Value students' voices/proposals.

Criteria of the Joint Quality Monitoring

Through a careful analysis of the criteria developed for the 1st monitoring by the three parties, we proposed the framework for the second joint monitoring consisting of five criteria based on the core criteria jointly recognized by the three parties. Each of these criteria has two sub – criteria. As shown in the following table, the following information is contained:

Criteria	Sub – criteria	Criteria	Sub – criteria
1. Objectives and Implementation	1. 1 Objective Achievement	3. Student Support	3. 1 Students Admission
	1. 2 Organization and Administration		3. 2 Support for Learning and Living
2. Collaborative Development of Academic Program	2. 1 Curriculum Integration	4. Added – value of the collaborative program	4. 1 Student Satisfaction
			4. 2 Credit Transfer and Degree Awarding
	2. 2 Academic Staff and Teaching	5. Internal Quality Assurance	5. 1 Self – assessment
			5. 2 Continuous Quality Improvement

The criteria system places a great emphasis on the viewpoints as follows:

Consortium – wide goals reached, achievements, and good practice (s) worthy of promotion;

Collaboration of participating universities in each consortium in respect of joint management, resource integration and transnational quality assurance, etc;

Student support and added – value of CAMPUS Asia pilot programs;

Sustainability of quality improvement of each CAMPUS Asia pilot program;

Joint Monitoring Panel Composition and Responsibilities

The quality assurance agencies of the three countries select three experts respectively, at least one of which is quality assurance agency representative, to form a joint monitoring committee. The committee mainly fulfills the following three responsibilities: reviewing the self – assessment reports submitted by 10 consortiums; jointly agreeing on consortiums that needs to be visited on site; and finalizing a final joint monitoring report to fully reflect the monitoring of 10 pilot programs.

The three countries respectively select one to two experts from the joint monitoring committee to form a joint monitoring site visit team. The team mainly fulfills the following two responsibilities: conducting on – site visits according to the criteria of the second round quality monitoring; as well as finalizing a site visit report and submitting to the committee for deliberation upon the completion of survey.

Joint Quality Monitoring Timetable

We identified the year 2016 as the final period of "CAMPUS Asia" pilot programs. Joint monitoring was conducted by the following procedures:

Period	Procedure
April to June, 2015	Compiling a self – assessment report —Each consortium prepares a self – assessment report in English
June to November, 2015	Material review —The joint monitoring panel team members from China, Japan and South Korea conduct material review
November, 2015 to March, 2016	Joint site visit —The China – Japan – Korea joint monitoring panel experts from Renmin University of China (China), Tokyo University (Japan) and Dongseo University (South Korea) conduct a joint site survey
November, 2015 to March, 2016	Interview or site visit —Panel members of each country make an interview or site visit to their homeland universities
October, 2016 to 2017	Joint monitoring committee —Finalization and publication of the *Joint Monitoring Report*

Specific operation procedures are as follows:

Through mutual cooperation, the quality assurance agencies of the three countries offer identical or similar trainings on the purposes and implementation methods of quality monitoring of their participating universities.

Each consortium is required to compile and submit one common (joint) self-assessment report by all participating HEIs in the consortium and summarize program quality in terms of good practices and issues for improvement.

Monitoring Panel members conduct document reviews based on the submitted self-assessment reports.

Monitoring Panel members conduct site visits to interview the officials responsible for the program, faculty and staff involved in the program, and participating students about the matters that are not clear in the document reviews.

Monitoring Panel members produce a draft monitoring report in English on a consortium respectively based on the results of their document review and site visit.

Evaluation agencies supervise and urge the consortium to review the draft monitoring report to ensure the report is free from any factual error. If any factual error is identified, the Monitoring Panel Sub-committee will conduct deliberations.

Monitoring Panel members share the draft monitoring report completed by the consortiums of evaluation agencies of the three countries. Evaluation agencies draw up the draft of final evaluation report based on the monitoring reports submitted by all consortiums. The quality assurance agencies make the finalized monitoring report widely available to the public in the forms of book, network and symposia.

Different from the first round of quality monitoring in which quality evaluation is conducted by three countries on their universities, the second round of quality monitoring adopts a joint mode. Specifically, quality assurance agencies of the three countries recommended or selected high-level experts to form a panel team, which conducted joint document review and site sampling visits on 10 consortiums of participating programs and produced a final quality evaluation report based on the joint evaluation criteria formulated together. The whole process fully reflected the "joint" of the three countries in several aspects and explored a set of new model suitable for quality assurance of "CAMPUS Asia" pilot programs. ①Joint evaluation criteria. Based on the core indicators recognized by the three parties, they proposed a framework for joint quality evaluation criteria including five first-class indicators and ten second-class indicators. This evaluation criteria system especially established for "CAMPUS Asia" initiative highlights the cooperation and consistent quality improvement of the three parties involved in the program. ②Joint self-assessment and self-inspection. By reference to the joint evaluation criteria, participating universities of the three countries sought problems together, conducted self – assessment on the overall program implementation and highlighted the joint management, resource integration and quality assurance of programs. ③Joint Evaluation Panel Team. Quality assurance agencies of the three countries recommended or selected experts and scholars who have the knowledge of internationalization of higher education and representatives of the agencies to form a joint panel team. The team conducted joint document review on the self – assessment reports of programs, formed comprehensive review comments, selected some programs for joint site visits and produced the final quality report.

For 5 years, under the support and guidance of the Ministry of Education, through self – assessment and self – building of participating universities and with the guarantee of the two rounds of quality assurance, participating universities of "CAMPUS Asia" programs have made positive explorations in terms of resource integration, talent training patterns, quality assurance, mutual credit transfer and mutual degree granting by exploiting their advantages and making innovations, and have accumulated valuable experience, thus achieving good phased results.

Chapter II

Cross-border Quality Monitoring Result and Analysis of "CAMPUS Asia" Initiative

Quality Report of "CAMPUS Asia" Cross-border Higher Education Programs

By integrating the joint quality monitoring self – assessment report, panel team site visit report, site investigation report and materials regarding work experience exchange meeting of participating universities, HEEC, together with Japanese and Korean evaluation institutions, fully discussed the good practices of "CAMPUS Asia" pilot programs and made an in – depth analysis of issues for improvement.

I. Objectives and Implementation

1. Experience Summary

During the design stage of "CAMPUS Asia", participating universities within the consortiums discussed the establishment of program objectives and basic framework in combination with their academic and resource advantages and shared them among students, faculty and staff members. The objectives of most programs clearly describe the requirements for students' knowledge, ability and quality; fully reflect the characteristics and additional value of multinational cooperation programs and provide guidance for program operation.

In terms of system building, from the perspective of quality assurance, consortiums specified in the written cooperation agreement the talent training level, cross – university cooperation mode, organization management mechanism, division of responsibilities as well as supporting personnel, funds, site facilities and other systems. All participating universities formulated special management measures on the "CAMPUS Asia" pilot programs or incorporated the programs into the existing teaching management systems and specifications and managed them strictly according to the unified standards. Detailed provisions were formulated in the management measures on course setting, teaching management, student service, etc., with clear responsibilities as well as feasible and practical solutions. The multi – layer working and collaboration mechanisms were built to provide guarantee for the normal advancement of programs, facilitate the effective achievement of program objectives and offer necessary support to participating students for effectively maintaining their rights and benefits. In terms of organization and management, "CAMPUS Asia" programs were highly appreciated by the university – level leaders of most

First 10 "CAMPUS Asia" Pilot Programs

Chinese Higher Institution	Japanese Higher Institution	Korean Higher Institution	Program Name	Program Abbreviation	Program Type
Peking University	Hitotsubashi University	Seoul National University	BEST (Beijing – Seoul – Tokyo) Alliance Asia Business Leaders Program (ABLP)	ABLP	With a focus on Short – term Exchange Program (Master)
Peking University	The University of Tokyo	Seoul National University	BESETO Dual Degree Master's Program on International and Public Policy Studies (BESETO DDMP)	BESETO DDMP	Master Semester Exchange Program
Tsinghua University	National Graduate Institute for Policy Studies (GRIPS)	KDI School of Public Policy and Management	Northeast Asian Consortium for Policy Studies	Policy Consortium Program	Master Semester Exchange Program
Tsinghua University	Tokyo Institute of Technology	Korean Institute of Science and Technology	TKT Campus Asia Program (Tsinghua – KAIST – Tokyo Tech)	TKT Program	Dual Master Degree Program
Jilin University	Okayama University	SungKyunKwan University	Program for Core Human Resources Development: For the Achievement of Common Good and the Re – evaluation of Classical Culture in East Asia	Traditional Culture Program	Master and Doctor Semester Degree Program

continude

Chinese Higher Institution	Japanese Higher Institution	Korean Higher Institution	Program Name	Program Abbreviation	Program Type
Renmin University of China/Tsinghua University/Shanghai Jiao Tong University	Nagoya University	SungKyunKwan University/Seoul National University	Training Human Resources for the Development of an Epistemic Community in Law and Political Science to Promote the Formation of "jus commune" in East Asia	Legal Talent Program	Long – term Undergraduate Exchange Program
Nanjing University/Shanghai Jiao Tong University	Nagoya University/Tohoku University	Seoul National University/POSTECH	A Cooperative Asian Education Gateway for a Sustainable Society: Expanding the Frontiers in Science and Technology of Chemistry and Materials	Chemistry and Materials Program	Master Semester Exchange Program
Shanghai Jiao Tong University	Kyushu University	Pusan National University	Co – operational Graduate Education Program for the Development of Global Human Resources in Energy and Environmental Science and Technology	EEST Program	Dual Master Program
Fudan University	Kobe University	Korea University	Program for Careers on Risk Management Experts in East Asia	Public Risk Management Program	Dual Master Program
Guangdong University of Foreign Studies	Ritsumeikan University	Dongseo University	Plan for a Joint Campus representing Korea, China and Japan which will foster leaders in East Asian humanities for the next generation	Mobile Campus Program	Undergraduate Tri – degree Program

participating universities. Led by these leaders, special working teams were organized and resources including personnel, property and materials were provided, basically forming a management system featuring joint participation by stakeholders and two – stage implementation mechanisms involving universities and schools. On the one hand, perfect systems and standard management ensure that program operation is under the guidance of the overall development planning of universities and program implementation can be guaranteed by fully exploiting on – campus and off – campus resources; on the other hand, they guarantee the quality and level of program implementation and facilitate the improvement of universities in terms of international education cooperation.

2. Good Practices

1) Jointly Identify the Objectives and Implementing Framework of Programs, and Clarify Expected Requirements for Knowledge, Ability and Accomplishments

For Public Risk Management Program, by taking advantage of the academic strength in government and public governance, three partner universities made a full discussion on training objectives of the program. According to characteristics of frequent natural and urban disasters in the three countries of Northeast Asia, it was agreed by the three parties that the program objectives would be positioned as training trilateral experts who are familiar with risk management of Asia and could promot the internationalization development of emergency management disciplines in the three countries. The objectives specifically describe the knowledge, ability and accomplishments of students. Students are required to learn risk management knowledge and conduct master's thesis research in a systematic manner, obtain a complete and in – depth understanding of basic principles of risk governance in different countries and acquire solid abilities of academic analysis and practice, thus laying a foundation for their future risk management at public emergency departments both at home and abroad. The consortium brings the academic strength of the three universities into full play: Kobe University offers risk management education in terms of natural disaster and disaster reduction; Korea University offers risk management education regarding safety and energy issues; Fudan University offers risk management education in terms of public policy.

In terms of talent training mode, the Mobile Campus Program made a breakthrough in the traditional bilateral cooperation of multinational education and presented a new pattern of trilateral cooperation, making it a pioneer in China. This new teaching pattern combines "student mobility" and long – distance multimedia teaching. Forming an international class, participating students live and study together on "mobile campuses" of China, Japan and South Korea in four semesters of two academic years and appreciate the demeanor of teachers under different cultures. The university – runnign mode strengthens the international cooperation and exchange of universities in China, Japan and South Korea, ensures mutual complementation of advantages and joint cooperation of strong strengths, and meanwhile fully reflects multilateral characteristics. The mode has a profound influence over our exploration of the integrated development of higher education in the three countries.

Schematic Diagram of Mobile Campuses

中日韩移动（两年间）	Flow among China, Japan and South Korea in Two Years
东西大学校	Dongseo University
立命馆大学	Ritsumeikan University
广东外语外贸大学	Guangdong University of Foreign Studies
各大学的学生	Students of the Three Universities

In the program, Chinese, Japanese and Korean students are organized to flow across universities of different countries, learn the courses jointly offered in universities of the three countries and specialty courses set by these universities, improve foreign language skills and deepen understanding of politics, culture, history, etc. of the three countries. The program aims to train students' ability to analyze and solve problems in the fields of culture, history, politics and education research, making them leading talents in humanity in East Asia. The talent training objectives of the program can be clearly summarized as the following four points in terms of knowledge, skills, communication ability and practical ability: ①Training talents who understand basic knowledge about traditional cultures of East Asia and have great abilities to understand and control the constantly changing situation and status quo of East Asia (level of cognition); ②training the talents who have the great ability of interpreting documents and understand the social, living, historical and media conditions of China, Japan and South Korea by learning their modern cultures (literature, films and TV series, animation, language, etc.) (skills, etc.); ③training talents who are highly capable of communication and could be active on the future international stage through acquisition of Chinese, Japanese and Korean languages, overseas internship and practice (international communication skills); ④ training talents who can solve all problems faced by East Asia in a peaceful way (practical skills).

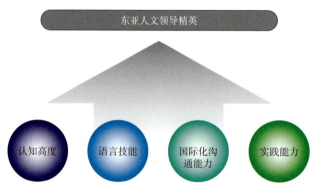

Talent Training Objectives of Mobile Campus Program

东亚人文领导精英	Leaders in East Asian Humanities for the Next Generation
认知高度	Level of Cognition
语言技能	Language Skills
国际化沟通能力	International Communication Skills
实践能力	Practical Skills

Highlighting student exchanges among six universities of China, Japan and South Korea, the Legal Talent Program selects excellent undergraduates and postgraduates for exchanged learning among partner universities of the three countries. The program aims to cultivate human resources for the development of an epistemic community in Law and Political Science to promote the formation of "jus commune" in East Asia. Requirements for students' learning achievements of the program are as follows: As the next-generation legal professionals, participating students should acquire necessary knowledge and skills and actively participate in the formation of "jus commune"; they should be ready to initiate the new trend of research on comparative research and to facilitate the sharing among law information regions; they should have the ability to apply the results to the growth of other Asian countries, especially those seeking for system transformation, and to offer more assistance to these countries in legal cooperation and assistance programs.

The Traditional Culture Program aims to facilitate the mutual understanding among Chinese, Japanese and Korean youths and strengthen the building of human resources cooperation and common values. The three participating parties, namely Jilin University, Okayama University and SungKyunKwan University, are located in the core belts of Northeast Asia, with geographical, historical and cultural proximity. There exists a basis of cooperation among the three parties for teaching, research and exchanges of students & teachers for consecutive years. By taking the "traditional culture" factor into full account, the consortium builds an academic framework for participating students to understand Chinese, Japanese and Korean realities and culture. A global education course system of Humanities in East Asia was developed through discussions among the three. The system was completed by the three universities through division of labor: Okayama University organized practice and investigation; Jilin University offered the international relations course; and SungKyunKwan University offered courses in terms of classical and traditional cultures of East Asia.

For the EEST Program, clear visions and objectives have been identified by the three participating universities: to integrate quality educational resources of the three universities, strengthen exchange and interaction of excellent postgraduates of the three universities while offering dual degree education in the fields of energy and environment sciences as well as engineering, expand the influence and benefits of the program, train distinguished professionals with global vision in the fields of energy and environment sciences and engineering based in Asia, and explore the building of an exemplary education system featuring advancement and diversity in science and engineering related fields. The clear visions and objectives have played a vital role of guidance in the implementation and continuous development of the program.

2) Sharing of Program Objectives among Universities

In the ABLP, program objectives are shared among participating universities via agreement and memorandum of understanding and are regarded as guidelines for education. The memorandum of understanding clearly describes the objectives and vision for human resources development and declares "in order to enhance economic links, business leaders, professors and students from China, Japan and South Korea should learn about economics, society, culture and other important fields of partner countries" and "participating universities will jointly cultivate business leaders who will make great contributions to the common prosperity of East Asia in the future."

The Chemistry and Materials Program shares its objectives through regular meetings held among consortium members. Six universities from the three countries have agreed to hold an annual "CAMPUS Asia" seminar by turns, on which the initial objectives of the program are restated as "to train leading talents with global vision in chemistry and materials". Partner universities make joint efforts to push forward student exchanges and improvement of program operation.

The International Relations Program shares its objectives in the student and teacher selection links. In the program, strict English interview was conducted on the students and teachers to be sent abroad. It is required that both students and teachers should be aware of talent training objectives and graduation requirements of the program and clearly understand learning and teaching objectives. A committee composed of the faculty and staff members who participate in enrollment and course development was established in the program. The committee organizes teaching and research activities according to program objectives.

3) Formulation of Implementation Measures according to Program Objectives

The TKT Program establishes its objectives of training innovative youth pioneers who have good knowledge of language, cultures and customs of the three countries in Asia's technology and humanity areas by bringing the talent training strength of consortium members into full play. The consortium has formulated complete, practical and feasible implementing measures based on program objectives, covering organization and implementation, exchange forms, student qualifications, enrollment plans, application procedures, appointment procedures, training plans, research plans, student performance record, financial liabilities, learning result certificates, mutual credit recognition, quality monitoring, etc.. In consideration of the differences among the three countries in education policy, the implementing measures make detailed explanations on some links. For example, the slight differences of the three countries in mutual credit recognition and credit transfer policies are listed in details in the measures:

Policies on Mutual Credit Recognition and Transfer of TKT Program

Tsinghua University	Korea Advanced Instituteof Science and Technology	Tokyo Institute of Technology
The similar or related courses and credits completed or acquired in any partner university may be transferred and recognized upon approval of the academic office of relevant department.	The transfer of credits of similar courses is subject to the approval of the professor that teaches the course (pass/fail) or competent department.	Before leaving from the visiting university, a student should consult from head or academic consultant of the advisory department on mutual credit recognition. After returning to his/her home university, the student must submit his/her academic performance record and other documents, such as the syllabus and curriculum schedule issued by the visiting universities. Credits obtained from a partner university are recognized by the principal according to the decision made at the teachers' meeting. The grade of credit recognition is "pass".

4) Building a Working Mechanism Linking the Three Parties

In order to ensure smooth operation of the EEST Program, three participating universities establish a Plan – Do – Check – Adjust (PDCA) Leadership Committee, which is responsible for planning, implementation, self – assessment and continuous improvement of the program. A closed loop work system linking three parties is formed. The PDCA Leadership Committee and "CAMPUS Asia" Program Office are established under the Leadership Committee at each university within the consortium, which provides daily support for students (PDCA is the combination of the initial letters of Plan, Do, Check and Adjust. This is a process of cycle. PDCA cycle is also called a quality loop and represents a universal model in management.)

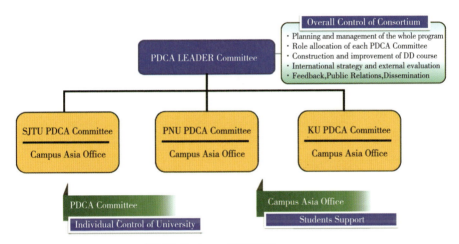

PDCA System of EEST Program

The Mobile Campus Program adopts international good practice in curriculum management. Three participating universities jointly established a "CAMPUS Asia" Academic Affairs Website in Chinese, Japanese and Korean to publish course information. Students may check curriculum plans, their grades and information about their teachers. Students may also sign up for courses independently on the website; teachers may publish information about courses on the website at any time, check students' information and courses selected. All these are helpful for timely exchange of information between teachers and students.

5) Building a Multi – level Negotiation and Communication Collaboration Mechanism

The Legal Talent Program improves quality assurance construction of the project through building a coordination mechanism among school – program – student.

School Level: Coordination Mechanism of "Law School Deans' Meeting on CAMPUS Asia Project"

The program has gained strong support from leadership of six universities of the three coun-

Teacher Management page of "CAMPUS Asia" Academic Affairs Website

Course List of All Programs on "CAMPUS Asia" Academic Affairs Website

tries since it was launched, and formed a coordination mechanism of "Deans' Meeting on Campus Asia Project" consisting of deans of laws schools of the six universities. The "Deans' Meeting on Campus Asia Project" has been held for seven times till 2017, and has conducted in-depth communication in development trend of legal education, reform measures, talents training standards, institution building and other related issues of Asia area, especially of East Asia area. It has become an important platform for legal education and policy reform of East Asia area. Also, it plays a vital role for development and quality assurance of the program.

Program Level: Quality Assurance Committee of CAMPUS Asia Project"

In order to establish a regular coordination mechanism for program operation and solve the issues arising from program operation, program heads and teaching staff in charge formed a "Quality Assurance Committee of CAMPUS Asia Program". Since December 2011, the Committee has held nearly 20 working meetings in Nagoya, Shanghai, Beijing and Seoul. At the meetings, the Committee shared the living and study of the received students, proposed sugges-tions on the selection of next – term students and also made an in – depth discussion of the exist-ing curriculum setting and program development plan. Regular negotiation mechanism is vital to refine student management and implementation of program design in place.

Student Level: "Alumni Association of CAMPUS Asia (law) Project"

In order to further promote the exchange of students from six universities of the three coun-tries and improve the enthusiasm of students to participate in the project and exchange relevant learning feelings and experience, "Alumni Association on CAMPUS Asia (law) Project" com-posed of students from "CAMPUS Asia" project has been formed under the efforts of the Project Quality Assurance Committee in February 2014, and has elected its administrators, which was helpful to improve long – term mechanism for the exchange of students learning. Upon the estab-lishment of the alumni association, the "CAMPUS Asia Program Student Seminar" is held on an annual basis to provide students with a platform of learning and exchange. The association not only share gains from participating programs and make suggestions on program development, but also conduct academic exchanges on the topic of Eastern Asian laws, producing a significant effect. In March 2017, partner universities proposed to increase tutoring on students' career development and to extend the student seminar to exchanges in terms of students' career development. They al-so invited Chinese, Japanese and Korean scholars, attorneys and outstanding people from all in-dustries (including enterprises) to conduct joint exchanges with students and to provide a useful guidance for students' career development upon their graduation. The establishment of the alum-ni association can build a good platform for students' exchanges and learning, enhance inter-action and bring the subjective initiative of students. It also can motivate students' enthusiasm for participation in the program so as to enable them to maintain close interaction after comple-ting exchange learning and facilitate the improvement of their academic performance.

3. Problem Analysis

In terms of objectives setting, "CAMPUS Asia" differs from most student exchange or joint training programs. It makes a breakthrough in traditional mode of bilateral cooperation, highlights multilateral cooperation among China, Japan and South Korea, builds the awareness of community in Asia through closer and more frequent student exchanges, explores the possi-bility of regional education integration, and creates conditions for free flow of more students in Asia in order to train distinguished talents of next generation. However, the uniqueness and ne-cessity of "CAMPUS Asia" Initiative failed to be understood by some participating universi-ties. Few of their program objectives highlight the innovation in terms of system (such as multi-lateral cooperation, mutual credit recognition and joint degree granting), and most of them are still limited to the objectives of traditional point – to – point cooperation. Due to macro objectives setting, some programs fail to reflect the integration of multilateral advantages that is different from bilateral cooperation, and are described with no focuses. For example, no clear and detailed descriptions are provided regarding students' learning outcome in some programs.

In terms of organization and implementation, for a few programs, no balanced roles and complete communication mechanism are available among China, Japan and South Korea, no mechanism of link has been built and forms of cooperation are highlighted more than content. Some programs are poorly managed; although multiple departments (schools) and functional departments are involved, there is no clear division of responsibilities. The lack of program executives and the difficulties in coordination and arrangement have affected program implementation. Some other programs are under the jurisdiction of single department or school; however, due to the lack of emphasis at the university level and cooperation by relevant departments, they are poorly implemented. Both conditions mentioned above have caused certain impacts on the achievements of expected program results. As there is a big difference among the three countries in terms of program investment form (for Japan and South Korea, annual special fund allocation was adopted; for China, provision of government scholarships to the students that visit China was adopted), some programs failed to take effective measures to raise funds for program operation and the advancement of program activities was limited to some extent. For some programs, no adequate efforts were made in terms of enrollment; no clear description was given concerning student selection policies and methods; the number of expected students to be involved in exchange was not guaranteed, with an unbalance in the number of sending and receiving students.

II. Advantages of Cooperation among Academic Programs

1. Experience Summary

The consortiums of "CAMPUS Asia" programs have formulated a frontier value – added curriculum system with international characteristics based on program objectives jointly established and fully integrated resources as well as the academic strength of participating universities. Due to the difference of programs in terms of academic level and discipline field involved, consortiums pursued innovation of different forms in terms of curriculum type, teaching content, connection among core courses, teaching methods, course management, etc.. Useful explorations have been made on curriculum development of international programs.

The cooperation among high – level universities ensures the teaching and research level of teachers participated in the "CAMPUS Asia" programs. International teacher teams are available in most programs for teaching and tutoring and can ensure effective achievement of teaching objectives. In order to reflect the advantages of cooperation among multinational programs, most programs adopt the methods of joint teaching, mutual teacher sending, long – distance teaching, themed lecture, etc. to integrate teacher resources and ensure the effective achievement of teaching tasks. Multi – language teaching environment of "CAMPUS Asia" Initiative provides added value for students and lays a solid foundation for students to actively get engaged in the development of East Asia in the future. Diversified teaching forms enabled by information technology further contribute to the achievement of teaching objectives.

2. Good Practices

1) Jointly Developing the Curriculum System Applicable to Multinational Education Cooperation Based on Cooperation Advantages

The Mobile Campus Program integrates effective resources of Chinese, Japanese and Korean universities. It is expressly specified that the program aims to train interdisciplinary innovative talents who have rich accomplishments in East Asian culture, have a good knowledge of international rules and are able to directly get involved in international governance. A complete circumlunar system was jointly designed by the three countries and special faculty and management teams were formed. In terms of teaching content and curriculum system, the "embedded" curriculum system applicable to multinational education cooperation was developed. The four – and – a – half – year curriculum system, jointly developed by three universities in China, Japan and South Korea, regards "Mobile Campus" (Semesters 4 to 7) as the core and short – term research (Semesters 1 to 3) and joint internship program (semesters 8 to 9) as compulsory courses (see the chart below). In the unified curriculum system, the three universities offer disciplines of Humanities and Sociology in terms of society, economics, history, literature, culture, region/country research in addition to required language course covering listening, speaking, reading, writing, translation/interpretation and other knowledge and skills training. The three universities mutually provide assisted curriculum modules that can support talent training objectives and implement the policy of mutual credit transfer. Also, by making use of the long – distance devices and technologies of each university, they offer long – distance teaching subjects to share other education resources of third parties. The program is intended to train excellent talents who would play key roles in politics, foreign affairs, society, culture, economics & technology exchanges and cooperation, education and research. Through the curriculum training of flow and embedded type, the three universities share teaching resources and make breakthroughs in getting rid of the barriers in territory, culture and discipline. Through the "immersive" learning pattern, young students with different cultural backgrounds from different countries could fully exchange on the same platform, acquire relevant knowledge and skills and obtain three – party academic degrees, thus laying a solid foundation for them to become interdisciplinary talents with common value in East Asia and even much broader international stage.

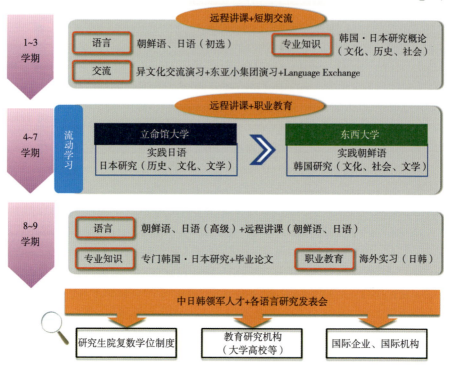

Four – and – a – half – year "Embedded" Curriculum System of Mobile Campus Program

1 – 3 学期	Semesters 1 to 3
4 – 7 学期	Semesters 4 to 7
8 – 9 学期	Semesters 8 to 9
远程讲课 + 短期交流	Long – distance lecture + short – term exchange
语言	Language
朝鲜语、日语（初选）	Korean and Japanese（junior）
专业知识	Professional knowledge
韩国·日本研究概论（文化、历史、社会）	Overview of Korean and Japanese Researches（Culture, history and society）
交流	Exchange
异文化交流演习 + 东亚小集团演习 + Language Exchange	Foreign culture exchange exercise + East Asian small group exercise + language exchange
流动学习	Mobile learning
远程讲课 + 职业教育	Long – distance lecture + occupational education

continued

立命馆大学	Ritsumeikan University
实践日语 日本研究（历史、文化、文学）	Practical Japanese: Japanese researches (history, culture and literature)
东西大学	Dongseo University
实践朝鲜语 韩国研究（文化、社会、文学）	Practical Korean: Korean researches (culture, society and literature)
语言	Language
朝鲜语、日语（高级）+远程讲课（朝鲜语、日语）	Korean, Japanese (advanced) + long – distance lecture (Korean and Japanese)
专业知识	Professional knowledge
专门韩国·日本研究+毕业论文	Professional Korean and Japanese researches + graduation thesis
职业教育	Occupational education
海外实习（日韩）	Overseas internship (in Japan and South Korea)
中日韩领军人才+各语言研究发表会	Leading talents of China, Japan and South Korea + language research presentations
研究生院复数学位制度	Multi – degree system adopted at the Graduate School
教育研究机构（大学高校等）	Education and research institutions (universities, etc.)
国际企业、国际机构	International enterprises and institutions

In the Public Risk Management Program, the Degree Program of Master in Public Administration was offered in English by the School of International Relations and Public Affairs in 2012. In addition to Korean and Japanese degree and exchange students involved in the "CAMPUS Asia" initiative, the program also enrolls students from the rest of the world. The "CAMPUS Asia" initiative positions itself as training trilateral experts who are familiar with the management of Asian risks. The students are required to understand basic principles of risk management and relevant practices in Northeast Asia by systematically learning risk management and conducting master's thesis research. The School has a long – term foundation for internationalized operation. Nearly 30 English courses are offered in the master program, including 6 foundation courses, 8 core courses and about 15 elective courses. Also, Chinese language courses are customized for international students (six levels). The courses of the "CAMPUS Asia" programs are embedded into the degree courses. Also, the following specialized courses are offered such as Emergency Management in China, China's Environmental Policy and Sustainable Development, Public Innovation, Technical Integration and New Public Operation, Public Policy, Research Method, Chinese Society, Program Evaluation and Policy Analysis. Also, the risk management degree education is incorporated into the basic teaching systems including public management and international relations, thus contributing to the interdisciplinary teaching advantages. In terms of overall architecture of curriculum system, in combination with the overall positioning of the program, all courses are divided into three categories: cooperation courses, joint courses and extended courses. The Chinese party has also communicated and exchanged with Japanese and Korean parties and made a thorough deployment and overall negotiation on curriculum setting and system building. Also, the requirements of different countries for emergency response practice are taken into account while the integrated risk management system building of East Asia is facilitated in combination with the operation characteristics of each university.

2) Training Talents through University – enterprise Cooperation in an In – depth Manner

"Doing Business in Asia" Project (DBIA) is a sub – project of Asia Business Leaders Program (ABLP), whose main participants are students majoring in Business School Management (MBA) project and Executive Education project. DBIA lasts for three weeks in three countries. Its contents, objectives and group assignments are jointly developed by Guanghua School of Management of Peking University, Business School of Seoul National University and Strategic Enterprise Institute of Hitotsubashi University. The courses training, corporate site visits, case studies and discussions and other exchange activities are conducted in Beijing, Tokyo and Seoul.

University – Enterprise Cooperation—top business schools of China, Japan and South Korea are responsible for practical implementation of this project. Project Directing Committee and relevant enterprises are responsible for developing the courses, lecture handouts and corporate cases cooperatively, which will integrate the hottest topics about three countries' economy and other aspects of recent years, the latest researches of joint faculties, to train future business leaders for three countries from the perspective of Asian business models and business leadership styles. This project will last for two weeks and will be conducted in three universities. There will be course learning, enterprises visits, cultural experiences and activities in each university, and students will be sent to the headquarters of well – known enterprises to talk with responsible people.

Program – based teaching—The program class has 30 students. Each party is responsible for the selection of their 10 students. During the learning that lasts two weeks in three places, 30 students are allocated to 5 groups. Each group is composed of two Chinese, Japanese and Korean students and conducts program research based on a common topic. Each group gives a report upon the completion of courses. Some characteristic program courses are listed as follows:

Cross – culture Management Program. The group research program was established by professors from the three parties. In the program, customs relations management and talent management in cross – culture management were studied in the case of Starbucks. Starbucks Asia – pacific Region gave a great support to the research program and received students in Beijing, Tokyo and Seoul divisions respectively. Also, the company sent heads of each region to have an interview with students and share their years of experience in the industry.

Competition and Cooperation Program—Teaching of East Asian Manufactoring Industry. Students paid visits to headquarters of Hyundai (Beijing), UNIQLO (Tokyo) and Samsung (South Korea). By sharing their stories, executives presented not just academic knowledge in class and on textbooks but vivid cases that reflect the cooperation and competition game.

As for project – based teaching on aging issues in East Asia, the proportion of the aging population and the evolution of this figure have shown directly that it would bring great challenges to economic development. Students gradually found problems and sought solutions under the guidance of professors.

Two Weeks in Three Countries—with the collaboration of three countries, the project has set clear goals, course contents with clear theme and sent students to three countries for cultural experience in just two weeks. The short – time and concentrated training form solved the traditional superficial communication problems in short – term projects. Embedded learning and experience of different cultures enhances students' understanding on Asian economy, government, social system, as well as cultural and commercial activities. Their working skills and team spirit have been developed in transnational teams, and it is helpful to form a correct understanding of East Asian business and leadership model.

3) The Multi – language Teaching Environment Provides Added – value for Programs

The consortium of Legal Talent Program specially designed six joint courses, which covers the learning of language, politics and culture of the three countries. The six courses include: Chinese/Japanese/Korean in Social Sciences (I), Chinese/Japanese/Korean in Social Sciences (II), Overview of Chinese/Japanese/South Korean Laws, Politics of China, Japan and South Korea, Comparative Laws of East Asia and Comparative Politics of East Asia. The six universities of the three countries jointly discussed curriculum design and teaching at the program working conference and explored the possibility of cooperation in textbook compilation and long – distance teaching. In addition to the six joint courses, exchange students also accepted one – year local language training to improve their language skills and laid a solid foundation of language skills for their further study and research. Also, the program offered all English course systems so as to satisfy students' learning demand. For example, based on the Program of Master in Chinese Laws in English offered by Law School of Renmin University of China, students who visit China may select multiple Chinese department laws offered in English, which would facilitate their overall learning and understanding of Chinese laws.

In offering the Mobility Campus Program, each university offers Chinese, Japanese and Korean languages to students. Participating students studied using local languages in classroom and lived together after class. In view of the advantage of learning languages in the local, students' language skills were greatly developed and improved. Currently, participating students of the three countries can communicate with each other using proficient Chinese, Japanese and Korean and get engaged in topic research and study. The program facilitates cultural exchanges through language training. During the Mobile Campus program learning period, cultural experience courses were offered at three universities, such as Chinese Handwriting, Chinese Martial Arts and Lingnan Culture offered at Guangdong University of Foreign Studies. During the process, participating students learned from each other and made comparisons, thus laying a solid foundation for their research and discussion on history, culture and other aspects. According to the statistics 2012 – 2015, Chinese, Japanese and Korean students totaled 30. Among them, all the 10 students from Guangdong University of Foreign Studies passed the Japanese Language Proficiency Test Level 1 (top level), 7 passed the Korean Language Proficiency Test Level 6 and 2 passed Level 5 (the top level is 6); 5 students from Ritsumeikan University passed Korean Language Proficiency Test Level 6 and 8 passed HSK5; 8 students from Dongseo Uuniversity passed the Japanese Language Proficiency Test Level 1, 1 passed the HSK6 and 8 passed the HSK5.

4) Integrating Teacher Resources via Multiple Approaches

While ensuring teacher resources, the Mobile Campus Program combines the "immobile teachers and mobile students" and long – distance multimedia teaching in an organic manner. In terms of teacher resources guarantee, each university participating in the Program selects experienced teachers to give lectures. Before the start of lectures, student archives are distributed to teachers so as to enable teachers to fully understand student conditions and teach them according to actual circumstances. In the Program, teacher resources are shared by the three participating universities from the three countries. As of 2017, Guangdong University of Foreign Studies had 7 full – time faculties, 2 foreign tutors and 2 administrative secretaries; Ritsumeikan University had 6 full – time faculties and 3 administrative secretaries; Dongseo University had 6 full – time faculties and 2 administrative secretaries. There is a reasonable structure of professional titles for faculties and all of them have the background of overseas studies. During the learning period, administrative secretaries conduct regular communication with faculties, understand classroom conditions and give a feedback of students' comments so as to guarantee the achievement or completion of classroom teaching quality and teaching tasks to a high standard. The "international class" formed by students is divided into three semesters each year. They live and study together on the "mobile campuses" of the three universities (Guangdong University of Foreign Studies, Ritsumeikan University and Dongseo University) by following the order of China, Japan and South Korea and appreciate the charm of faculties under different cultures.

In addition, completing basic courses according to training plans of their universities, students that participate in the TKT Program would participate in one year's scientific research and learn at the joint lab of the partner university. Upon graduation, they may be entitled to dual master degrees. Currently, ten phases of students have been admitted and 158 students been sent to each other, with over 110 students graduated. Additionally, each year, Tokyo Institute of Technology sent senior professors to give lectures and guidance to Tsinghua University for a medium and long term. Also, young and middle – aged backbone teachers were sent to Tsinghua University for intensive teaching (short – term). The facilities for core courses of the Program offered by Tsinghua University are listed as follows:

Opened subjects with a focus of nano:

Solid Physics, taught by one permanent teacher of Tokyo Institute of Technology

Nano Electronic Materials, taught by two teachers of Tokyo Institute of Technology

Selected Topics in Nanoscience, taught by two teachers of Tokyo Institute of Technology

Quantum Chemistry, taught by one teacher of Tokyo Institute of Technology

Flexible Materials, taught by two teachers of Tokyo Institute of Technology

Nano Material Performance Test, taught by two teachers of Tokyo Institute of Technology

Opened subjects with a focus of biology and chemistry:

Selected Topics on Biotechnology, eight – week lectures by one teacher of Tsinghua University + short – term lectures by one teacher of Tokyo Institute of Technology

Selected Topics on Life Science, eight – week lectures by one teacher of Tsinghua University + short – term lecture by one teacher of Tokyo Institute of Technology

Selected Topics on Biomolecular Science, eight – week lectures by one teacher of Tsinghua University + short – term lectures by one teacher of Tokyo Institute of Technology

Opened subjects with a focus of humanities and social sciences:

Technology and Society, full – semester lectures by one teacher of Tsinghua University + short – term lectures by three teachers of Tokyo Institute of Technology

Additionally, with three discipline orientations as units, an academic seminar of mutual visit type, attended by senior professors and young scholars, is held each year in the Program. Up to now, more than 70 supervisors have sent and received students and over 300 person – time have attended various forms of academic seminars in terms of the three orientations, including academic activities held with other Chinese universities. Teachers applied for topics based on their joint interests in research and conducted diversified in – depth exchanges in the forms of mutual

**Professor of Tokyo Institute of Technology
Was Giving Lectures at Tsinghua University**

visit and teaching, joint teaching, etc. , thus contributing to the mutual study and joint research across territories.

In addition to guaranteeing sufficient qualified faculty and reform of teaching method, in the curriculum system of Mobile Campus Program, the three universities shared their education resources by means of long – distance teaching. The three universities selected excellent teachers or invited academic experts to give special lectures by remote teaching video for "CAMPUS Asia" participating students and other students of the universities. Also, the program opened

**Mobile Campus Program Students Were Attending Lectures
in the Long – distance Simultaneous Interpretation Classroom**

long – distance teaching subjects by taking advantage of long – distance devices of each universi-ty, thus realizing the sharing of education resources and education internalization of the three universities.

Mobile Campus Program Students Were Attending the History Class Given by Dongseo University by Long – distance Device

Mobile Campus Program Students Were Publishing Their Researches under the Guidance of Their Teachers by Long – distance Device

In the Public Risk Management Program, the three – party "Comparative Public Adminis-tration" video course was opened through cooperation with Victoria University of Wellington (New Zealand) and National Institute of Development Administration (Thailand) and was quite popular among students from Japan, South Korea, Singapore and Thailand. The three – party video courses opened through cooperation among the school, Japan and South Korea in-clude traditional courses such as Global Governance, Economics and Politics in Northeast Asia and International Relations of Northeast Asia, from which the students of the "CAMPUS Asia" programs benefit a lot.

5）Multiple Teaching Platforms that Contribute to the Achievement of Program Objectives

Information technology lab platform for social sciences

The Public Risk Management Program actively absorbs advanced teaching experience from China and the rest of the world, respects the education and learning concepts of students from different countries. The program adopted the education mode that combines discussion type teaching and real-time interaction. The accomplishments of the School of International Relations and Public Affairs, Fudan University on international teaching research were also applied to classrooms of the "CAMPUS Asia" Initiative. The scene where participating students attended classes at the Public Policy Making Lab was shown as follows:

"Public Policy Making Lab" Teaching Platform

With an organic combination of personnel, machine, internet and database and by focusing on "national urgently needed, world – class" topics, the lab conducted research, consultation and service tasks, aiming to build a first – class computer simulation and display platform of government performance management and public policy making. With quantitative analysis and technical methods of experiment as major characteristics, the lab devoted itself to facilitating discipline crossing and resources integration regarding government governance, public policy performance, foreign relations and international relations. The computer simulation and display platform of the lab represents an effective tool of studying public issues and an effective and low – cost policy experiment platform. Decision – makers may make policy experiments on the platform and observe beforehand the optional decision – making results and their comparisons by visualization technology. In the class, teachers are providers, organizers and guiders of the platform while students play the roles of active explorers, participants and partners, thus enabling the transformation of teaching mode. The lab enjoys multiple powerful functions including scene experience, case analysis, scene simulation, brain storming, collaboration work, emergency drill, complicated policy making, simulation, innovative experiment, behavior analysis, etc.. It is an open, parallel, two – way, real – time, flexible and interactive lab and teaching platform, reflecting the frontier and international level of the program.

Supervisor System Lab Teaching Platform for Science and Engineering

The EEST Program pays special attention to the combination of lab learning and classroom theory study. Adopting common practices, Chinese, Japanese and Korean universities allocated in a random manner the first – year postgraduates to study at different labs. Each teacher who is familiar with lab environment took charge of a lab so that every postgraduate can be rapidly acquainted with the lab environment under the guidance of the teacher. During the learning at the lab, the teacher in charge would spend half a day in introducing the research background of their topics and development of the field for postgraduates; then select specific research topics for postgraduates and organize experiments in groups; and finally give relevant evaluation comments according to the experiment performance of postgraduates. Through joint learning and group discussion, postgraduates would make their learning results available to the public and listen to comments from other teachers and students. The three universities organized students on an irregular basis to visit the plants, enterprises, government and non – government institutions that relate to their specialties, and continuously enhanced the linkage to the industry circle, local governments and other non – government organizations.

Research Debate Type Teaching Platform for Humanities

In terms of teaching method, the Mobile Campus Program highlights the training of students' abilities of research, thinking and practice. The talent training method that focuses on discussion and debate in class and practical investigation after class and regards teacher guidance as assistance is encouraged. The program brings the guiding role of teachers, motivates students' ability to observe and analyze problems and trains students' abilities of collaboration, innovation and practice. Normally, teachers would organize students to make a discussion and debate on hot topics of East Asia, including politics, history and humanities and guide students to obtain more in-depth understanding through the exchange and collision of thought.

3. Problem Analysis

In terms of curriculum system, some participating universities who send and receive fewer students have not designed special courses for the "CAMPUS Asia" programs. The current courses combination of those universities is not systematic and targeted, and fails to effectively support the achievement of the training objectives of "CAMPUS Asia" programs and implement the requirements of "CAMPUS Asia" for students' knowledge, ability and accomplishments. Some programs are insufficient in teaching students in accordance with their aptitude. The percentage of credits for elective courses over the total credits is lower; students are not flexible in selecting courses on their own and do not have much space for independent learning. Due to insufficient communication and negotiation, some partner universities have not reached a consensus on relevant systems including performance assessment, credit transfer, practice and internship, credit recognition, etc. , which affects students' enthusiasm and academic development to some extent. The cooperation within the same consortium is not enough. Although the curriculum system development through bilateral cooperation is in an in – depth way, the resources of the trilateral universities are insufficiently integrated. The participating universities of some pilot programs fail to convert the advantages of discipline, research and teaching resources into talent training advantages and fail to fully reflect the innovation and high level for talent training in the "CAMPUS Asia" pilot programs.

In terms of faculty and teaching, the number and structure of teachers for some programs is still unable to satisfy program requirements. In most programs, there is a lack of systems and measures to encourage teachers to make efforts in teaching, research and student tutoring, the reward and support system for teachers is not built, and the enthusiasm of teachers to guide students' studies, practice and internship and employment is not effectively motivated. The exchange system for some programs at the teacher level is incomplete. Teachers of the three parties have not conducted in – depth cooperation in terms of curriculum setting, textbook selection and editing, joint teaching, collaborative research, etc. . Some programs are still limited to the traditional teaching form and do not sufficiently apply multimedia interactive teaching. Teachers' practices in multiple teaching methods such as situational teaching, discussion type teaching and task – oriented teaching are not enough, which has little effect on inspiring students' creative thinking.

III. Student Support

1. Experience Summary

In "CAMPUS Asia" programs, enrollment systems are formulated and specific requirements are proposed on selection, admission, dispatching, etc. . Most programs are able to strictly control students' application qualification, learning motivation, learning plan, language proficiency, moral quality, etc. according to the high requirements for high starting point and high standards. Multiple approaches such as written test, interview and learning ability test are used to select outstanding students. Relevant systems are available to ensure the fairness and transparency of the selection. In most programs, the system for attracting outstanding students is formulated. The programs attract excellent students and guarantee the enrollment scale by launching program publicity, enhancing university – enterprise cooperation, perfecting scholarship and aid system and student service, regulating academic linkage system and enriching extracurricular activities. Some universities that send students provide pre – travel tutoring for students on folk culture and campus culture of overseas study destination and guarantee that students could adapt to the living and study abroad faster.

Most programs create good learning environment and provide accurate and timely living service information. Some programs offer students necessary language tutoring and help students to solve the difficulty in language and specialty learning. For most programs, rich extracurricular, internship and practice activities are conducted to facilitate students' cross – culture exchanges and learning. All participating universities can fully respect the national culture, emotion and religious relief of international students, organize diversified exchange activities and enhance students' understanding and acceptance of different cultures. Also, they avoid the tendency of guiding students in politics, religion and values.

2. Good Practices

1) Programs Have Policies and Measures to Attract Outstanding Students

With the joint efforts of the three universities, the EEST Program developed unique training plans for participating students in a creative manner and established a better linkage to the life and study of students from the three countries. Through flexible design and arrangement of "semester exchange", "spring seminar", "international summer vacation school", "autumn academic forum", the program can basically guarantee the postgraduates that participated in the dual degree program to satisfy the degree application requirements of the Chinese, Japanese and Korean universities and lay a solid foundation for building an advanced and diversified demonstrating education system in science and engineering related fields.

Since the normalized implementation of the Mobile Campus Program, a lot of students signed up for the program each year. Due to rigorous program selection, only a few outstanding students could participate in the program through selection. The reasons why the "CAMPUS Asia" initiative is so charming among students lay in the following aspects: first, characteristics of "CAMPUS Asia" program at Guangdong University of Foreign Studies or Mobile Campus. During their study at the university, students may visit Korean and Japanese partner universities for mobile learning for two years. During the period of mobile learning, a unique matching curriculum system is provided and they may live and study together with Korean and Japanese students, which are attractive for Chinese students. Second, as the program led by the ministries of department of the three countries, a certain amount of financial support is provided to the three countries and universities. For example, students of Guangdong University of Foreign Studies are funded by the Innovation Program of the China Scholarship Council when they study abroad. Starting from 2018, the university will also establish special funds to support students of "CAMPUS Asia" programs to study abroad. For students who visit China, the "CAMPUS Asia" special scholarship is set by the State. For students, their study abroad with scholarship not only means receiving financial aid but also honor. Thus, excellent students would actively participate in the program.

The Traditional Culture Program attaches great importance to the advancement of "CAMPUS Asia" initiative. Jilin University, Okayama University and SungKyunKwan University list each other as important strategic partners in the global strategies. Under the framework of "CAMPUS Asia" program, each university provided financial aids to the teachers and students sent by other parties and encouraged outstanding students and teachers to exchange and learn from each other. The three universities selected key cooperation disciplines, made efforts to facilitate bilateral or trilateral substantive research cooperation and joint talent training, and facilitated young students to freely flow among the three universities so as to enhance their understanding.

2) Programs Have Perfect Student Selection Mechanisms

The Mobile Campus Program adopts the on – campus freshman selection system and follows the process of signing up, initial review, written test and interview. Take Guangdong University of Foreign Studies for an example. Each year, the CAMPUS Asia Education Center of the university would make CAMPUS Asia enrollment information available to the students via its official website, admission website, website of Teaching Affairs Division, official WeChat, etc. and publish the information of student selection about "CAMPUS Asia" Program. Before freshmen are admitted, the CAMPUS Asia Education Center would acquire freshman data from the university and determine sign – up conditions after analyzing admission scores in different regions, number of enrollments and other data. After the deadline of sign – up, the Center would review the qualifications of candidates according to sign – up conditions. Qualified students may attend the written test. The questions for written test are prepared by related experts of the university and schools. Questions cover politics, history, humanities and other content relating to East Asia and mainly test candidates' abilities of humanistic accomplishments, critical thinking, writing, etc.. In the written test, students are selected based on the percentage of 2∶1 at least. That means 40 to 50 excellent students are admitted to the interview link. Interview teachers are teachers of Japanese and Korean specialties of the CAMPUS Asia Education Center of the university and interview topics cover politics, history, language, culture, etc.. Students' skills of language expression and critical thinking as well as comprehensive skills are mainly tested. Through the above tests, 20 students would be finally admitted to the "CAMPUS Asia" initiative.

In the EEST Program, decisions are made through negotiation among participating universities. Each party may send 5 postgraduates to the other parties each on an annual basis to participate in the dual degree program. That means the three universities would select 30 postgraduates in total every year to participate in the joint training of dual degree program. The first – year master's degree candidates are listed as major enrollments. Each university is encouraged to make enrollment publicity in the receiving university. In terms of student selection, students' accomplishments would be fully invested and their academic innovation ability would be highlighted. For example, at Shanghai Jiao Tong University, students who apply for dual master degree programs would be reported to the Graduate School for review after they pass the interview organized by departments (schools) . They may become dual master degree program students after their admission is finally confirmed by partner universities. Students from the other universities who apply for studying master degree programs at Shanghai Jiao Tong University must also pass the review and selection of their home universities, which would recommend these students to relevant departments or schools of the university. The university may decide whether to admit these students after assessment. Additionally, in order to expand the benefits of the program, the Spring Seminars, Summer Vacation Schools and Autumn Academic Forums designed in the program are open to the students who are not studying dual degree programs and are attended by the students selected by the three universities.

3) Highlighting Student Service, Building a Scientific Guidance System for Student Development

The student groups that the Mobile Campus Program targets at include two types. Take Guangdong University of Foreign Studies for an example. The first type is undergraduates of the university and the second type is international students that are sent by partner universities to the university. For original students of the university, a guidance system composed of head teacher supervisors and peer supervisors was built at the "CAMPUS Asia" Education Center of the university. Head teacher supervisors mainly guide students in terms of specialty recognition, academic planning, exchange abroad, etc. ; and peer supervisors mainly exchange with junior schoolmates in terms of learning experience, scholarship application and overseas study experience. For visiting students from Japan and South Korea, in addition to head teacher supervisors, who are responsible for academic planning and learning guidance, psychological guidance teachers who speak students' native languages are also available at the "CAMPUS Asia" Education Center of Guangdong University of Foreign Studies. The latter are mainly responsible for psychological health of Japanese and Korean students. Teachers would often exchange with international students and learn about their living and study at the university so as to promptly understand students' mental status and better help international students to complete their learning tasks at the university.

The Mentor system was built for International Relations Program, Legal Talent Program, Traditional Culture Program, TKT Program and EEST Program each. That means each Japanese or Korean student is provided with a Chinese student with a good foundation of language and similar specialty background as learning companion. The system aims to help these international students to adapt to the study and living in China, get familiar with social environment, improve their Chinese language level, discuss with their companions about the issues in life and study, enhance the communication among youths of the three countries in ideology, culture and vision and achieve joint learning and growth.

4) Enhancing University – enterprise Cooperation, Providing Students with Internship and Practice Support as well as Employment Guidance

The Public Risk Management Program aims to train risk management experts in Asia. Students are required to systematically learn risk management knowledge, get much involved in risk management practice and conduct master's theses research so as to make contributions to the risk management practice and regional cooperation of Northeast Asia. Focusing on the training objectives, Fudan University made efforts to allocate and integrate on – campus, domestic and international risk management teaching, academic and practice resources to contribute to a complicated system that trains international risk talents. The system features in practical operation, practical training and practice resources and regards specialty courses in English as its theory foundation, with international seminars regularly held as useful supplement:

Field risk investigation. With the support from the program team, international students visited and investigated Hanwang Dongfang Steam Turbine Works (DFSTW) Earthquake Relics, Hanwang Residential Area Earthquake Relics, Wenchuan Earthquake Relics and Mianzhu Earthquake Memorial. In the factories and residential areas that were seriously damaged by earthquake, students carefully checked the damage of earthquake to different building materials and frames, heard from others about the situation of the earthquake and casualties caused, as well as detailed introduction to post – earthquake self rescue and aids provided by different provinces to the building of the area. Through field investigation, students further considered the reasons for earthquake, personnel casualties and material damage caused by different levels of earthquake as well as huge impact caused to the living and production of the earthquake stricken area.

Practical Emergency management training: In the program, international students were organized to attend the International Disaster Reduction and Security Exhibition. Students paid visits to top – level emergency equipment in multiple sub – exhibition areas such as emergency rescue in earthquake, fire rescue, urban safety emergency response, emergency backup supplies and logistics preparation, etc.. Also, they experienced in person the guiding role of emergency rescue command vehicles in the central policy making at the natural disaster rescue site. Students thus obtained an initial understanding of the requirements for management ability in the disaster environment as well as the timeliness and urgency of emergency policy – making.

Students of Public Risk Management Program Participated
in the Investigation of Sichuan Earthquake Relics

Emergency rescue practice. During the period when the Urban Search and Rescue Skills Training in Developing Countries was held in China, international students of the program participated in theory training by taking the opportunity of training officials from the three countries in terms of emergency management system building and policy – making training. Additionally, they paid visits to China Earthquake Network Center, participated in the emergency rescue practice training offered by the national emergency rescue team, experienced each process for emergency rescue of China and emergency rescue management organization system of the country, and sensed the gaps between empirical emergency management training and college emergency management education highlighting theory.

In the Mobile Campus Program, internship bases are shared by partner universities of China, Japan and South Korea. Currently, there is 1 domestic signing base at the "CAMPUS Asia" Education Center of Guangdong University of Foreign Studies, which can receive up to 20 interns. There are 6 internship sites in Japan and South Korea, namely Pasona (Guangzhou) Talent Service Co., Ltd., Pricewaterhouse Coopers, Asahi Shimbun, Kyoto Shiyakusho Cultural Promotion Office, Ward Office, Fuji Xerox, Mynavi, Kinokuniya Shoten, Hyatt Regency Kyoto and Nara Hotel based in Japan, as well as Shinsegae Duty Free Shop based in South Korea. Students may select internship sites based on their advantages and future career plans during the fourth – year overseas internship. 9 students of the university have been sent to Japan and South Korea for internship during their overseas internship stage. Additionally, with active international exchanges in Guangdong, various types of trade fairs held in the region also offer plenty of internship opportunities for students of the program. While studying at the university, Korean students have participated in the China Cosmetic Trade Show together with

Chinese students and provided interpretation service on site. Due to their proficient Chinese, Japanese and Korean and good communication skills, program students are well reviewed by employers. With the economic growth of Guangdong as well as further expansion of China's cooperation with Japan and South Korea, the number of internship sites and methods that may be provided to students would gradually increase. In order to guarantee the effect of students' internship and social practice, it is required by this specialty that students should submit the Internship Evaluation Forms provided by their employers as well as internship reports summarized by students so as to learn about employers' evaluation on program students as well as students' internship results promptly.

3. Problem Analysis

In terms of student selection, the scale of student exchanges in some programs fails to reach the expected target and there is an imbalance between the number of sent students and that of received students. One of the important reasons is insufficient publicity of the program. That is to say, no diversified measures, forms and channels are adopted to advertise the program; focused publicity at related schools or departments is not emphasized; and no consensus is reached among teachers and students of the university. Some programs do not have rigorous selection mechanisms. No strict assessment on students' foreign language level is conducted. Students fail to satisfy the requirements for attending lectures and the university fails to offer language tutoring service, thus leading to poor learning results of students. For some programs, there are no sufficient measures and efforts to attract outstanding students; no sufficient measures to create development opportunities for students via university – enterprise cooperation and no enough efforts to raise funds for students' study and development by various means. Although most programs provide pre – travel guidance, they usually focus on the guidance on students' living and cultural cognition but ignore the tutoring on academic planning. Training plan, content of learning (curriculums and syllabus), credit transfer, degree granting system and other important information are not notified in advance. In some programs, participating students are not clear of their rights and obligations and no mechanism for expression and feedback of students' comments is built.

In terms of learning and life support, some programs fail to effectively solve the problem of students' living and study together and participating students do not have an in – depth extracurricular communication and integration. As some programs are incomplete in the overall organization building, there is a lack of personnel in terms of student support and service; student consultation service is only limited to handling of daily affairs and administrative formalities, and academic consulting, provision of internship opportunities, employment support and tutoring, etc. are rather weak. Some pilot programs are characterized by "more life service, less learning support". Except having classes, students have fewer opportunities in obtaining language tutoring, additional courses, post – class tutoring and assistant support.

IV. The Added – Value of Program

1. Experience Summary

In some programs, students' satisfaction level and added value of programs are surveyed by means of questionnaire, interview, etc., which provides a reference for continuous improvement of these programs. Mutual credit transfer and mutual degree granting represent the special demand of multinational education cooperation programs. A well – developed mutual credit transfer and mutual degree granting system is the driving force to increase the attractiveness of multinational education cooperation programs and to promote regional education cooperation integration. Through full communication and negotiation, some partner universities have proposed the mutual credit transfer system and reached a consensus on credit recognition criteria. Also, all programs adopt specific methods such as core course linkage, credit hour conversion, research credit system, score/rating conversion and management of upper limit for credits, which ensures the substantive equivalence of transferred credits and the quality of obtained credits.

In degree education programs, partner universities have basically reached a consensus on general guidelines on degree granting, academic degree quality review method, etc. through full consultation. With full collaboration and linkage, the partner universities of the three countries have formulated complete degree training systems as well as unique working mechanisms and management procedures; formulated systems and specifications in terms of fiscal expenditure, admission criteria, language tutoring, mutual credit transfer, quality assurance, thesis review, degree granting, etc. Distinctive program characteristics, powerful organization and implementation system, international teaching and practice arrangement, regulated student exchange and management system, as well as the student service and development system with a blend of emotion and reasoning have been formed. And the strategic objectives of facilitating the mutual trust and understanding among students and scholars of the three countries and promoting knowledge exchange and practical innovation have been achieved. Some well – developed degree or exchange programs have satisfied the conditions of being expanded to multilateral cooperation and joint degree granting.

2. Good Practices

1) Student Satisfaction Survey and Analysis

In ABLP, the three universities formulate the evaluation plan for the program, and the Joint Academic Committee is responsible for specific implementation. Procedures include design and implementation of student questionnaires as well as collection of evaluation and improvement comments on the program from students, teachers and administrative personnel. The evaluation system will collect the comments relating to curriculum quality, service content and quality as well as administrative efficiency and perfect the shortcomings that exist in the joint exchange plan.

CAMPUS Asia Joint Meeting
Friday, June 28, 2013
Questionnaire

L Quality Assurance	To be answered by either professor or administrator. Please choose from the dropdpwn list. If you are practicing any of the examples, choose "yes."				Please write any comments. (Examples, reasons why not, etc)
Criteria	Examples of good practice	PKU	SNU	UT	Any Comment from Each School
Contents of Academic Programs: Is a framework for achieving the program goals established and functioning effectively among the participating institutions?					
1 Contents of Academic Programs	The educational contets are configured in line with expected leaming outcomes (e.g. student kn owledge, skills, attitudes) —such as a need for global talent within East Asia. and have been systematically analyzed by the institution.				
2 Contents of Academic Programs	Information on the program contents, especially on curriculum stru cture and courses offerings, is shared among the participating institutions, with each program component inte grated and systematically structured.				
3 Contents of Academic Programs	It is clear that through intemational collaboration. the program adds value to education in the particlpating institutions and enhances their international competiveness.				

Three – party Joint Evaluating Questionnaires of ABLP

In the EEST Program, annual questionnaire surveys were made on students that participate in degree courses and summer vacation courses. Results indicate that most students are quite satisfied with course content and lab research and training. Also, students' comments and suggestions were collected in the questionnaire survey. The survey results were shared among participating universities for continuous improvement of programs.

In addition to conducting and analyzing student questionnaire survey and student course evaluation, the Policy Consortium Program provided deans/vice deans with an opportunity to talk with students. Students were encouraged to build an exchange and communication network so that their comments and suggestions on the program can be widely collected.

2) Building a Credit System of Substantive Equivalence through Core Course Linkage, Credit Hour Conversion, Research Credit System, Score/rating Conversion, Management of Upper Limit for Credits, etc.

For the BESETO DDMP that offers dual degree courses, a comparison list of core courses was created. It is expressly specified what courses offered by the partner university are substantively identical with the core courses offered by the original university of the students. This list may be used as a reference for students' credit transfer. By using the comparison list or "mapping table", students may avoid selecting core courses repeatedly.

Mapping Table of BESETO DDMP Courses

	University A	University B
	Introduction to Public Administration	Global Business Strategies
	Policy Process and Negotiation	Multilateral Trade Negotiations or International Negotiation Simulation Games
	Japanese Politics Under Public Policy	Japanese Politics and Diplomacy
	Modern Japanese Diplomacy	Theories and Issues in Contemporary Japanese Politics
Selecting 4 courses (8 credit hours)	Comparative Analysis of Japanese Economic Decision – making Process	Comparative Study of Korean and Japanese Enterprises
	International Politics of East Asia	International Relations of East Asia
	Governance and Development	International Development Issues and Cooperation, or Global Social Governance, or International Cooperation
	Study of International Conflict	International Cooperation, or Case Study of International Conflict Management, or International Business Seminars
Selecting 2 courses (10 credit hours)	Macro Economy of Public Policy	International Economic Relations, or Exchange Rate and International Macro Economics
	Statistical Method	Study Method and Skills, or Comparative Method
Compulsory courses (8 credit hours)	Case Study (International Politics and Economy) Case Study (Foreign Economic Policies of Japan) Case Study (Macro Economic Policies of Japan: Evaluation on Monetary and Fiscal Policies) Case Study (Macro Economic Policies of Japan: Solutions to Monetary and Fiscal Policy Challenges) Case Study (East Asian Policies of Japan)	Business Negotiation Research Project Special Research on International Cooperation: Cooperation and Peace Structure of East Asia Comparative Study of East Asia International Business Research Project International Relations

Since the implementation of the EEST Program, the partner universities have committed themselves to building a quality joint credit and degree granting system and jointly issued the graduation certificate in Energy and Environment Science and dual master's degree according to students' accomplishments. In order to achieve the goal of joint dual master degree training, tens of trilateral meetings have been held among Shanghai Jiao Tong University, Kyushu University and Pusan National University. Through joint teaching and unified teaching method and formulation of the measures and systems on credit transfer among the three universities, a rigorous degree granting policy featuring graduation upon joint review was formed in the meetings. During the cooperation among the three universities, student exchanges are conducted via dual master's degree joint training program, international summer vacation program and international forum. In the dual degree program, a complete credit system is established. The total credits required for application for the degree shall not be less than 24 and are basically in the form of "$10 + 6 + X = 24$". "10" means Japanese and Korean students should complete courses of at least 10 credits at Shanghai Jiao Tong University; "6" indicates that as the program adopts learning and research credit systems, students will obtain 3 credits (6 credits in total) by participating in each of the two phases of international summer vacation schools; "X" means the courses completed by Japanese and Korean students at their home universities may be incorporated into the academic program by means of credit transfer. The credits composition of

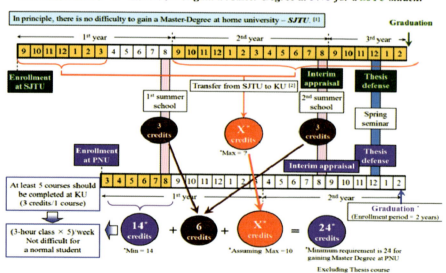

**Credits Composition of EEST Dual Master Degree Program
(PNU & SJTU)**

the EEST dual master degree program provided through the cooperation between Shanghai Jiao Tong University and Pusan National University is as follows:

In order to regulate the recognition of students' transcripts for the courses learned at universities abroad and the credit transfer, the program formulates detailed provisions on the requirements and procedures of participating students' credit recognition and transfer in strict accordance with universities' systems and specifications. If the performance achieved by Japanese and Korean students at their home universities share the same grading criteria with Shanghai Jiao Tong University, the performance will be directly registered; in case of hundred – point system, the performance will be converted into that of Shanghai Jiao Tong University before being registered. Each participating university specifies the upper limit for students' convertible credits. The *Score/Rating Conversion Table* was developed in the program and it shows how to convert different rating criteria among participating universities into their hundred – point system. It is required by the programs that Japanese and Korean students may be entitled to credit transfer qualifications only when they achieve the result of at least B – at their home universities. The conversion criteria are as follows:

EEST Program Score/Rating Conversion Table

Korean University		Pusan National University		Shanghai Jiao Tong University	
Score	Rating in word	Score	Rating in letter	Score	Rating in letter
90 – 100	Outstanding	95 – 100	A⁺	96 – 100	A⁺
		90 – 94	A	90 – 95	A
80 – 90	Excellent	85 – 89	B⁺	85 – 89	A⁻
		80 – 84	B	80 – 84	B⁺
70 – 80	Good	75 – 79	C⁺	75 – 79	B
		70 – 74	C	70 – 74	B⁻
60 – 70	Average	65 – 69	D⁺	67 – 69	C⁺
		60 – 64	D	63 – 66	C
				60 – 62	C⁻
<60	Bad	<60	F	0 – 59	D

The dual master degree students who achieve credits may start to make an application for master's degree of the Chinese university in the spring semester of the third year and finally obtains the dual master degree. The first batch of dual master degree students of the program obtained their dual master degrees in March 2015. Additionally, the three countries involved in the program also try to establish an international joint graduate school. The school will adopt unified admission, curriculum and foreign exchange system, explore the innovation mechanism and build an advanced and diversified demonstrative education system in the fields of Science and Engineering.

For the Legal Talent Program, partner universities were required to provide syllabuses in advance. After discussing in details the credit system, teaching hours and credit related regulations of the other universities, these universities adopted mutual credit transfer and recognition system. Heads, teachers and staff members that participate in programs of the three universities attended regular quality assurance (QA) meetings, on which they exchanged ideas on planned courses and quality assurance and determined the mutual credit transfer method by comparing the length of lectures per credit. According to the mutual transfer method determined at the QA meetings, it was decided that one credit obtained in Japan is equal to one credit obtained in China and 3 credits obtained in South Korea is equal to 4 credits obtained in Japan. In the "Legal Talent in East Asia" Program of Renmin University of China, the management of upper limit for mutual credit transfer was adopted in overseas study by visit. For example, a student who is sent from Japan to China may at most transfer 22 credits in half a semester (compulsory and elective subjects) ; and a student who goes to Korea from Japan for study may at most transfer 21 credits in half a semester (compulsory and elective subjects) .

In the Mobile Campus Program, according to training objectives of the program, the courses offered in the program were compared and adjusted among participating universities of China, Japan and South Korea. After adjustment, the courses completed by students at other universities would be recognized as language or special courses completed at their home universities. Additionally, due to different curriculum schedule and credit accreditation criteria at each university, participating universities also made efforts to adjust teaching hours for better linkage. Also, courses were supplemented to ensure students receive suitable credit accreditation at their home universities. The results of these adjustments among universities are listed in the student manual of "CAMPUS Asia" Program Guideline.

In the rules of each participating university, the TKT Program also identified the transfer of credits obtained in the place of overseas study or upper limit for mutual transfer. Also, there are core courses jointly taught by tutors of both parties. Through friendly negotiation, it is agreed by both parties that the program credits may be regarded as those obtained by students at Tsinghua University or those obtained at Tokyo Institute of Technology. Regarding credit granting for research activities, one policy was adopted at Tsinghua University in this program: for an undergraduate who studies abroad on summer and winter vacations, one credit may be added to his/her research results (at most 5 credits) .

The lab activities at partner universities may also be deemed as research internship in the Chemistry and Materials Program that also highlights lab research activities. When the period of students' overseas study overlaps with the academic period at their home universities, they may obtain credits and recognition at their home universities. For students who participated in international internship, their credits may be confirmed according to the reports submitted after returning to their homelands.

3) Complete Graduation and Degree Granting Policies

In the EEST Program, the consortium specified the policies for dual degree granting in the memorandum of understanding (MoU), including student selection, admission procedures, provision of courses, credit transfer, dual degree courses, scholarship and insurance, Plan – Do – Check – Action (PDCA) Committee and problem solving. After students complete the required credits, academic personnel of the three universities would conduct a joint review of master's theses of dual degree candidates. In addition to receiving joint thesis review, students may also need to pass thesis review according to the conventional criteria at their home universities and satisfy the requirements for degree granting.

The Public Risk Management Program specified high requirements for students' graduation. It is specified that the score of less than "C" (GPA2.0) will not be counted into total credits. After completing at least 30 credits and passing mid – term assessment, they are required to complete papers under the guidance of the Master's Degree Thesis Steering Committee. If a student has obtained necessary credits and passed oral thesis defense at his/her home university and visiting university, the academic degrees of the two universities will be granted according to the result of degree granting and review of the two universities. The policy is established based on the dual degree agreement signed among participating universities and rules of each university.

3. Problem Analysis

In terms of student satisfaction, each participating university created better living and study environment for students through input and guarantee of expenditure, personnel and resources. Students were basically satisfied with their on-campus learning and cultural experience. However, some universities appear simple in information collection and evaluation methods, they fail to understand students' learning and living experience and added value (i. e. the value can not be achieved by participating in similar specialty programs) obtained by participating in the "CAMPUS Asia" programs in a thorough and in – depth manner, and fail to supplement satisfaction from the perspectives of participating teachers and employers. Although students were generally satisfied with their learning experience and employment conditions, some of them expected to perfect relevant systems including credit transfer and to enhance employment tutoring. As each program differs in operation mode and talent training mode, there is a huge imbalance in the satisfaction of participating students among different programs. Most programs need to further effectively apply the student satisfaction evaluation result to facilitate teaching and improve the quality of learning and study experience.

In terms of credit transfer and degree granting, some consortiums do not conduct full negotiation and communication. Performance evaluation, mutual credit transfer as well as recognition of practice and internship credits do not match each other. The consistency and equivalence of the trilateral curriculum system remain to be further improved. Currently, most programs adopt mutual degree granting and fewer ones explore joint degree granting. As different requirements for degree granting are proposed by ministries of education of China, Japan and South Korea, although the joint training mode and results tend to be developed in some programs, joint degree granting in the current stage is not available. The joint granting of degrees by the three universities not only can further expand the influence of the three universities in China, Japan and South Korea but also encourage more universities to explore the new mode of operation through international cooperation and facilitate higher education institutions of the three countries in cooperative operation, thus promoting the integrated development of Northeast Asian education. The information regarding credit transfer and degree granting should be further shared among participating students so as to enable them to plan their study in a rational way.

V. Internal Quality Assurance

1. Experience Summary

Improving the quality of "CAMPUS Asia" programs and exploring an effective operation mechanism for university exchanges and quality assurance are specific requirements proposed in the *Guideline on University Exchange and Cooperation with Quality Assurance in China, Japan and South Korea*. For universities specifically responsible for pilot programs, they have reached a consensus on establishing an effective internal quality assurance system.

Some participating universities incorporated "CAMPUS Asia" programs into quality assurance of their daily teaching process including teaching and learning evaluation. Most universities also considered the special characters of multinational education cooperation programs and highlighted the improvement of overall program quality and students' learning experience. Most programs collected and analyzed students' learning results and effect via consortium self-assessment, student questionnaire, regular meetings of university – school – department committee, information exchange platform for officers, joint meeting for teachers and staff members, students' learning outcome testing mechanism, etc., regularly reviewed important matters including teaching resources configuration, course setting, teaching content, etc. , continuously corrected program issues and guaranteed the effective achievement of teaching quality and objectives. These measures reflect the emphasis of universities from the three countries on integrated management and overall quality improvement of the programs, as well as basic principles of "student – orientation" and highlighting students' learning experience, outcome achieving and satisfaction.

Despite its limited scale, the "CAMPUS Asia" programs have received obvious effect and accumulated rich experience. Some universities took multiple measures to make the programs widely available to the public. For example, the content and effect of the programs were made widely known to the public by brochure, themed website, newspaper, radio, other media, special magazine and newspaper, publicity video, etc. . These publicity measures can increase the attractiveness of programs, increase enthusiasm of all participating parties, facilitate universities to summarize program implementation experience and promote the sustainable development of programs.

2. Good Practices

1) Program Consortium Self – assessment

In order to establish a regular coordination mechanism for program operation and timely discuss and solve issues arising from program operation, the CAMPUS Asia Project Quality Assurance Committee was organized by program heads and personnel in charge of teaching affairs of the Legal Talent Program. Since December 2011, the Committee has held nearly 20 working meetings in Nagoya, Shanghai, Beijing and Seoul. At these meetings, living and study conditions of received students were shared and suggestions were proposed on the selection of students of the next phase. And the current course setting and program development plan were also discussed in an in – depth way. The regular coordination mechanism plays a vital role in refining student management and implementing program design.

It is required in ABLP that after completing the intensive courses offered by the consortium, students should submit comments and suggestions on the program. The Curriculum Committee, consisting of academic personnel of the three countries, will review students' comments and suggestions and make full discussions so as to help to improve the curriculums of the next phase.

During the operation stage of the Traditional Culture Program, program quality and implementing effect were focused on and evaluated; seminars would be held on a regular basis to report and discuss program progress and issues highlighted by each party and to negotiate on the formulation of the program implementation plan of the next step. The three universities would conduct the program test from the perspective of international standards and development of faculties and staff members to guarantee program quality and qualifications of program participants. Also, peer review system was introduced by the three universities from the three countries to guarantee teaching quality when teaching experience is exchanged. Relevant organizations have also incorporated teaching and management of "CAMPUS Asia" project into regular and institutionalized operation process. Quality assurance of program links is enhanced while program details are identified and previous experience is summarized. In terms of specific regulation, the presidents in charge lead teaching quality monitoring of the "CAMPUS Asia" programs and both universities and schools are responsible for this aspect. The teaching management organization coordination system is built. The Graduate School, Teaching Affairs Division, International Cooperation and Exchange Division as well as relevant teaching and research units conduct management and monitoring of classroom teaching and special teaching and timely solve problems arising from teaching so as to better adapt to students' demands in the program.

2) Implementation of On – campus and Off – campus Quality Assurance Measures

Internal Quality Assurance Measures of Mobile Campus Program

(1) Each semester, Guangdong University of Foreign Affairs timely tracks the teaching evaluation by students and learning evaluation by teachers held at the university. For courses relating to Japanese and Korean students, data is shared with partner universities to jointly analyze evaluation results so as to timely discover and solve problems. Additionally, the CAMPUS Asia Education Center has active interviews with students and teachers, gets engaged in communication in terms of curriculum arrangement, teaching methods, extracurricular tutoring, etc. and collets comments from teachers and students so as to gradually improve teaching patterns and talent training effect. Upon graduation of pilot program students, the CAMPUS Asia Education Center will track these students and promptly understand their career development and evaluation by their employers and graduates' satisfaction with the program so as to gradually perfect program operation.

(2) The program leading group and functional departments of the university review on a regular basis the project operation, classroom teaching and office work, listen to the work reports from the CAMPUS Asia Education Center, interview with teachers and program students, learn about student training results as well as issues arising from program advancement, and offer guiding opinions.

External Quality Assurance Measures of Mobile Campus Program

(1) When any competent departments at the upper level or any identical university pays a visit, the university will report the program advancement, introduce the results of program operation, arrange experts to observe lectures, communicate with teachers and students, distrib-

ute program reports and jointly discuss the method of sustainable program development. The Higher Education Evaluation Center of the Ministry of Education, Chinese Scholarship Council of the Ministry of Education, Trilateral Cooperation Secretariat, etc. conducted program inspection and investigation on the CAMPUS Asia Education Center of Guangdong University of Foreign Studies several times. While affirming the operation result of this operation, they also pointed out possible issues in program operation and offered guiding opinions on the long – term development and demonstration and promotion of the program.

(2) The CAMPUS Asia Education Center of Guangdong University of Foreign Studies promptly sorts working materials and operation results, translates Chinese, Japanese and Korean documents and receives the evaluation by the ministries of education of China, Japan and South Korea together with Japanese and Korean universities. At the mid – term evaluation by the ministries of education of China, Japan and South Korea held in 2014, the program was awarded Level S (top level) by the Ministry of Education, Culture, Sports, Science and Technology (MEXT, Japan), top 3 by the Korean Ministry of Education and excellent operation program by the Ministry of Education of China. In the final evaluation on pilot program operation conducted by the Ministry of Education of China in 2016, the program was awarded Level S (top level) and the three universities were evaluated as excellent pilot operation units. During the university collection stage of expanding "CAMPUS Asia" Program implemented by the Ministry of Education, the Ministry of Education announced that there was no need for this program to participate in selection and the program may be directly operated as formal program continuously.

By the top – down and combined internal and external supervision methods, the operation of the Mobile CAMPUS Program has been advanced under the scientific and normative quality assurance. Both student training quality and program operation mode have been improved all the time.

The TKT Program jointly trains postgraduates and has formed the on – campus and off – campus quality assurance mechanism facilitated by several measures through years of practice. In the on – campus link, a multi – level management and supervision mechanism covering education management department at the upper level, university, school or department is built to control education quality, program effect as well as teacher and student involvement. In the off – campus link, as joint training and teaching by professors are adopted in some programs, student training quality evaluation and control are conducted by the university. The result and quality of the program are also supervised by students, parents and relevant public departments. With the Joint Operation Working Committee as support, the plenary meeting is held once every year to discuss major issues arising from joint training and provide guarantee for smooth implementation of the program. Based on the existing student training platform, the evaluation and feedback mechanism of students and supervisors on program effect and results is built. The school or department concerned manages teaching arrangement for students and its daily quality and test students' learning quality by regular inspections, examinations, etc.. Also, for the exchange program with mutual credits recognition provided, transcripts will be issued to partner universities for recognition. It is specified by the university that students should submit a learning summary, including learning outcome and related thoughts as well as suggestions on the program.

3) Sustainable Development and Teaching Quality Monitoring

Since the establishment of "Public Risk Management Program", a series of management methods and systems for "CAMPUS Asia" project has been formed, and this has been integrated with overseas students' management system of universities. The project ensures the sustainable development of the project through effective funds-using mechanisms regular information reporting. In addition, the project also highly regarded improvement and management of teaching quality and formed complete teaching quality monitoring measures.

Financial Support—Through involving "CAMPUS Asia" project into the "Public Administration" master degree program taught in English and enrolling self – funded overseas students for the later, School of International Relations and Public Affairs of Fudan University uses such tuition to finance operating of "CAMPUS Asia" project, providing a long – term financial planning and financial assurance for sound operation and sustainable development of the project.

Information Transparency—The project has established a special report system for its development. It provides regular special report of "CAMPUS Asia" project to the Ministry of Education through the International Student Office of university; so far it has submitted a total of fifteen special reports.

Teaching Quality Monitoring—In addition to inviting administrators of universities and project directors to attend the class, the project has also developed a Degree Program Evaluation Form. It helps to carry out comprehensive self – evaluation and mutual evaluation on project design, source of students and admission, curriculum and training, teaching staff as well as 5 first – class indicators and 16 second – class indicators of the project, and adjusts and improves relevant measures on teaching quality monitoring based on the above evaluation results. The project has established a regular meeting system, analyzing problems and adjustments in the project as well as priorities and requirements of the next step. Three universities have also formed a cooperative mechanism and mutual trust through regular meetings. At the end of each semester, students are required to give comprehensive assessment on teachers' teaching time, teaching content, teaching methods and curriculum design, and teachers will receive a comprehensive teaching assessment based on students' feedbacks, thereby ensuring communication of needs and benign interaction between teachers and students.

4) Focusing on Publicity of Program Achievements

"Mobile Campus" Program ensures the effective organization and implementation of the project and operation quality through tripartite cooperation, and attaches importance to inspection of students' learning outcomes. It also focuses on project information disclosure and achievements publicity so as to enhance the attraction of the project.

Trilateral Cooperation—Three universities have set up a "CAMPUS Asia" office respectively; communication platform such as group mail, file transfer station and other forms have been established between offices for timely sharing of information and working together. To grasp the operation direction of the project, administrative staff and main participating teachers of three offices hold regular remote video conference on a monthly basis, reporting on project operations, students' learning and activities, and summarizing problems encountered during the implementation of the project; meanwhile, every year, three universities regularly hold Joint Meeting of Staff of Three Countries three times a year, summarizing last year's project operation, and discussing on the next year's curriculum design, teaching activities, student services and other contents so as to jointly promote and improve the project's operation.

Outcomes Inspection—Three universities test students' language ability through holding speech contests. Currently, students of the three countries can conduct communications skillfully in Chinese, Japanese and Korean. The project is to promote cultural exchange through language learning. In addition, the project often holds irregular Elite Leadership Talent Forum, Humanities Study Forum, "CAMPUS Asia" Forum and other academic activities and arranges students to publish papers on special subject so as to test their professional academic level, group cooperation ability and other aspects.

Project Publicity—the unique operating system of the project and its outstanding achievements in students' training are widely and highly recognized by education sectors and educational institutions of three countries. The project focuses on sharing the project's content to the public in an appropriate manner and achieving results and other information, which enhances the attraction of the project. All the three countries have jointly given a wide and influential report on contents and achievements of the project. The following are part of representative reporting materials on key newspapers and social media such as TV and online magazines in China, Japan and South Korea between 2011 and 2016.

Guangzhou Daily **Vigorously Promoted Mobile Campus Program**

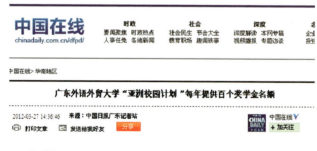

China Daily **Reported Mobile Campus Program**

List of "CAMPUS Asia" Media Reports

Country	Media	Date	Content
China	Guangzhou Daily	7 Nov. 2011	Degrees will be mutually recognized among Guangdong University of Foreign Studies and Two Japanese and Korean Universities
China Japan	China Daily Kyoto Shimbun	27 Mar. 2012 19 Jun. 2012	One hundred scholarships are offered each year by the "CAMPUS Asia" Initiative of Guangdong University of Foreign Studies
Japan	Kyoto Shimbun	2 Aug. 2012	Trilateral University Operation: Field Surveys and Visits
Japan	Asahi Shimbun	7 Jun. 2013	Introduction to Mobile Campus Program
South Korea	The Chosun Ilbo	4 Sept. 2013	Trilateral Mobile Campus Program offered at Dongseo University
Japan	Yomiuri Shimbun	6 Sept. 2013	Internship at Disaster – stricken Areas
Japan	[TV] Mainichi Broadcasting System (MBS) Report	6 Sept. 2013	Mobile Campus: Study in Japan (Special Column)
Japan	Nikkei Business Daily	14 Oct. 2013	Word – class Universities (Special Column)
South Korea	Financial News	29 Nov. 2013	Final Lecture of CAMPUS Asia South Korea in Summer A Special Lecture by Dr. Jekuk Chang, President of Dongseo University
Japan	Nihon Keizai Shimbun	19 Jun. 2014	Introduction to Mobile Campus Program
South Korea	Dong – A Ilbo	20 Nov. 2014	A Hot Debate Beyond Nationality that Broadens Vision and Increases Understanding
Japan	Asahi Shimbun	7 Apr. 2015	Trilateral Cooperation International Forum
China	People's Daily Online	17 Jan. 2016	With normalized implementation, "CAMPUS Asia" Initiative may grant three – countries certificates to students upon their graduation

3. Problem Analysis

In terms of self – assessment, the quality self – assessment management system of most programs remains to be further improved; institutions, personnel, funds, rights and responsibilities are not implemented in place; and quality criteria are short of pertinence and rigid implementation, which affects the high – quality performance of programs. Consortiums fail to make enough efforts to conduct self – assessment and fail to monitor the resource integration and trilateral cooperation within consortiums, thus causing inconsistency in the emphasis by the three countries. The method of program self – assessment is quite simple; teaching evaluation and questionnaire forms are intensive; and there is a lack of in – depth survey on students' learning experience and satisfaction towards study. The major responsibilities, quality awareness and culture of participating universities remain to be enhanced.

In terms of continuous quality improvement, some programs lack the mechanism of reviewing teaching resources configuration, curriculum setting and teaching content. The feedback and continuous improvement of quality monitoring are not in place and there is a lack of linkage of closed loop system covering policy making, implementation, evaluation, feedback and improvement. Most programs are not active enough to accept peer evaluation and external review or with weak consciousness. A long – acting mechanism to provide quality assurance of programs from the outside has not been established. Universities make public the program content and effect in a more appropriate manner and do not make enough efforts in increasing the attractiveness and sustainable development of programs.

Chapter III

Suggestions on Quality Improvement of " CAMPUS Asia " Initiative

Quality Report of "CAMPUS Asia" Cross-border Higher Education Programs

With the globalization of higher education and increasingly frequent cross – border education cooperation and exchanges, the flow of education elements including students, faculty, concepts, management, system, etc. become active day by day in the region and in the world. They cause influence to and integrate with each other and gradually move towards the direction of win – win cooperation. It is pointed out in the *Ideas on the Opening of Education to the outside in the New Era* that we should further facilitate win – win cooperation in the education sector, enhance regional education cooperation and exchanges, push forward the building of university consortiums, and further promote the in – depth education cooperation among friendly cities and universities and deepen bilateral and multilateral education cooperation. The "CAMPUS Asia" Initiative is an education exchange initiative with great significance for facilitating higher education cooperation and exchanges in East Asia and deepens the mutual benefit and win – win cooperation of all countries in the East Asia. Implementation of the initiative represents a useful exploration of transnational education cooperation and education integration in East Asia. Over five years since the implementation of the "CAMPUS Asia" initiative, under the vigorous promotion, support and guidance of the Department of International Cooperation and Exchange of the Ministry of Education, careful planning, organization and implementation by relevant universities, HEEC have provided professional quality monitoring and evaluation service, which is well received in general. By overcoming the limitations of system, culture and custom differences, participating universities have summarized a series of good practices that can be referred to and promoted in terms of talent training mode, course teaching, faculty resources, mutual credit recognition and mutual degree granting, quality assurance, etc. . These programs are of great significance and play demonstrating role in facilitating sustainable development of pilot programs and exploring multilateral education cooperation mode and education integration of East Asia.

The active exploration and good practices of "CAMPUS Asia" Initiative participants build confidence for further improving the overall quality of programs, expanding project scale and deepening program construction. In the future continuous development of programs, we should make our efforts to deepen, implement, strengthen and perfect the good programs so as to make them produce effect in a more widely and effective way. Also, continuous improvements should be made in response to program shortcomings. Substantive breakthrough and innovation should be pursued in terms of advancement of multilateral cooperation, core course linkage, mutual credit transfer and recognition, curriculums as well as joint degree granting and certification by reference to international advanced concepts and experience. Based on the analysis above, the following suggestions are proposed on the quality improvement of "CAMPUS Asia" initiative.

Ⅰ. Highlighting Whole – process Management and Perfecting Advancing and Eliminating Mechanism

"CAMPUS Asia" programs are implemented every five years. Each period covers program publicity, program selection, cooperation plan, implementation and operation, quality control, assessment and evaluation, and other important links. It is of great significance for improvement of the program quality to enhance management of each link, conduct whole – process monitoring and guidance on programs and facilitate sustainable development of programs. In the program publicity link, government departments should make full use of various resources and channels, encourage and attract universities to participate in programs, make programs widely available to officers, at the levels of university, school and department, teachers and students and enhance the attention and focus of universities on programs. In the program selection link, "high starting point", "characteristics" and "cooperation basis" of programs should be further controlled to ensure that candidate programs do not stay at the general forms of traditional exchange learning and joint training, specialty fields covered by programs are highlighted, trilateral academic advantages are exploited and the objectives of "training outstanding talents for Asia" is achieved, and to ensure that trilateral universities have some basis for cooperation and university leaders pay attention to education cooperation. Relevant departments should strictly control programs according to the above point and disapprove the programs that are not consistent with requirements. In the cooperation plan drafting link, government departments should give corresponding guidance, check if partner universities conduct full communication on program objectives and formulate explicit and detailed requirements for talent training in terms of knowledge, ability and accomplishments. Participating universities should guarantee the quality benchmark of programs and ensure program objectives are recognized, supported and facilitated by related parties in the universities. In the implementation and operation link, the universities should further perfect the organization mechanism building of programs, appoint designated personnel and posts to take charge of specific work, enhance negotiation among related functional departments, schools and departments, specify the responsibilities of all parties and jointly perform organization and implementation, teaching management, student service and other tasks of programs. In the quality monitoring link, we should, according to program quality criteria, establish and perfect internal quality management system, perfect quality monitoring systems including teaching evaluation, student satisfaction survey, graduates quality tracking and investigation, actively accept external quality evaluation on a regular basis, make continuous improvements according to internal and external evaluation feedback comments and form a closed – loop quality assurance system. In the program assessment and evaluation link, it is advised to introduce the program advancement and withdrawal mechanism. For those programs that are not paid attention to (no designated staff for post transfer, seriously insufficient personnel, property and material support, poor enthusiasm of both teachers and students) or not well implemented (there is a large gap in the expected enrollment of programs all the year round; teaching activities fail to be organized normally; and student service system is not built), relevant parties should be urged to make rectification according to the requirements for quality monitoring and evaluation. In case of ineffective rectification, fiscal funds should be immediately stopped and the program qualifications of the parties should be cancelled by the Committee through negotiation. For programs that are positively built and receive obvious effect, policies should be inclined to them, such as provision of more special activity funds to guarantee the implementation of characteristic programs.

II. Exploring the Building of Mutual Recognition System for Cross – border Higher Education Learning Outcome

The mutual recognition system for learning outcome represents a key link of ensuring cross – border education quality and a precondition for mutual education recognition among different countries and implementation of education internationalization. Currently, the credit systems in different universities vary from country to country, such as length of study, years of completion, length of academic term, score calculation method, etc.. No clear learning outcome mutual recognition management entity is specified by participating universities of "CAMPUS Asia" initiative and poor management is conducted in practice. University – level education departments or foreign affairs management departments should manage in a unified way and conduct quality monitoring of mutual credit recognition and degree granting involved in exchange learning and joint training. Alternatively, they should supervise and urge program partners to sign the learning outcome mutual recognition agreements concerning special circumstances and form the final management plans. Partners are encouraged to sign development agreements regarding mutual degree granting, joint degree granting, dual degrees or multiple degrees, etc. and explore various strategies that may be adopted in mutual recognition of cross – border education at the university level. Participating universities should perfect systems, specify responsible parties, recognition criteria and procedures, and make credit transfer and score evaluation scientific, equivalent, procedure – based and transparentin in order to effectively transfer the credits obtained by students of different education systems in their visiting universities, make a substantively equivalent evaluation of learning performance and reduce barriers during the mutual recognition of learning outcome, thus facilitating student flow in the region. A complete learning outcome mutual recognition system can also ensure the quality of students' learning and exchange activities, make the personnel flow in the region more substantively significant and meanwhile enhance the attractiveness of programs. Related departments and personnel should cooperate closely so as to effectively supervise and guarantee the operation and implementation of the learning outcome mutual recognition system.

Ⅲ. Deepening Cross – country Collaboration Training Mechanism among Chinese, Japanese and Korean Universities

"CAMPUS Asia" Initiative differs from the traditional bilateral cooperation mode in the region. It regards Chinese, Japanese and Korean universities as a consortium and realizes mutual advantage supplement and union within the consortium. Such multilateral cooperation mode is far more difficult than the traditional mode. There will be inconsistency in culture, language, education system, etc.. Once difficulties are conquered, with in – depth and perfect implementation, program influence and the added value brought to students will far surpass the traditional mode. The three parties should further integrate competitive resources of Chinese, Japanese and South Korean universities and train talents through cooperation with three governments, non – government organizations, enterprises, research institutions and other social forces; make innovation in talent training mode, facilitate the joint development of curriculum system, fully explore teacher resources, promote joint teaching of teachers, enhance university – enterprise collaboration, arrange students to participate in internship or career experience on sites of enterprises and enhance their social practice ability; and build the multinational training collaboration systems at the university, school, student and teacher levels so as to ensure the common understanding, common development, common pace and common voicing in each link of programs, finally contributing to the effect of $1 + 1 + 1 > 3$.

Ⅳ. Establishing an Incentive Support Mechanism, Improving Enthusiasm of Teachers and Students

Teacher input and student participation are important factors to ensure the continuous advancement of "CAMPUS Asia" programs. It is shown from the two rounds of quality monitoring for "CAMPUS Asia" programs that some teachers and students are not highly positive in participating in the programs, mainly due to the lack of incentive support mechanism. For teachers, the existing teacher resources are exploited to teach courses for "CAMPUS Asia" participating students in most programs. In addition to completing basic tasks, teachers should also spend a lot of research time in teaching of "CAMPUS Asia" programs. Therefore, relevant incentive support mechanisms should be established and the work relating to "CAMPUS Asia" programs should be incorporated into teacher evaluation and assessment so as to form competitions, increase teachers' enthusiasm for participation and attract more excellent academic talents and high – level teachers to participate in curriculum research and program teaching. For students, there are differences in length of study, years of completion and term period of the three parties, and barriers in credit recognition and transfer; the credits obtained by students when studying abroad are not recognized and they have to spend a lot of efforts in reaching the requirements for credits of their home universities; students participate in research, academic publication and social practice during their study abroad but there are no related systems to transfer learning activities outside these courses to equivalent credits; and the added value presented by programs remain to be further improved. Thus, credit transfer and social activity credit recognition systems should be built and incentive support mechanisms and measures that differ from traditional score sheets and aim to improve students' comprehensive employment competitiveness should be provided so as to allow students to actively participate in programs with assurance and make great achievements.

Chapter IV

Guidelines on Quality Monitoring of "CAMPUS Asia" Transnational Joint Education Academic Programs

Quality Report of "CAMPUS Asia" Cross-border Higher Education Programs

Ⅰ. Introduction

"CAMPUS Asia" (Collective Action for Mobility Program of University Students in Asia) is a program launched based on a trilateral summit agreement among the governments of China, Japan, and Korea, and is designed to carve out a better future for Asia. Its objectives are to promote exchange and cooperation in the area of quality assurance among higher education institutions (HEIs) in the three countries, to create a shared sense of community in terms of history and culture in Northeast Asia, and to nurture the future leaders a vision of regional peace and coexistence through trilateral educational exchanges.

Three quality assurance agencies, i. e. , the Higher Education Evaluation Center of the Ministry of Education in China (HEEC), the National Institution for Academic Degrees and University Evaluation (NIAD – UE, currently the National Institution for Academic Degrees and Quality Enhancement of Higher Education) in Japan, and the Korean Council for University Education in Korea (KCUE – KUAI) —set up the China – Japan – Korea Quality Assurance Council. Recognizing the gurantee model of quality assurance in international education as a common issue, the Council agreed to carry out quality monitoring of the CAMPUS Asia pilot programs.

This monitoring was intended not to confirm attainment of minimum quality standards, but to monitor the current stages and overview of the programs to be visited, identify good practices from the standpoint of educational quality and disseminate them at home as well as abroad.

The three quality assurance agencies conducted monitoring activities for the 10 pilot programs in two rounds. The first round monitoring was conducted independently in each country from 2013 to 2014, taking into account of the country's relevant regulations, quality assessment system, and methods. After that, the monitoring criteria and each country's methods were comparatively analyzed. From 2015 to 2016, the three agencies jointly established a common framework for quality assurance, which includes criteria, principles, and processes, before conducting the second round monitoring. In the second round monitoring, panel members from the three countries jointly performed document reviews and site visits, based on common self – as-

sessment reports provided by the consortium for each CAMPUS Asia program. The monitoring results were compiled into a report featuring examples of good practices, which was widely disseminated.

Following the completion of the pilot period in 2015, in the autumn of 2016, the three
governments promoted CAMPUS Asia as a full – fledged program taking the second – round monitoring mode as the template. Based on the vision of long – term development, they also agreed
to continue discussing the feasibility of further expansion to the whole ASEAN region. Meantime,
the three quality assurance agencies plan to conduct monitoring on the full – fledged programs as
well. In so doing, they are expected to refer to these guidelines and further expand their monitoring efforts based on the experience gained in the pilot period and the structure of close cooperation established among the three countries while collaborating with the national governments and
the participating HEIs.

We hope that these monitoring activities and the ongoing dissemination of good practices
can contribute to the enhancement of the quality of international cooperative academic programs
including CAMPUS Asia, to the fostering of excellent students who acquire appropriate learning
outcomes with respect to the goals of the respective programs, and to strengthening international
cooperation among the quality assurance agencies.

II. Objectives of the Guidelines

The three quality assurance agencies formulated these joint guidelines based on experiences
gained through the establishment of a common quality assurance method for future quality assurance initiatives on CAMPUS Asia programs.

The first objective of the guidelines is to specify a method of monitoring international cooperative academic programs (CAMPUS Asia) so that the three agencies and the reviewers can
clearly understand the monitoring criteria, processes, and methods and, thereby, carry out
the monitoring of CAMPUS Asia programs in a consistent fashion.

The second objective is to serve as a helpful model for other quality assurance agencies conducting monitoring or evaluation of international cooperative academic programs, especially
when working with partner agencies in other countries, and for HEIs in their internal quality assurance work with regard to international cooperative education.

Through their experience of joint monitoring of CAMPUS Asia, the three quality assurance
agencies developed the unified quality assurance framework described here and also built a sense
of mutual trust. In this sense, it encourages them to apply a common quality framework. When a
certain quality assurance agency conducts quality monitoring, the Joint Monitoring Committee
can make the final decision.

We hope that these guidelines will contribute to the improvement of quality assurance initiatives both within and beyond the three participating countries. The three quality assurance agencies involved will review these guidelines periodically and improve them as needed in light of global trends in quality assurance and the circumstances of international collaborative education at each institution.

Ⅲ. Quality Monitoring Guidelines

1) General Principles

- Promote quality enhancement of international collaborative academic programs
- Conduct monitoring based on joint criteria and procedures of three countries
- Review consortium – wide progress and achievements to identify each program's good practices
- Examine the degree of cooperation among participating HEIs with respect to resource integration and quality assurance activities as international collaborative academic programs
- Examine each program's continuous quality improvement
- Value students' opinions and ideas regarding CAMPUS Asia

2) Implementation System

The Joint Monitoring Committee is the decision – making body for conducting the monitoring. A Monitoring Panel is set up under the Committee to carry out the actual process.

Members of the Joint Monitoring Committee and the Monitoring Panel shall have no right to make decisions on the programs that are related to such members.

Consisting of 3 experts (including one from quality assurance agency), the Joint Monitoring Committee is designated by quality assurance agencies of the three countries. The committee is responsible for:

—Identifying and finalizing the final joint monitoring report;

—Making the final official joint monitoring report available to the public;

It is preferable that members of the Joint Monitoring Committee have knowledge and experience in terms of joint international cooperation program and quality assurance.

Members of the Monitoring Panel are designated by quality assurance agencies of the three countries. The panel is responsible for:

—Reviewing self – assessment reports and preparing material review reports;

—Conducting site surveys;

—Compiling consortium monitoring reports;

It is preferable that Monitoring Panel experts should have knowledge and experience in terms of joint international academic program, quality assurance and professional fields of each program.

It is preferable that each quality assurance agency designates at least one member of the Monitoring Panel. When members fail to be designated by each quality assurance institution, the Monitoring Panel had better arrange members that understand relevant countries.

It is preferable that Monitoring Panel members arrange relevant training so that Monitoring Panel members understand the criteria for implementation of quality assurance activities. When Monitoring Panel members of all countries offer training, quality assurance agencies of the three countries should cooperate with each other so as to ensure identical training content.

Monitoring Panel members (such as president and coordinator) shall give descriptions.

3) Procedures

The overall procedures for monitoring are as follows:

• The quality assurance agencies hold an orientation program for Monitoring Panel members to enable them to deepen their knowledge and understanding of the goals and implementation methods of quality assurance (monitoring) activities. When holding different orientation programs separately in different countries, the three quality assurance agencies should cooperate for same or similar content at all the programs.

• Each consortium is required to produce and submit one common (joint) self-assessment report produced by all participating HEIs in the consortium, describing its good practices and issues for improvement in the ten standards under each criterion.

• Monitoring Panel members conduct document reviews based on the submitted self-assessment reports.

• Monitoring Panel members conduct site visits to ask about matters that are not clear from document reviews. Interviews with the officials responsible for the program, with faculty and staff members involved in the program, and with students are included in the site visit schedule. An exchange of views and opinions with the officials responsible for the program takes place at the end of the visit. It is preferable to conduct site visits at a time when representatives of the participating HEIs in each country can be present.

• Monitoring Panel members produce a draft monitoring report on a consortium based on the results of their document review and site visit. If the draft report is produced in the local language, a version in English should also be prepared.

• Before finalizing the draft monitoring report on a consortium, the consortium itself has the opportunity to review it and ensure that there are no factual errors. If any errors were to be identified, Monitoring Panel members would conduct deliberations and revise the report where necessary.

• Monitoring Panel members then share finalized monitoring reports on a consortium with the three quality assurance agencies, which will draw up a draft joint monitoring report based on the monitoring reports on each consortium.

- The Joint Monitoring Committee finalizes the joint monitoring report.

- The quality assurance agencies make the finalized joint monitoring report widely available to the public in book form, online, and at symposia.

4) Criteria and Viewpoints

To ascertain the current status of each program and its quality enhancement initiatives, the following monitoring criteria on quality should be applied. When monitoring with respect to each criterion, refer to the viewpoints listed thereunder.

However, the envisioned viewpoints are not limited to those listed below.

Objectives

The vision for talent training is clearly defined via discussion among the participating institutions.

The goals are clearly articulated, including expected learning outcomes in terms of students' knowledge, skills, and attitudes. Participating institutions exhibit a shared recognition of these program goals.

The program goals are shared among the staff members and students of the participating institutions and are understood in the same, unequivocal way at each institution.

The program goals function as guidelines for developing and implementing the academic program.

Program objectives are realized according to the five – year plan. And excellent activities and results may be generated from programs.

Organization and Administration

Basic policies on the multi – institutional operational structure, institutions' responsibilities with regard to students, and the allocation of expenses are clearly articulated in a written agreement signed and put into effect by the participating institutions.

Periodic meetings are held among the participating institutions; a mechanism for reviewing program implementation and related issues is established, and responsibility for addressing common issues is shared.

Where academic supervision is applicable, an appropriate supervisory system is established and implemented cooperatively among the participating institutions.

Within each institution, responsibility for conducting the international collaborative academic program is clearly defined along with a suitable support system involving other divisions (e. g. , international, student support, and quality assessment).

The participating institutions have agreed to sustain the program based on the experience of the past five years, and the operational structure and plans for sustaining the program are actively reviewed. Also, institution – wide approval to sustain the program is obtained from the management of each institution.

Curriculum Integration

The curriculum is jointly designed by the participating institutions.

Information on curriculum and courses at each institution is shared by and across the participating institutions.

The educational content is suited to achieving the program goals.

The educational content complies with the expected learning outcomes (e. g. , students' knowledge, skills, and attitudes) .

The educational content and methods are suited to international collaborative education.

The relationship between the program methods/content and the expected learning outcomes is clarified.

Academic Staff and Teaching

A sufficient number of qualified faculty and staff members are deployed for the sustained implementation of the international collaborative academic program.

The system for the provision of educational content (e. g. , joint supervision by dispatching faculty, distance learning) which faculty members of partner institutions join is implemented.

Faculty and staff development and capacity building for attaining international competencies are conducted.

Incentives and a support for the work environment are provided to attract faculty and staff members who are skilled in international education and can contribute to the sustainability of the program.

The teaching methods used are acceptable and suitable for international students (e. g. , bilingual textbooks, classes taught in English and access to after – class or extracurricular tutorials) .

Student Admission

Information on the program is disseminated widely in order to recruit motivated students.

The student selection process (selection criteria and system) is suited to the educational objectives and content and is jointly established and carried out by the participating institutions.

The expected number of students has been secured.

The academic level of admitted students is appropriate for the program's objectives and curriculum.

Support for Learning and Living

Participating institutions share with students the information necessary for course selection and enrollment, including sufficient guidance prior to participating students' departure from their home countries.

Various types of learning support are provided for participating students, including language training, supplemental classes, and support from teaching assistants.

Various types of living support are provided for the participating students, including orientation, counseling, disaster risk management, and career support.

A sufficient learning environment is provided for participating students, including libraries, information technology, and laboratory facilities.

Sufficient scholarships and accommodation support are provided appropriately for participating students.

Participating institutions support exchange and interaction among students and alumni.

Learning Outcomes

Based on the expected learning outcomes, an appropriate method for measuring learning outcomes is established, and learning outcomes are measured regularly.

The relationship among students' course enrollment, credit acquisition, and learning outcomes is analyzed.

Appropriate learning outcomes aligned with the program objectives are achieved.

Students are highly satisfied with the program content and exhibit high levels of achievement.

The results of a student satisfaction survey and student achievement survey are shared across participating institutions.

Learning outcomes (added – value outcomes) resulted from the international collaborative program are obtained.

The status of graduates is tracked regularly and is shared among the participating institutions.

Credit Transfer, Grading Methods and Degree Awarding

The credit systems of the partner institutions are mutually understood, and a program – based credit transfer system is established.

As regards a program that awards two degrees upon completion, criteria for awarding degrees and methods of review at each institution are shared, and the criteria and methods of review are discussed periodically among the participating institutions.

Grading methods are coordinated among the participating institutions with each institution conducting strict assessments so as to ensure the validity of the awarded credits.

As regards a program that awards two degrees upon completion, the achieved learning outcomes are appropriate for a CAMPUS Asia program.

Internal Quality Assurance

Feedback from students is periodically gathered in multiple ways, in such manners as through questionnaires, interviews, and student participation in review committees, and is incorporated into the program review.

A program review is carried out based on an analysis of information gathered on the learning progress of students, learning outcomes achieved, curriculum, teaching and its contents, and other information.

External review methods, including inputs from an advisory committee, are conducted.

The results of program reviews are shared and discussed among the participating institutions to contribute toward further program improvement and development.

Participating institutions discuss and consider measures for quality improvement and future initiatives based on the self – assessment results.

The results of the review are appreciated by the international affairs, quality assurance, and student support divisions of each institution, and necessary measures are taken at the institutional level.

The participating institutions agree to sustain and enhance the program through quality improvement according to the experience accumulated in the last five years. Also, institution – wide approval from the management of each institution to sustain the program is obtained.

Some effects of the program's implementation on students who are not in the program are recognized.

5) Considerations When Conducting Monitoring

Considerations for the quality assurance agencies

(1) Adequate and appropriate resources, both human and financial, should be available to carry out consistent monitoring. It is preferable to obtain financial support from the government in one's own country.

(2) Objectivity, transparency, and independence of the quality assurance agencies should be maintained. The independence of the reviewers should be ensured to carry out objective and fair monitoring.

(3) Active communication and cooperation among quality assurance agencies from the three countries, participating institutions, and organizations concerned should be ensured in all monitoring activities.

(4) Systems leading to continuous improvement through quality assurance activities should be developed.

Considerations for the reviewers

(1) Active communication and cooperation: Reviews are to be conducted with active communication and cooperation among the reviewers from the three countries.

(2) Monitoring documents and information: Documents and information obtained during monitoring are not to be used or provided for purposes other than monitoring activities.

(3) Liaison and coordination: If uncertainties or inquiries about the CAMPUS Asia programs are recognized during the document review and the preparation of reports, the quality assurance agency in charge of queries should be contacted. Directly contacting the HEIs is discouraged.

(4) Objective and unbiased review: Reviews are to be conducted objectively and in an unbiased manner.

(5) Interview during site visit:

• Before each interview, the reviewers should hold a meeting to thoroughly discuss the facts to be confirmed and remarks to be made during the interview.

• Regarding inquiries from the HEIs during the site visit, the reviewers carrying out the sitevisit should, in principle, be unanimous on their responses. Should you wish to offer your personal opinions, it would be appropriate to convey to the interviewees that the views are personal and not those of the review team.

• The reviewers should refrain from asking interviewees about personal issues.

• The reviewers should take care so that interviewees are not detrimentally affected by their responses but ensure confidentiality.

• The reviewers should not debate with interviewees or criticize the HEIs.

• Should the interviewees criticize CAMPUS Asia initiatives or the monitoring process, it would be advisable to listen for the reasons behind their opinions and avoid making any counter-arguments.

However, if there are misunderstandings, correct information should be conveyed.

• At the end of the site visit, the reviewers should thoroughly discuss the facts to be included in the report.

(6) Points to keep in mind when producing each report (document review report, site visit report, and final report):

• Reports should be produced with objectivity and fairness based on the facts verified in the document review and the site visit.

• Especially when making negative observations, care should be taken to provide detailed and objective reasoning in regard to observation result.

• Any contradictions should be avoided within a report.

Appendixes

Quality Report of "CAMPUS Asia" Cross-border Higher Education Programs

Appendix Ⅰ
Guidelines for Exchange and Cooperation among Universities in China, Japan and South Korea with Quality Assurance

(Approved at the 2nd Committee Conference, December 2010, Beijing)

In line with meeting of the leaders of China, Japan and South Korea and also *Trilateral Cooperation Vision* 2010, the three countries would promote exchanges among universities and cooperation among quality assurance agencies in education to assure the quality of exchanges. In this sense, the guidelines are elaborated, based on the discussion in the China – Japan – Korea Committee for Promoting Exchange and Cooperation among Universities (hereinafter referred as the "Committee")

Ⅰ. Introduction

1. Objective

The guidelines aim to encourage exchanges and cooperation among universities in China, Japan and South Korea with quality assurance and jointly improve international competitiveness of universities. The purposes of guidelines are to establish an effective operational mechanism for university exchange and quality assurance, to protect students and other stakeholders as well as to urge relevant stakeholders to fulfill the responsibilities and promote collaboration, thereby contributing to comprehensive educational cooperation and a good – neighborly partnership of mutual trust among people of these three countries.

2. Connotation

Exchanges and cooperation among universities as mentioned in these guidelines could be carried out through "CAMPUS Asia" (Collective Action of Mobility Program of University Students) program with the consent of the three countries. The framework and detailed programs would be stated in other documents. In addition, the proposed guidelines do not force any particular educational and exchange activities, as these activities should be conducted autonomously by themselves.

3. Principles

Considering each other's characteristics and legal system, exchanges and cooperation among universities and quality assurance activities must adhere to the principles of openness, extensiveness, progressiveness, flexibility and demonstrativeness. Enough respect for mutual benefit should be given in jointly exploring a common framework while recognizing each other's differences and characteristics in system, customs, and cultures and so on.

4. Scope

The guidelines are applicable for governments, universities, quality assurance agencies and other stakeholders including the industries to implement. It is expected that all involved bodies work together to conduct exchange programs among universities and guarantee the quality of credits and degrees conferred.

II. Specific Provisions

(I) Guidelines for Governments

1. Establishment of a Comprehensive, Coherent and Transparent Quality Assurance Framework

It is imperative that the governments should clarify what higher education system entails in terms of school types, academic level, diploma issued and the connection with other education systems including secondary education systems, vocational education systems, and other non – formal education systems, in accordance with their laws and regulations. In addition, the governments should define the national prerequisite for students to be admitted into universities, detailed requirements for them to obtain degree and quality assurance standard in higher education (or qualification framework) as well as prepare the information package of quality assurance in higher education.

2. Encouragement for Relevant Universities to Participate in the Exchange Programs

The governments, in their assured authorities and policies, should support universities in conducting exchange programs through various resources and means. The governments should also give supports through financial and other means to the Pilot Program to be launched.

3. Support for the Quality Assurance Agency to Conduct Activities

The governments should encourage quality assurance agencies to exert positive effects on quality improvement and support relevant activities conducted independently by the China – Japan – Korea Quality Assurance Council (hereinafter referred to as the "Council") through financial and other means.

(II) Guidelines for Universities

1. Establishment of Internal Quality Assurance System

Relevant universities should establish an effective internal quality assurance system to ensure the quality of exchange program. Here the meaning of "internal quality assurance" varies according to the differences of the education system and academic practices of the three countries, but the following could be assumed to be applicable for all universities of three countries to implement.

(1) to publish basic information of school education and teaching, and provide detailed information of exchange program;

(2) to construct systematic curriculum and pay due consideration for maintaining the standards and consistency for writing syllabus and grade evaluation;

(3) to confirm, under the comprehensive teaching system and appropriate administration, that the process of conferring credits, giving academic grade, and processing credits transfer is in accordance with the laws and regulations of the country.

2. Effective Implementation of Exchange Programs

Universities participating in the exchange programs should formulate operational regulations and emergency preplan. These universities should also make an agreement about important items and the details in the exchange programs, which is available to the public and then take periodical follow – up. While paying attention to quality assurance, it is also necessary for universities to probe into the establishment of credit transfer system, which would lay a foundation for establishing credit transfer and accumulation system in China, Japan and South Korea and even in Southeast Asia. It is also important for universities to offer educational support in collaboration with a partner university through learning agreement, under which both universities and students confirm whether learning outcomes (including credits and diploma and so on) can be certified or not so that they can further their learning after returning to their own country.

3. Good Services for Exchange Students

It is important to provide students including applicants with adequate and correct information resources for decision – making of their academic career. Implementation procedure and requirements of exchange programs should be maintained clear, transparent and readable, and it is recommended for universities to offer "one – stop service" as much as possible, through which international students can use various services such as information service, application service and other consultation, so that they can concentrate on preparing their academic career. Upon implementation of the program, necessary language training and continuous support, guidance and opportunities of "cultural exchanges" are recommended to be provided for exchange students. And in order to provide better service, it is also recommended to maintain communication with international students through counselors, teaching assistant, volunteers and all available forces of the school.

(III) Guidelines for Quality Assurance Agencies

1. Maintaining Clarification and Visibility of Procedure

It is important to understand that the role of quality assurance agencies is different in the three countries, even though these three countries have similar system of university evaluation. In this sense, the quality assurance agencies should pay attention to the diversity and variety of quality assurance mechanism in each country, while making efforts in exchanging and sharing information in the three countries through information platform of the Council.

2. Seeking for Common Standards and Joint Evaluation

While strengthening quality assurance of exchange program, the quality assurance agencies in these three countries should pay attention to common practices and features such as index system and evaluation measures. These agencies should find out certain common index framework in exchange program among universities in the three countries and jointly conduct university evaluation.

3. Capacity Building for the Staff

Capacity building for the staff in charge of evaluation activities plays a very important role in improving university evaluation. From the perspective of international exchange program, it is necessary for the relevant staff to have adequate knowledge and experience in the cross – border nature of exchange program. It is recommended to conduct staff exchange and capacity building through the Council so that the outcomes will be shared in exchange and cooperation among universities for capacity building.

(IV) Guidelines for Other Stakeholders

Exchange programs among universities aim to cultivate international talents with communication and working abilities, who are the potentials for the future economic development in the East Asia, thereby having far – reaching significance in terms of economic development and prosperity of China, Japan, and Korea as well as the whole East Asia. Therefore, it is expected that other stakeholders including industries can offer necessary support for university exchange programs in the three countries, such as cooperation for establishing internship courses, joint scientific researches projects, and so on.

III. Supplementary Articles

1. Validity of the Guidelines

These guidelines were approved, based on the discussion at the second meeting for the Committee held in Beijing, December 10th, 2010. The texts were written in four languages, namely, Chinese, Japanese, Korean and English. In the event of any divergence of interpretation between any of the texts, the English text shall prevail. The terms of the guidelines may be altered with the consent of the Committee. All relevant bodies have access to these guidelines for reference in conducting exchange and cooperation. It should be noted that each higher education system has its own characteristics, and the proposed guidelines never intend to force any change of the rules or regulations of any countries.

2. Dissemination of the Guidelines

It is important that the governments should make efforts in disseminating the guidelines and "CAMPUS Asia" framework as non – binding but significant material for the society both domestically and internationally. Through such process, it is also recommended that the governments should publish good practices implemented in the universities and quality assurance agencies, including the Pilot Exchange Program to be carried out.

Appendix Ⅱ

Agreement of the 4th Meeting of "the China – Japan – Korea Committee for Promoting Exchange and Cooperation among Universities"

At the 4th meeting of "the China – Japan – Korea Committee for Promoting Exchange and Cooperation among Universities" (hereafter referred to as the Committee) held on August 6th, 2013 in Tokyo, the following consensus was reached:

Ⅰ. The "CAMPUS Asia" Extended Committee jointly identified the great significance, openness and development potential of "CAMPUS Asia" in Asian higher education. In order to implement the spirit of the *Joint Declaration* made at the 5th Trilateral Summit Meeting among the People's Republic of China, the Republic of Korea and Japan held in Beijing in May 2012, it was acknowledged by the Committee that the development of "CAMPUS Asia" would be further facilitated based on pilot programs in the future so as to further expand the scale and scope of such pilot programs and train more and better talents for the region.

Joint Declaration on the Enhancement of Trilateral Comprehensive Cooperative Partnership, made at the 5th Trilateral Summit Meeting (May 13, 2012, Beijing, China) said, "We encouraged the three countries to make contribution to the establishment of a shared quality assurance framework in Asia through the pilot programs and to further expand the scale and scope of the programs so as to cultivate more and better talents for the region."

Ⅱ. Quality Monitoring of "CAMPUS Asia" Pilot Programs

The Committee identified the significance and importance of quality monitoring of the on – going pilot programs, and monitored and facilitated the quality assurance of "CAMPUS Asia". It will also formulate a set of criteria that is of importance for the expansion and future sustainable and effective implementation of programs. The basic system and schedule arrangement of monitoring activities are identified by the Committee as follows:

1. In the monitoring, quality assurance agencies of the three countries identify university

quality assurance activities and select good practices for promotion based on teaching quality.

2. Quality assurance agencies of the three countries conduct two rounds of monitoring, aiming to compare and analyze quality assurance activities of the three countries and formulate a joint guideline that orients towards quality assurance agencies and relates to quality assurance of international education cooperation.

Ⅲ. The 5th Meeting of the China – Japan – Korea Committee for Promoting Exchange and Cooperation among Universities will be held in Shanghai, China in the fall of 2014.

Appendix Ⅲ

Agreement of the 5th Meeting of "the China – Japan – Korea Committee for Promoting Exchange and Cooperation among Universities"

The 5th Meeting of the China – Japan – Korea Committee for Promoting Exchange and Cooperation among Universities (hereafter referred to as the Committee) was held on April 10th, 2015 in Shanghai, China. The consensus reached is as follows:

I. Quality Assurance and Monitoring of the CAMPUS Asia Programs

1. In line with the *Guidelines for Exchange and Cooperation among Universities with Quality Assurance* and the *Trilateral Consensus of the 4th meeting of the Committee*, the 1st (midterm) quality monitoring of the 10 pilot programs of CAMPUS Asia was carried out separately by quality assurance agencies of the three countries, based on their own criteria and procedures which are mutually recognized. The Committee accepted the quality monitoring results given by three agencies.

2. The good practices of CAMPUS Asia pilot programs identified by quality assurance agencies of the three countries, were highly regarded by the Committee, and will be disseminated and made available within the three countries and beyond, in order to facilitate the expansion and quality enhancement of CAMPUS Asia Programs.

3. The Committee adopted the framework of the final term joint quality monitoring standards and implementation framework of CAMPUS Asia Pilot Programs, and showed support for the quality assurance agencies of the three countries to jointly conduct final quality monitoring before the pilot programs end (from 2015 to 2016) according to this framework, and to develop the final quality report.

4. The Committee agreed to make the full use of the website of "China – Japan – Korea

Quality Assurance Council", to improve the information exchange and sharing in CAMPUS Asia program quality assurance and monitoring, and make timely reports to the public regarding the quality monitoring criteria, procedure and results, thereby ensuring the transparency and access to quality information, and strengthening the public support and oversight to the programs.

Ⅱ. Expansion and Sustainable Development of CAMPUS Asia Program

1. Echoing the mission of CAMPUS Asia Program which is open, flexible, progressive, the Committee supported the three – mode expansion scheme. Mode 1 is to enhance the openness of the programs, to allow more flexible student mobility, such as among programs. It will be decided by member universities. Mode 2 is to select more China – Japan – Korea universities to join in CAMPUS Asia Program. Mode 3 is to expand participating countries beyond China, Japan and South Korea in Asia.

2. To ensure the sustainable development of CAMPUS Asia Program, the Committee agreed to implement the expansion scheme in the following three stages. From 2015 to 2016, Mode 1 will be adopted. The quantity of student mobility will be enlarged for the programs which have demonstrated outstanding performances and development potentials during pilot period. During 2015 and 2016, the admission criteria and procedure with more flexibility and diversity for new programs will be studied and formulated, and additional participating universities will be selected. Mode 2 will be launched in September 2016. After the implementation of Mode 2, the Committee will summarize experience and discuss the practicable implementation scheme of Mode 3.

3. To further facilitate sustainable development of "CAMPUS Asia" and to provide services for authorities, teachers and students, the committee agreed to further discuss a specialized website of "CAMPUS Asia Information Platform" after fully implementing Mode 2, in order to release events and activities of the Committee, to provide information of the China – Japan – Korea exchange programs, to gather and publish the exchange development status and experiences, and to produce data analysis result. Detailed scheme shall be discussed at the working – level meeting of Working Group for University Exchange.

4. To provide better environment for more flexible student mobility and to strengthen the development capacity of CAMPUS Asia, the Committee agreed to establish cooperation mechanism for mutual recognition of qualifications and credits among China, Japan and South Korea. The Committee encouraged participating universities to regularly hold seminars for rectors, teachers and students to exchange views on experience of university exchanges and quality assurance, in order to ensure the sustained attractiveness, and to promote visibility and influence of CAMPUS Asia.

Ⅲ. The Next Meeting

The Committee decided that the 6th Meeting of the China – Japan – Korea Committee for Promoting Exchange and Cooperation among Universities woule be held in Korea in the year of 2016.

Appendix IV

Agreement of the 6th Meeting of "the Korea – China – Japan Committee for Promoting Exchange and Cooperation among Universities"

(Draft)

The 6th Meeting of the Korea – China – Japan Committee for Promoting Exchange and Cooperation among Universities (hereafter referred to as the Committee) was held on 23 November 2017 in Seoul, Korea. As a result, the following consensus was reached:

I . Sustainable Development and Expansion of CAMPUS Asia

1. (Continued Promotion of CAMPUS Asia) In line with the Guidelines for Exchange and Cooperation among Universities and the Trilateral Consensus of the 6th Meeting of the Committee, the Committee highly appreciated the successful launching of full – fledged program in 2016 and China – Japan – Korea's joint – selection work for the full – fledged program based on the criteria of each country. The Committee agreed to work more closely to pursue the continued development of CAMPUS Asia based on the successful outcome of its pilot programs. To this end, the outcomes of the programs were shared among the three countries, while the ways to further improve them were discussed. Furthermore, the Committee confirmed that further in – depth discussion is required to set the pathway for the future of the programs through various means, including the 2nd Trilateral Education Ministers' Meeting.

2. (Expansion of Mode 3) At the previous Meeting of the Committee, the three countries agreed to expand CAMPUS Asia Program by introducing the three – mode expansion scheme. The Committee also reaffirmed their consensus to continue to pursue the program to promote mobility in higher education even after this current period of CAMPUS Asia Programs (Mode 2), and decided to discuss about the Mode 3 in more details at the next meeting.

II. Quality Assurance and Monitoring of CAMPUS Asia

(Common Principles) To support the active exchange of students among the consortia, the Committee agreed to draw up the Common Principles for implementing CAMPUS Asia Progrem. The Common Principles will include various matters relevant to the operation of the program, including the period of exchange, the principle of balanced student exchange, the parties responsible for the provision of funding, and the scope of scholarship. The three countries also consented to actively inform the consortia of the Common Principles to assist their successful operation of the program.

(Monitoring) The outcome of the 2nd Monitoring, which was distributed at the 1st Trilateral Rectors' Forum, was shared once again at the 6th Meeting of the Committee, and was adopted by its members. Based on the outcome, the Committee decided to establish the framework of the 3rd quality monitoring of CAMPUS Asia Program. The overall direction of the upcoming 3rd monitoring, including the monitoring criteria and guidelines, was discussed and it was decided to be conducted in 2018. The specifics of the monitoring will be determined by government assigned agencies later on through further discussion.

III. Creation of Conducive Environment for Active Student Exchange and Capacity – building

1. (Launching of Joint Policy Research) Based on the agreement of the 5th Meeting of the Committee, the members of the Committee agreed to support the active exchange among CAMPUS Asia consortia, and to start discussion on launching joint research project on the higher education systems of the three countries and their recognition of qualifications to promote mobility in the field of higher education. Moreover, the Committee shared views that this research should contribute to the promotion of dual/joint degrees and mobility in higher education among the three countries.

2. (Expansion of Relevant Exchange Activities) At the 5th Meeting of the Committee, it was agreed that more seminars should be held on a regular basis, inviting rectors, faculty and students to exchange views on their experiences of exchanges with other universities and of their efforts to achieve quality assurance. The members of the Committee also confirmed to work harder to take note of the positive outcome of CAMPUS Asia, and to proliferate its progress by conducting these activities including through organizing regular meetings for the consortia and alumni of the three countries.

IV. The Next Meeting

The Committee decided that the 7th Meeting of the Committee will be held in Japan in the year of 2019.

Appendix V   Statistics on Student Exchange in Pilot Programs on "CAMPUS Asia"

1. ABLP

Inbound Activities (Japan/Korea→China)

No.	Program Duration		Students Participation	Type of Mobility Program	Contribution to Double-degree Awarding	Maximum Credits (to be) Recognized in Home University	Number of Inbound Students
	Begins	Ends	(From Japan/Korea)				
1	Feb. 2012	Jun. 2012	Korea	Semester Exchange Program (MBA, 4 months)	No	18	2
2	Sept. 2012	Dec. 2012	Japan	Semester Exchange Program (MBA, 4 months)	No	18	2
3	Sept. 2012	Dec. 2012	Korea	Semester Exchange Program (MBA, 4 months)	No	18	1
4	Sept. 2013	Dec. 2013	Korea	Semester Exchange Program (MBA, 4 months)	No	18	1
5	Sept. 2014	Dec. 2014	Japan	Semester Exchange Program (MBA, 4 months)	No	18	1
6	Sept. 2015	Jun. 2016	Korea	Double Degree Program (MBA, 1 year)	Yes	36	4
7	Sept. 2013	Jun. 2014	Japan	Double Degree Program (MBA, 1 year)	Yes	36	1
8	Sept. 2014	Jun. 2015	Japan	Double Degree Program (MBA, 1 year)	Yes	36	1
9	20 Aug. 2012	1 Sept. 2012	Japan and Korea	Summer Program (2-week, MBA)	No	2	20
10	15 Aug. 2013	30 Aug. 2013	Japan and Korea	Summer Program (2-week, MBA)	No	2	20
11	12 Aug. 2014	28 Aug. 2014	Japan and Korea	Summer Program (2-week, MBA)	No	2	20
12	11 Aug. 2015	26 Aug. 2015	Japan	Summer Program (2-week, MBA)	No	2	8

Outbound Activities (China→Japan/Korea)

No.	Program Duration		Students Participation (To Japan/Korea)	Type of Mobility Program	Contribution to Double-degree Awarding	Maximum Credits (to be) Recognized in Home University	Number of Outbound Students
	Begins	Ends					
1	Sept. 2013	Jun. 2014	Japan	Double Degree Program (MBA, 1 year)	Yes	22	2
2	Sept. 2012	Jun. 2013	Korea	Double Degree Program (MBA, 1 year)	Yes	22	1
3	Sept. 2013	Jun. 2013	Korea	Double Degree Program (MBA, 1 year)	Yes	22	1
4	Jan. 2015	Jun. 2015	Korea	Double Degree Program (MBA, 5 months, two modules)	Yes	22	5
5	Feb. 2014	Jun. 2014	Japan	Semester Exchange (MBA, 4 months)	No	18	1
6	Sept. 2015	Dec. 2015	Japan	Semester Exchange (MBA, 4 months)	No	18	2
7	20 Aug. 2012	1 Sept. 2012	Japan and Korea	Summer Program (2-week, MBA)	No	1	8
8	15 Aug. 2013	30 Aug. 2013	Japan and Korea	Summer Program (2-week, MBA)	No	1	8
9	12 Aug. 2014	28 Aug. 2014	Japan and Korea	Summer Program (2-week, MBA)	No	1	8
10	11 Aug. 2015	26 Aug. 2015	Japan	Summer Program (2-week, MBA)	No	1	10

2. BESETO DDMP

Inbound Activities（Japan/Korea→China）

No.	Program Duration		Students Participation		Type of Mobility Program	Contribution to Double－degree Awarding	Maximum Credits（to be）Recognized in Home University	Number of Inbound Students
	Begins	Ends		（From Japan/Korea）				
1	1 Sept. 2012	1 May 2015	Korea		Exchange Program（Graduate，6 months）		9	17
2	1 Sept. 2012	1 May 2015	Japan		Exchange Program（Graduate，6 months）		9	9
3	1 Sept. 2012	1 May 2015	Japan		Double Degree Program	Yes	10	5

Outbound Activities（China→Japan/Korea）

No.	Program Duration		Students Participation		Type of Mobility Program	Contribution to Double－degree Awarding	Maximum Credits（to be）Recognized in Home University	Number of Outbound Students
	Begins	Ends		（To Japan/Korea）				
1	1 Sept. 2012	1 May 2015	Korea		Exchange Program（Graduate，6 months）		9	27
2	1 Sept. 2012	1 May 2015	Japan		Exchange Program（Graduate，6 months）		6	25
3	1 Sept. 2012	1 May 2015	Japan		Double Degree Program	Yes	24	4

3. Policy Consortium Program

Inbound Activities (Japan/Korea→China)

No.	Program Duration		Students Participation	Type of Mobility Program	Contribution to Double–degree Awarding	Maximum Credits (to be) Recognized in Home University	Number of Inbound Students
	Begins	Ends	(From Japan/Korea)				
1	20 Feb. 2012	15 Jul. 2012	Korea	Exchange Program	No	9	1
2	1 Mar. 2013	15 Jul. 2013	Korea	Exchange Program	No	9	1
3	1 Mar. 2013	31 Jan. 2014	Korea	Exchange Program	No	9	1
4	21 Feb. 2014	30 Jun. 2014	Korea	Exchange Program	No	27	3
5	7 Aug. 2013	3 Sept. 2013	Japan	Summer Program	No	–	2
6	7 Aug. 2014	3 Sept. 2014	Korea	Summer Program	No	15	5
7	22 Sept. 2014	31 Jan. 2015	Korea	Exchange Program	No	9	1
8	22 Sept. 2015	31 Aug. 2015	Korea	Exchange Program	No	9	1
9	1 Mar. 2015	31 Aug. 2015	Korea	Exchange Program	No	18	2
10	28 Jul. 2015	25 Aug. 2015	Korea	Summer Program	No	15	5
11	31 Aug. 2015	31 Jan. 2016	Korea	Exchange Program	No	9	1
12	1 Mar. 2016	15 Jul. 2016	Korea	Exchange Program	No	27	3

Outbound Activities (China→Japan/Korea)

No.	Program Duration		Students Participation (To Japan/Korea)	Type of Mobility Program	Contribution to Double – degree Awarding	Maximum Credits (to be) Recognized in Home University	Number of Outbound Students
	Begins	Ends					
1	13 Jul. 2013	31 Oct. 2013	Japan	Exchange Program	No	9	1
2	1 Aug. 2013	31 Aug. 2013	Korea	Summer Program	No	9	4
3	7 Aug. 2013	22 Aug. 2013	Japan	Summer Program	No	9	5
4	1 Oct. 2013	31 Mar. 2014	Japan	Exchange Program	No	9	1
5	1 Oct. 2013	30 Sept. 2014	Japan	Exchange Program	No	9	1
6	4 Aug. 2014	5 Sept. 2014	Korea	Summer Program	No	9	5
7	12 Aug. 2014	25 Aug. 2014	Japan	Summer Program	No	9	4
8	30 Jul. 2015	23 Sept. 2015	Japan	Summer Program	No	9	4
9	1 Oct. 2015	5 Feb. 2016	Japan	Exchange Program	No	9	2

4. TKT Program

Inbound Activities （Japan/Korea→China）

No.	Program Duration		Students Participation (From Japan/Korea)	Type of Mobility Program	Contribution to Double-degree Awarding	Maximum Credits (to be) Recognized in Home University	Number of Inbound Students
	Begins	Ends					
1	1 Sept. 2012	31 Jul. 2013	Japan	Long-stay (Graduate)		10	1
2	1 Sept. 2012	1 Feb. 2013	Japan	Long-stay (Graduate)		10	1
3	1 Sept. 2012	31 Jul. 2013	Japan	Long-stay (Undergraduate)		60	1
4	3 Sept. 2012	30 Jan. 2013	Korea	Long-stay (Graduate)		36	3
5	1 Mar. 2013	31 Jan. 2014	Japan	Long-stay (Graduate)	Yes	10	1
6	1 Sept. 2013	31 Jul. 2014	Japan	Long-stay (Graduate)	Yes	10	2
7	1 Mar. 2013	31 Jul. 2013	Korea	Long-stay (Graduate)		18	1
8	1 Sept. 2013	31 Jan. 2014	Korea	Long-stay (Undergraduate)		36	4
9	1 Sept. 2013	31 Jan. 2014	Korea	Long-stay (Graduate)		18	1
10	1 Jan. 2014	31 Mar. 2014	Japan	Short-stay (Graduate)		10	1
11	1 Feb. 2014	30 Jun. 2014	Japan	Long-stay (Graduate)		10	1
12	1 Sept. 2014	30 Nov. 2014	Japan	Short-stay (Graduate)		10	1
13	1 Sept. 2014	31 Jan. 2015	Japan	Long-stay (Graduate)		10	1
14	1 Sept. 2014	31 Aug. 2015	Japan	Long-stay (Graduate)		10	1
15	1 Sept. 2014	15 Jul. 2015	Korea	Long-stay (Undergraduate)		36	3
16	27 Feb. 2015	26 Jun. 2015	Korea	Long-stay (Graduate)		18	1

Outbound Activities（China→Japan/Korea）

No.	Program Duration		Students Participation（To Japan/Korea）	Type of Mobility Program	Contribution to Double–degree Awarding	Maximum Credits（to be）Recognized in Home University	Number of Outbound Students
	Begins	Ends					
1	1 Jul. 2012	31 Aug. 2012	Japan	Summer Program		No limit	3
2	1 Aug. 2012	31 Jan. 2013	Japan	Long–stay（Graduate）		11	2
3	1 Oct. 2012	28 Feb. 2013	Japan	Long–stay（Undergraduate）		No limit	2
4	1 Sept. 2012	31 Dec. 2012	Korea	Long–stay（Undergraduate）		No limit	4
5	1 Jul. 2013	31 Aug. 2013	Japan	Summer Program（Undergraduate）		No limit	4
6	1 Sept. 2013	28 Feb. 2014	Japan	Long–stay（Graduate）		11	1
7	1 Sept. 2013	30 Sept. 2014	Japan	Long–stay（Graduate）	Yes	11	3
8	1 Jan. 2013	20 Feb. 2013	Korea	Short–stay（Undergraduate）		No limit	2
9	1 Aug. 2013	31 Aug. 2013	Korea	Summer Program		No limit	6
10	1 Sept. 2013	31 Dec. 2013	Korea	Long–stay（Undergraduate）		No limit	8
11	1 Dec. 2013	19 Feb. 2014	Korea	Short–stay（Graduate）		11	5
12	1 Jan. 2014	28 Feb. 2014	Korea	Short–stay（Undergraduate）		No limit	1
13	1 Jan. 2014	28 Feb. 2014	Korea	Short–stay（Graduate）		No limit	1
14	1 Dec. 2013	16 Feb. 2014	Korea	Short–stay（Undergraduate）		No limit	1
15	1 Jul. 2014	31 Aug. 2014	Japan	Summer Program（Undergraduate）		No limit	3
16	1 Oct. 2014	28. Feb. 2015	Japan	Long–stay（Graduate）		11	2

229

continued

No.	Program Duration		Students Participation	Type of Mobility Program	Contribution to Double-degree Awarding	Maximum Credits (to be) Recognized in Home University	Number of Outbound Students
	Begins	Ends	(To Japan/Korea)				
17	1 Sept. 2014	30 Sept. 2014	Japan	Short – stay (Graduate)	Yes	11	1
18	1 Sept. 2014	1 Aug. 2015	Japan	Long – stay (Graduate)	Yes	11	2
19	1 Mar. 2015	1 Aug. 2015	Japan	Long – stay (Graduate)	Yes	11	1
20	1 Aug. 2014	29 Aug. 2014	Korea	Summer Program (Undergraduate)		No limit	4
21	1 Aug. 2014	29 Aug. 2014	Korea	Summer Program (Graduate)		11	9
22	3 Mar. 2015	9 May 2015	Korea	Short – stay (Graduate)		11	1

5. Traditional Culture Program

Inbound Activities (Japan/Korea→China)

No.	Program Duration		Students Participation	Type of Mobility Program	Contribution to Double-degree Awarding	Maximum Credits (to be) Recognized in Home University	Number of Inbound Students
	Begins	Ends	(From Japan/Korea)				
1	Mar. 2012	Feb. 2013	Japan	Long – stay			4
2	Mar. 2012	Feb. 2014	Japan	Long – stay			5
3	Mar. 2014	Aug. 2014	Japan	Long – stay			1
4	Mar. 2014	Feb. 2015	Japan	Long – stay			4

continued

No.	Program Duration		Students Participation	Type of Mobility Program	Contribution to Double – degree Awarding	Maximum Credits (to be) Recognized in Home University	Number of Inbound Students
	Begins	Ends	(From Japan/Korea)				
5	Mar. 2015	Feb. 2016	Japan	Long – stay			5
6	1 Mar. 2012	31 Aug. 2012	Korea	Long – stay			2
7	1 Mar. 2012	28 Feb. 2013	Korea	Long – stay			1
8	4 Aug. 2012	2 Sept. 2012	Japan	Summer Program			10
9	4 Aug. 2012	3 Sept. 2012	Korea	4 – Week Chinese Program			10
10	1 Sept. 2012	28 Feb. 2013	Korea	Long – stay			4
11	1 Mar. 2013	31 Aug. 2013	Korea	Long – stay			1
12	1 Mar. 2013	28 Feb. 2014	Korea	Long – stay			3
13	5 Aug. 2013	31 Aug. 2013	Japan	Summer Program			10
14	1 Sept. 2013	28 Feb. 2014	Korea	Long – stay			2
15	1 Mar. 2014	31 Aug. 2014	Korea	Long – stay			2
16	1 Mar. 2014	28 Feb. 2015	Korea	Long – stay			3
17	7 Aug. 2014	31 Aug. 2014	Japan	Summer Program			10
18	1 Sept. 2014	28 Feb. 2015	Korea	Long – stay			2
19	21 Sept. 2014	27 Sept. 2014	Japan	Workshop			22
20	1 Mar. 2015	31 Aug. 2015	Korea	Long – stay			5
21	24 Aug. 2015	27 Aug. 2015	Japan	Short – stay			10
22	Sept. 2015	28 Feb. 2016	Korea	Long – stay			3

Outbound Activities（China→Japan/Korea）

No.	Program Duration Begins	Program Duration Ends	Students Participation (To Japan/Korea)	Type of Mobility Program	Contribution to Double－degree Awarding	Maximum Credits（to be）Recognized in Home University	Number of Outbound Students
1	Oct. 2012	Mar. 2013	Japan	Long－stay			6
2	Oct. 2013	Mar. 2014	Japan	Long－stay			5
3	Apr. 2013	Sept. 2013	Japan	Long－stay			5
4	Oct. 2014	Mar. 2015	Japan	Long－stay			5
5	Oct. 2015	Mar. 2016	Japan	Long－stay			5
6	Apr. 2015	Sept. 2015	Japan	Long－stay			5
7	1 Sept. 2C12	28 Feb. 2013	Korea	Long－stay			6
8	4 Aug. 2013	24 Aug. 2013	Korea	3－Week Korean Program			10
9	6 Aug. 2013	20 Aug. 2013	Japan	Summer Program			5
10	1 Sept. 2C13	28 Feb. 2014	Korea	Long－stay			7
11	1 Mar. 2014	31 Aug. 2014	Korea	Long－stay			2
12	Apr. 2014	Sept. 2014	Japan	Long－stay			5
13	3 Aug. 2014	16 Aug. 2014	Japan	Summer Program			5
14	1 Sept. 2C14	28 Feb. 2015	Korea	Long－stay			3
15	1 Mar. 2015	28 Feb. 2016	Korea	Long－stay			5
16	9 Aug. 2015	18 Aug. 2015	Japan	Summer Program			10

6. Legal Talent Program

Inbound Activities（Japan/Korea→China）

No.	Program Duration		Students Participation (From Japan/Korea)	Type of Mobility Program	Contribution to Double-degree Awarding	Maximum Credits（to be）Recognized in Home University	Number of Inbound Students
	Begins	Ends					
1	1 Sept. 2012	30 Jun. 2013	Japan	Exchange Program（5 Undergraduates，1 year，4 to Renmin University，1 to Shanghai Jiao Tong University）		34	5
2	1 Sept. 2012	30 Jun. 2013	Korea	Exchange Program（4 Undergraduates，1 year & 1 Graduate，1 semester）		36	5
3	1 Sept. 2013	30 Jun. 2014	Japan	Exchange Program（5 Undergraduates，1 year，3 to Renmin University，2 to Shanghai Jiao Tong University）		28	5
4	1 Sept. 2013	30 Jun. 2014	Korea	Exchange Program（4 Undergraduates，1 year & 1 Graduate，1 semester；4 to Renmin University & 1 to Shanghai Jiaotong University）		36	5
5	1 Sept. 2014	30 Jun. 2015	Japan	Exchange Program（5 Undergraduates，1 year；3 to Renmin University & 2 to Shanghai Jiao Tong University）		Not yet	5
6	1 Sept. 2014	30 Jun. 2015	Korea	Exchange Program（4 Undergraduates，1 year & 2 Graduates，1 semester；4 to Renmin University & 2 to Shanghai Jiao Tong University）		36	6

Outbound Activities (China→Japan/Korea)

No.	Program Duration		Students Participation (To Japan/Korea)	Type of Mobility Program	Contribution to Double-degree Awarding	Maximum Credits (to be) Recognized in Home University	Number of Outbound Students
	Begins	Ends					
1	22 Sept. 2012	30 Aug. 2013	Japan	Exchange Program (5 Undergraduates, 1 year; 4 from Renmin University, 1 from Shanghai Jiao Tong University)		38	5
2	28 Aug. 2012	1 Aug. 2013	Korea	Exchange Program (2 Undergraduates & 1 Graduate, 1 year)		22	3
3	5 Aug. 2012	31 Aug. 2012	Japan	Summer Program (5 Undergraduates & 4 Graduates, 5 from Renmin University, 2 from Shanghai Jiao Tong University & 2 from Tsinghua University)			9
4	22 Sept. 2013	30 Aug. 2014	Japan	Exchange Program (4 Undergraduates & 1 Graduate, 1 year; 3 from Renmin University & 2 from Shanghai Jiao Tong University)		26	5
5	28 Aug. 2013	1 Aug. 2014	Korea	Exchange Program (3 Undergraduates & 2 Graduates, 1 year; 4 from Renmin University & 1 from Shanghai Jiao Tong University)		11	5
6	5 Aug. 2013	23 Aug. 2013	Japan	Summer Program (5 Undergraduates & 4 Graduates, 5 from Renmin University, 2 from Shanghai Jiao Tong University & 2 from Tsinghua University)			9
7	22 Sept. 2014	31 Aug. 2015	Japan	Exchange Program (5 Undergraduates, 2 for 1 semster & 3 for 1 year; 1 Graduate, 1 year; 4 from Renmin University & 2 from Shanghai Jiao Tong University)		Not transferred yet	6

continued

No.	Program Duration		Students Participation	Type of Mobility Program	Contribution to Double – degree Awarding	Maximum Credits（to be）Recognized in Home University	Number of Outbound Students
	Begins	Ends	（To Japan/Korea）				
8	28 Aug. 2014	1 Aug. 2015	Korea	Exchange Program（5 Undergraduates, 1 semester; 1 Graduate, 1 year）		Not transferred yet	6
9	4 Aug. 2015	25 Aug. 2015	Japan	Summer Program（5 Undergraduates & 4 Graduates, 5 from Renmin University, 2 from Shanghai Jiao Tong University & 2 from Tsinghua University）			9

7. Chemistry and Materials Program

Number of Exchange Students（Korea/China→Japan）

No.	Exchange Period		Type of The Exchanges Program		Number of Credits Earnable	Number of Exchange Students
	From	To				
1	4 Mar. 2012	31 May 2012	China→Japan	Tohoku University	1	1
2	12 Jun. 2012	11 Sept. 2012	China→Japan	Tohoku University	1	1
3	20 Aug. 2012	23 Aug. 2012	Short – Stay China→Japan	Tohoku University	0	3
4	26 Sept. 2012	28 Oct. 2012	Short – stay China→Japan	Tohoku University	1	1
5	15 Oct. 2012	20 Dec. 2012	Short – stay China→Japan	Nagoya University	1	1

continued

No.	Exchange Period		Type of The Exchanges Program		Number of Credits Earnable	Number of Exchange Students
	From	To				
6	24 Oct. 2012	25 Nov. 2012	Short – stay	China→Japan Tohoku University	1	1
7	1 Nov. 2012	31 Jan. 2013		China→Japan Nagoya University	4	1
8	5 Nov. 2012	6 Feb. 2013		China→Japan Nagoya University	4	5
9	5 Nov. 2012	19 Jan. 2013		China→Japan Nagoya University	4	1
10	11 Nov. 2012	10 Nov. 2013		China→Japan Tohoku University	1	1
11	1 Apr. 2013	30 Jun. 2013		China→Japan Tohoku University	1	1
12	1 Jul. 2013	30 Sept. 2013		China→Japan Tohoku University	1	1
13	1 Aug. 2013	31 Oct. 2013		China→Japan Nagoya University	4	3
14	29 Aug. 2013	30 Aug. 2013	Short – Stay	China→Japan Tohoku University	0	1
15	3 Sept. 2013	5 Jan. 2014		China→Japan Nagoya University	4	1
16	3 Sept. 2013	5 Dec. 2013		China→Japan Nagoya University	4	1
17	1 Mar. 2014	28 May 2014		China→Japan Tohoku University	1	1
18	29 Mar. 2014	30 Mar. 2014	Seminar	China→Japan Nagoya University	0	2
19	1 Apr. 2014	30 Sept. 2014		China→Japan Tohoku University	1	1
20	7 May 2014	6 Aug. 2014		China→Japan Nagoya University	4	3
21	7 May 2014	6 Sept. 2014		China→Japan Nagoya University	4	1
22	7 May 2014	31 Aug. 2014		China→Japan Nagoya University	4	1

continued

No.	Exchange Period			Type of The Exchanges Program		Number of Credits Earnable	Number of Exchange Students
	From	To					
23	14 May 2014	13 Aug. 2014		China→Japan	Tohoku University	1	1
24	28 May 2014	31 Aug. 2014		China→Japan	Nagoya University	4	1
25	1 Jul. 2014	30 Sept. 2014		China→Japan	Nagoya University	4	1
26	1 Jul. 2014	30 Sept. 2014		China→Japan	Nagoya University	1	1
27	25 Aug. 2014	26 Aug. 2014	Short – Stay	China→Japan	Tohoku University	0	5
28	24 Sept. 2014	24 Dec. 2014		China→Japan	Nagoya University	4	1
29	24 Sept. 2014	23 Jan. 2015		China→Japan	Nagoya University	4	1
30	1 Oct. 2014	31 Dec. 2014		China→Japan	Nagoya University	4	1
31	26 Nov. 2014	27 Nov. 2014	CA Symposium	China→Japan	Tohoku University	0	12
32	2 Mar. 2015	2 Jun. 2015		China→Japan	Tohoku University	1	1
33	1 May 2015	31 Jul. 2015		China→Japan	Tohoku University	1	4
34	1 Jun. 2015	31 Aug. 2015		China→Japan	Nagoya University	4	4
35	27 Aug. 2015	28 Aug. 2015	Short – Stay	China→Japan	Tohoku University	0	6
36	24 Sept. 2015	23 Jan. 2016		China→Japan	Nagoya University	4	5
37	24 Sept. 2015	22 Dec. 2015		China→Japan	Nagoya University	4	1
38	30 Jul. 2012	25 Aug. 2012	Short – stay	Korea→Japan	Tohoku University	1	3
39	20 Aug. 2012	23 Aug. 2012	Short – Stay	Korea→Japan	Tohoku University	0	2

continued

No.	Exchange Period		Type of The Exchanges Program			Number of Credits Earnable	Number of Exchange Students
	From	To					
40	24 Sept. 2012	8 Feb. 2013		Korea→Japan	Nagoya University	4	1
41	13 Jan. 2013	13 Aug. 2013		Korea→Japan	Tohoku University	1	1
42	1 Jul. 2013	30 Sept. 2013		Korea→Japan	Nagoya University	4	1
43	1 Aug. 2013	3 Dec. 2013		Korea→Japan	Nagoya University	4	1
44	5 Aug. 2013	1 Sept. 2013	Short – stay	Korea→Japan	Tohoku University	1	2
45	29 Aug. 2013	30 Aug. 2013	Short – Stay	Korea→Japan	Tohoku University	0	2
46	1 Oct. 2013	28 Feb. 2014		Korea→Japan	Nagoya University	4	1
47	29 Mar. 2014	30 Mar. 2014	Seminar	Korea→Japan	Nagoya University	0	2
48	7 May 2014	31 Aug. 2014		Korea→Japan	Nagoya University	4	1
49	7 Jul. 2014	8 Oct. 2014		Korea→Japan	Tohoku University	1	1
50	7 Jul. 2014	6 Aug. 2014	Short – stay	Korea→Japan	Tohoku University	1	1
51	25 Aug. 2014	26 Aug. 2014	Short – Stay	Korea→Japan	Tohoku University	0	2
52	26 Nov. 2014	27 Nov. 2014	CA Symposium	Korea→Japan	Tohoku University	0	3
53	15 Dec. 2014	14 Mar. 2015		Korea→Japan	Nagoya University	4	1
54	7 May 2015	31 Dec. 2015		Korea→Japan	Nagoya University	4	1
55	27 Aug. 2015	28 Aug. 2015	Short – Stay	Korea→Japan	Tohoku University	0	1
56	1 Sept. 2015	23 Dec. 2015		Korea→Japan	Nagoya University	4	0

Number of Exchange Students（Japan – Korea/China）

No.	Exchange Period		Type of The Exchanges Program			Number of Credits Earnable	Number of Exchange Students
	From	To					
1	11 Mar. 2013	13 Mar. 2013	CA Symposium	Japan→China	Nagoya University/Tohoku University	0	19
2	11 Jun. 2013	11 Sept. 2013		Japan→China	Tohoku University	2	1
3	4 Sept. 2013	3 Dec. 2013		Japan→China	Nagoya University	4	1
4	13 Mar. 2014	15 Mar. 2014	Edu – Exchange	Japan→China	Nagoya University	0	10
5	14 Mar. 2014	14 Mar. 2014	Edu – Exchange	Japan→China	Nagoya University	0	12
6	1 Jun. 2014		Edu – Exchange	Japan→China	Nagoya University	0	2
7	25 Jun. 2014	24 Sept. 2014		Japan→China	Nagoya University	4	1
8	31 Aug. 2014	30 Nov. 2014		Japan→China	Tohoku University	2	1
9	25 Jun. 2015	24 Sept. 2015		Japan→China	Nagoya University	4	4
10	1 Sept. 2015	30 Nov. 2015		Japan→China	Tohoku University	2	1
11	5 Nov. 2015	5 Nov. 2015	JSTU Sympo	Japan→China	Nagoya University/Tohoku University	0	16
12	2 Jul. 2012	31 Jul. 2012	Short – stay	Japan→Korea	Tohoku University	1	5
13	9 Aug. 2012	13 Nov. 2012		Japan→Korea	Tohoku University	2	1
14	31 Aug. 2012	29 Aug. 2013		Japan→Korea	Tohoku University	2	1
15	20 Jan. 2013	25 Jan. 2013	Edu – Exchange	Japan→Korea	Nagoya University	0	5
16	5 Apr. 2013	5 Jul. 2013		Japan→Korea	Tohoku University	2	1
17	18 Jun. 2013	17 Sept. 2013		Japan→Korea	Nagoya University	4	1
18	19 Jun. 2013	3 Mar. 2014		Japan→Korea	Tohoku University	2	1

continued

No.	Exchange Period		Type of The Exchanges Program		Number of Credits Earnable	Number of Exchange Students
	From	To				
19	1 Jul. 2013	30 Sept. 2013	Japan→Korea	Tohoku University	2	1
20	8 Jul. 2013	5 Aug. 2013	Japan→Korea Short – stay	Tohoku University	1	3
21	19 Jul. 2013	19 Oct. 2013	Japan→Korea	Nagoya University	4	1
22	2 Sept. 2013	6 Dec. 2013	Japan→Korea	Tohoku University	2	1
23	7 Nov. 2013	9 Nov. 2013	Japan→Korea CA Symposium	Nagoya University/Tohoku University	0	18
24	25 Jun. 2014	24 Sept. 2014	Japan→Korea	Nagoya University	4	1
25	7 Jul. 2014	7 Aug. 2014	Japan→Korea Short – stay	Tohoku University	1	2
26	24 Jul. 2014	23 Oct. 2014	Japan→Korea	Nagoya University	4	1
27	17 Aug. 2014	23 Aug. 2014	Japan→Korea Summer School	Nagoya University	2	6
28	17 Aug. 2014	23 Aug. 2014	Japan→Korea Summer School	Tohoku University	0	3
29	1 Dec. 2014	28 Feb. 2015	Japan→Korea	Tohoku University	2	1
30	25 Feb. 2015	25 Mar. 2015	Japan→Korea Short – stay	Tohoku University	1	1
31	4 May 2015	4 Aug. 2015	Japan→Korea	Tohoku University	2	1
32	25 Jun. 2015	24 Sept. 2015	Japan→Korea	Nagoya University	4	4
33	5 Jul. 2015	11 Jul. 2015	Japan→Korea Summer School	Nagoya University	2	0
34	6 Jul. 2015	11 Jul. 2015	Japan→Korea Summer School	Tohoku University	0	0
35	6 Jul. 2015	4 Aug. 2015	Japan→Korea Short – stay	Tohoku University	1	1

8. EEST Program

Inbound Activities (Japan/Korea→China)

No.	Program Duration Begins	Program Duration Ends	Students Participation (From Japan/Korea)	Type of Mobility Program	Contribution to Double – degree Awarding	Maximum Credits (to be) Recognized in Home University	Number of Inbound Students
1	1 Sept. 2012	31 Jan. 2013	Korea	Exchange Program		0	2
2	1 Sept. 2012	31 Jan. 2013	Japan	Exchange Program		0	3
3	1 Sept. 2013	31 Jan. 2014	Korea	Double Degree Program	Yes	10	3
4	1 Sept. 2013	31 Jan. 2014	Japan	Double Degree Program	Yes	10	5
5	25 Nov. 2013	27 Nov. 2013	Japan	CSS International Conference		0	50
6	25 Nov. 2013	27 Nov. 2013	Korea	CSS International Conference		0	61
7	11 Aug. 2014	22 Aug. 2014	Korea	Summer School	Yes	3	28
8	11 Aug. 2014	22 Aug. 2014	Japan	Summer School	Yes	3	44
9	1 Sept. 2014	31 Jan. 2015	Korea	Double Degree Program	Yes	10	4
10	1 Sept. 2014	31 Jan. 2015	Japan	Double Degree Program	Yes	10	6
11	1 Sept. 2015	31 Jan. 2016	Korea	Double Degree Program	Yes	10	5
12	1 Sept. 2015	31 Jan. 2016	Japan	Double Degree Program	Yes	10	5
13	6 Apr. 2016	8 Apr. 2016	Korea	Spring Seminar		0	
14	6 Apr. 2016	8 Apr. 2016	Japan	Spring Seminar		0	
15	1 Sept. 2016	31 Jan. 2017	Korea	Double Degree Program	Yes	10	
16	1 Sept. 2016	31 Jan. 2017	Japan	Double Degree Program	Yes	10	

Outbound Activities (China→Japan/Korea)

No.	Program Duration		Students Participation (To Japan/Korea)	Type of Mobility Program	Contribution to Double-degree Awarding	Maximum Credits (to be) Recognized in Home University	Number of Outbound Students
	Begins	Ends					
1	16 Aug. 2012	24 Aug. 2012	Korea	Summer School		0	9
2	1 Sept. 2012	31 Jan. 2013	Korea	Exchange Program		0	3
3	1 Sept. 2012	31 Jan. 2013	Japan	Exchange Program		0	3
4	20 Nov. 2012	23 Nov. 2012	Japan	CSS International Conference		0	22
5	1 Feb. 2013	1 July 2013	Japan	Double Degree Program	Yes	10	5
6	22 Feb. 2013	26 Feb. 2013	Japan	Spring Seminar		0	10
7	17 Aug. 2013	29 Aug. 2013	Japan	Summer School	Yes	3	18
8	1 Sept. 2013	31 Jan. 2014	Korea	Double Degree Program	Yes	10	2
9	1 Feb. 2014	1 Jul. 2014	Japan	Double Degree Program	Yes	10	6
10	22 Feb. 2014	26 Feb. 2014	Japan	Spring Seminar		0	8
11	1 Sept. 2014	31 Jan. 2015	Korea	Double Degree Program	Yes	10	6
12	13 Nov. 2014	15 Nov. 2014	Korea	CSS International Conference		0	22
13	1 Feb. 2015	1 Jul. 2015	Japan	Double Degree Program	Yes	10	8
14	17 Aug. 2015	27 Aug. 2015	Japan	Summer School	Yes	3	33
15	1 Sept. 2015	31 Jan. 2016	Korea	Double Degree Program	Yes	10	8
16	13 Nov. 2015	15 Nov. 2015	Japan	CSS International Conference		0	
17	1 Feb. 2016	1 Jul. 2016	Japan	Double Degree Program	Yes	10	
18	17 Aug. 2016	27 Aug. 2016	Korea	Summer School	Yes	3	
19	1 Sept. 2016	31 Jan. 2017	Korea	Double Degree Program	Yes	10	

9. Public Risk Management Program

Inbound Activities（Japan/Korea→China）

No.	Program Duration		Students Participation	Type of Mobility Program	Contribution to Double-degree Awarding	Maximum Credits (to be) Recognized in Home University	Number of Inbound Students
	Begins	Ends	(From Japan/Korea)				
1	1 Sept. 2012	15 Jul. 2013	Korea	Double Degree Program (Graduate, 1 year)	Yes	10	2
2	1 Sept. 2012	15 Jul. 2013	Japan	Double Degree Program (Graduate, 1 year)	Yes	10	2
3	1 Sept. 2012	31 Jan. 2013	Korea	Exchange Program (Graduate, 6 months)		10	2
4	1 Sept. 2012	15 Jul. 2013	Japan	Exchange Program (Graduate, 1 year)		10	1
5	1 Sept. 2013	15 Jul. 2014	Korea	Double Degree Program (Graduate, 1 year)	Yes	10	3
6	1 Sept. 2013	15 Jul. 2014	Japan	Double Degree Program (Graduate, 1 year)	Yes	10	2
7	1 Sept. 2013	31 Jan. 2014	Korea	Exchange Program (Graduate, 6 months)		10	2
8	1 Sept. 2013	31 Jan. 2014	Japan	Exchange Program (Graduate, 6 months)		10	2
9	1 Sept. 2014	15 Jul. 2015	Korea	Double Degree Program (Graduate, 1 year)	Yes	10	1
10	1 Sept. 2014	15 Jul. 2015	Japan	Double Degree Program (Graduate, 1 year)	Yes	10	4
11	1 Sept. 2014	15 Jul. 2015	Japan	Exchange Program (Graduate, 1 year)		10	1
12	1 Sept. 2014	31 Jan. 2015	Korea	Exchange Program (Graduate, 6 months)		10	4
13	1 Sept. 2015	15 Jul. 2015	Korea	Exchange Program (Graduate, 6 months)		10	3
14	1 Sept. 2015	15 Jul. 2016	Korea	Double Degree Program (Graduate, 1 year)	Yes	10	3
15	1 Sept. 2015	15 Jul. 2016	Korea	Exchange Program (Graduate, 1 year)		10	1
16	1 Sept. 2015	31 Jan. 2016	Japan	Exchange Program (Graduate, 6 months)		10	1

Outbound Activities (China→Japan/Korea)

No.	Program Duration		Students Participation	Type of Mobility Program	Contribution to Double-degree Awarding	Maximum Credits (to be) Recognized in Home University	Number of Outbound Students
	Begins	Ends	(To Japan/Korea)				
1	1 Sept. 2012	15 Jul. 2013	Korea	Double Degree Program (Graduate, 1 year)	Yes	10	2
2	1 Sept. 2012	31 Jan. 2013	Korea	Exchange Program (Graduate, 6 months)		10	2
3	1 Sept. 2012	15 Jul. 2013	Japan	Double Degree Program (Graduate, 1 year)	Yes	10	3
4	1 Sept. 2013	15 Jul. 2014	Korea	Double Degree Program (Graduate, 1 year)	Yes	10	2
5	1 Sept. 2013	31 Jan. 2014	Korea	Exchange Program (Graduate, 6 months)		10	3
6	1 Sept. 2013	15 Jul. 2014	Japan	Double Degree Program (Graduate, 1 year)	Yes	10	2
7	1 Sept. 2013	31 Jan. 2014	Japan	Exchange Program (Graduate, 6 months)		10	4
8	1 Sept. 2014	15 Jul. 2015	Japan	Double Degree Program (Graduate, 1 year)	Yes	10	3
9	1 Sept. 2014	31 Jan. 2015	Japan	Exchange Program (Graduate, 6 months)		10	3
10	1 Sept. 2014	15 Jul. 2015	Korea	Double Degree Program (Graduate, 1 year)	Yes	10	1
11	1 Sept. 2014	31 Jan. 2015	Korea	Exchange Program (Graduate, 6 months)		10	4
12	1 Sept. 2015	31 Jan. 2016	Japan	Exchange Program (Graduate, 6 months)		10	4

10. Mobile Campus Program

Inbound Activities（Korea/Japan→China）

No.	Program Duration		Students Participation (From Japan/Korea)	Type of Mobility Program	Contribution to Double－degree Awarding	Maximum Credits（to be）Recognized in Home University	Number of Inbound Students
	Begins	Ends					
1	4 Aug. 2012	10 Aug. 2012（Japan）/11 Aug. 2012（Korea）	Japan/Korea	Short－stay		2/0	32
2	16 Feb. 2013	29 Apr. 2013（Japan）/30 Apr. 2013（Korea）	Japan/Korea	Long－stay（Undergraduate）		10/16	18
3	15 Feb. 2014	28 Apr. 2014（Japan）/29 Apr. 2014（Korea）	Japan/Korea	Long－stay（Undergraduate）		13/18	20
4	7 Mar. 2015	28 May 2015	Korea	Internship		0/0	7
5	19 Feb. 2012	24 Feb. 2012	Japan/Korea	Short－stay		2/0	29
6	18 Feb. 2014	22 Feb. 2014	Japan/Korea	Short－stay		2/2	23
7	31 Aug. 2013	12 Jul. 2014	Korea	Long－stay（Master）		0	2
8	9 Sept. 2014	25 Jul. 2015	Korea	Long－stay（Master）		0	1
9	9 Sept. 2014	25 Jul. 2015	Japan	Long－stay（Master）	Yes	10	1

Outbound Activities (China→Korea/Japan)

No.	Program Duration Begins	Program Duration Ends	Students Participation (To Japan/Korea)	Type of Mobility Program	Contribution to Double–degree Awarding	Maximum Credits (to be) Recognized in Home University	Number of Outbound Students
1	13 Aug. 2012	20 Aug. 2012	Korea	Short – stay		0	20
2	21 Aug. 2012	27 Aug. 2012	Japan	Short – stay		0	20
3	24 Aug. 2012	27 Jan. 2013	Korea	Long – stay (Master)		0	5
4	26 Feb. 2013	31 Dec. 2013	Korea	Long – stay (Master)		12	4
5	6 May 2013	8 Aug. 2013	Japan	Long – stay (Undergraduate)		14	10
6	3 Sept. 2013	7 Dec. 2013	Korea	Long – stay (Undergraduate)		14	10
7	27 Feb. 2014	31 Jul. 2014	Korea	Long – stay (Master)		6	4
8	1 May 2014	4 Aug. 2014	Japan	Long – stay (Undergraduate)		20	10
9	14 Sept. 2014	25 Dec. 2014	Korea	Long – stay (Undergraduate)		8	10
10	27 Aug. 2014	27 Jan. 2015	Korea	Long – stay (Master)		6	4
11	27 Feb. 2015	29 Jul. 2015	Korea	Long – stay (Master)		6	4
12	28 Jul. 2012	3 Aug. 2012	Japan	Short – stay		2	20
13	19 Feb. 2013	23 Feb. 2013	Korea	Short – stay		2	13
14	30 Jul. 2013	3 Aug. 2013	Japan	Short – stay		2	16
15	27 Jul. 2014	1 Aug. 2014	Japan	Short – stay		2	12
16	3 Feb. 2015	7 Feb. 2015	Korea	Short – stay		2	17

图书在版编目（CIP）数据

"亚洲校园"跨境高等教育项目质量报告／周爱军，
刘振天，郑觅主编.－－北京：社会科学文献出版社，
2018.6
ISBN 978 - 7 - 5201 - 2614 - 4

Ⅰ.①亚…　Ⅱ.①周…②刘…③郑…　Ⅲ.①国际教
育 - 高等教育 - 教育质量 - 研究报告 - 亚洲　Ⅳ.
①G649.1

中国版本图书馆 CIP 数据核字（2018）第 078220 号

"亚洲校园"跨境高等教育项目质量报告

主　　编／周爱军　刘振天　郑　觅

出 版 人／谢寿光
项目统筹／任文武
责任编辑／王玉霞　李艳芳

出　　版／社会科学文献出版社·区域发展出版中心（010）59367143
　　　　　地址：北京市北三环中路甲 29 号院华龙大厦　邮编：100029
　　　　　网址：www. ssap. com. cn
发　　行／市场营销中心（010）59367081　59367018
印　　装／天津千鹤文化传播有限公司

规　　格／开　本：787mm×1092mm　1/16
　　　　　印　张：16.25　字　数：295 千字
版　　次／2018 年 6 月第 1 版　2018 年 6 月第 1 次印刷
书　　号／ISBN 978 - 7 - 5201 - 2614 - 4
定　　价／88.00 元

本书如有印装质量问题，请与读者服务中心（010 - 59367028）联系

“
CAMPUS
Asia
”